SEVILLE
THE CELTIC MOVEMENT

David Faulds and Jim McGinley

CQN BOOKS
www.celticquicknews.co.uk

SEVILLE
THE CELTIC
MOVEMENT

Published by CQN Books, Quick News Media Limited, Glasgow
Copyright © Quick News Media, 2014.
All rights reserved.

First published in the United Kingdom in 2014 by CQN Books
ISBN 978-0-9576171-2-4

A catalogue for this book is available from the British Library

Design and typeset by Suzanne Waters (CQN Magazine)
Printed in the UK – Print and logistics by Tony Warrington

Edited by David Faulds (CQN Magazine)

Written by Jim McGinley and contributors and friends of Celtic Quick News.

**Special thanks to Paul Brennan for creating
www.celticquicknews.co.uk after he got back from Seville.**

CONTENTS

SPECIAL THANKS

The inspiration for this book came from the contributors to the Celtic fans blog www.celticquicknews.co.uk In May 2013. Ten years after Celtic took a travelling support of over 80,000 to Seville to contest the UEFA Cup Final, these contributors started to talk about Seville, some for the very first time. The result is SEVILLE – The Celtic Movement, a book that captures the unique bond between Celtic and her supporters. A very special CQN thanks to everyone who shared their Seville stories with us.

Thanks too to everyone who submitted photographs from Seville. These help us capture the supporter experience in Seville perfectly!

Thanks to the guys drafted in to write chapters for the book; accomplished journalist Alex Gordon (always a real friend to Celtic), CQN's intellectual heavyweight Setting Free the Bears, Joe Ruddy who was too young to be in Seville and for him it is the stuff of legend! Professor Richard Giulianotti for kindly granting his permission to quote from his detailed academic study on Celtic in Seville and Mike Maher, who tells the tale of how the Celtic support in New Zealand watched the match. Thanks too to L Monaghan and Blaise Plelan for their Seville stories and to St Patrick's Day 1956 for the excellent Seville poem. And special gratitude is due to Bill Houston for the excellent cartoons he has created especially for this book that feature the stories told by the CQNers in Chapter 22.

As always the women are crucial to any successful project. Suzanne Waters does a great job designing all the CQN projects: magazine, annual and books and in Seville – the Celtic Movement she maintains her superb standards, so thanks Suzanne. Thanks also my wife Karen who while abroad studying for six months in 2013, passed the time by subbing and proofing much of this book. After reading all the stories she has a great affinity to the CQNers and in particular has a soft spot for Bada Bing (don't tell him!)

And of course CQN Books would not be possible without Paul Brennan. Paul has had to take plenty of stick over the years for sticking up for Celtic through Celtic Quick News; much of this has gone unreported. As usual Paul gets the first word in this book and he also writes the epilogue on what happened to the Seville money. Then there is Jim McGinley – or Brogan Rogan Trevino and Hogan to his online friends. We are delighted to have persuaded Jim to write down all his Seville tales, some of which are absolutely hilarious!

We hope you enjoy SEVILLE – The Celtic Movement. It will in all probability move you to tears…

David Faulds
February 2014

FOREWORD

In the months afterwards I made a trip to the Celtic Superstore to buy the DVD of the match. I wasn't ready to watch it but needed to have it nonetheless, for when the time came. I've still not opened the box.

I watched the game from high up in the Porto end. The Porto fans were great, allowed us to celebrate with all the enthusiasm you could muster for goals in a European final, then wished us well as we made our way through them and out of the stadium. Had Celtic won while dropping like flies whenever an opponent coughed, it might have been different.

Porto were favourites and would go on to prove how good a team they were by winning the Champions League 12 months later. Their players would demonstrate their prowess across the world for the next decade. They had fabulous talent, so much so, that they should have aspired to better than the gamesmanship used during their run to the UEFA Cup and Champions League wins.

On the field it was a tale of great goals and heroic defeat, off the field, it was one of the most spectacular events in sport.80,000 Celtic fans made the pilgrimage to Seville and treated the world to a carnival. The city became the scene of one of the largest parties the game had ever known. For me the pre-match schedule involved a two hour trip north before a panicked dash across the city collecting match tickets. What a stress!

There were 10 in our party and collecting the tickets took priority. Once we had them we could afford time to eat, but what? Several restaurants were sold out but we eventually found a café with frozen chips and a meat-based slab of something or other. No choices. No beer, wine or cola either, it was diluting orange juice or water. An entire city was pretty much emptied of food and drink.

You could forget about motorised transport to get to the game, we had to walk from the city to the stadium on the very outskirts of town. It was hot and dry. An enterprising local was selling a retained stash of cola at the side of the road at a hugely inflated price. No one passed him without buying.

This was a journey to a football game that none of us were familiar with.

The long walk home from the game was memorable for the incredible reaction we got from the locals. They applauded each of us as we walked past their homes in recognition of what took place in their city throughout the day. Things like this don't happen but that day was different. Seville, like Lisbon, will always remember Celtic. FIFA and UEFA made their Fair Play Awards the following year to Celtic fans, a nomination normally reserved for clubs.

I met a German couple in the hotel elevator. "Are you disappointed?" they asked. "No. We were beaten by a good team". I had celebrated two Celtic goals in a European final and watched as we pushed a tremendously talented team to the brink. Disappointment comes a lot worse than this, although time brought regret.

Seville 2003 was not Lisbon 67 but it was a wonderful occasion in our very proud history. Let's do it again.

I hope that you enjoy reading SEVILLE – The Celtic Movement. This book, like the adventure in Seville in May 2003, has been put together by the collective efforts of the Celtic Movement and I would like to thanks everyone who has contributed either by telling is their stories or sharing photographs of Seville. Keep your copy safe, it is a part of Celtic's proud and unbroken history.

Written by Paul Brennan, Founder of Celtic Quick News.

CHAPTER 1

LISBON AND MILAN THE ROAD TO SEVILLE

LISBON was a kaleidoscope of vibrant, dazzling colours as the sun gleamed and welcomed the first of the green-and-white carnival. The image was flawless; a technicolour fusion of effervescent hues and vivid shades lighting up the Portuguese capital as the procession made its joyous way into the city. The many shades of green sat serenely among the local blooms of lavenders, pinks, violets, blues and yellows that adorned the pavement terraces and added to the festival atmosphere.

The glorious setting was perfection itself for a celebration. And the thousands of incoming supporters of Celtic Football Club weren't about to pass up the opportunity of playing their good-natured role in the party of a lifetime.

It was May 1967 and for many of the 10,000 or so who surfaced in Lisbon it was their first time abroad. A typical holiday destination was more likely to be Millport than Majorca, Rothesay rather than Rome. Obviously, the easiest route was to travel by charter flight. One company offered four full days in Lisbon for £57. To put that in context, the basic weekly wage of a Celtic first team player at the time was £65. A new Austin Morris saloon was £700 and the average semi-detached villa in Scotland cost £4,012. A two-piece suit from Burton's would set you back £16.50 (£16 10s) and a pint of beer was 10p (2s). So, for the majority desperate to watch their heroes in a far-off land, £57 represented a sizeable chunk of revenue. The fortunate among the travellers who managed to annex a centre stand seat had to fork out £2 7s 6d (£2.38) while a place in the terracing behind the goal was priced at 10s (50p).

The competition among the aircraft rivals was intense and one smart operator offered a half-bottle of whisky to each passenger as an inducement. Presumably, that airline did slightly brisker business than a rival who advertised "souvenir inscribed shillelaghs" as a lure to potential customers.

Hundreds, though, were enticed to dip into their life savings to take to the air for the first time in their lives. On one flight, an enterprising would-be entrepreneur, with a captive audience, managed to persuade the flight staff to allow him to utilise the aisle to sell some merchandise for part of the journey. In the unmistakable tones of an overworked and well-oiled larynx, more often heard around the Celtic End on match days, the future tycoon paced up and down, balancing a large cardboard box in his arms while rasping: "Errza macaroon bars and ra spearmint chewing gum."

For those of you too young to fully understand that little passage, I envy you your youth.

When one of the aircraft touched down in Lisbon airport, one supporter, in time-honoured fashion, got to his feet, removed his bunnet, threw a few shillings into it and began proffering it under the noses of the other passengers. "Let's have a whip-roon for the driver," he appealed, without a trace of irony. Goodness only knows what the 'driver' thought of this impromptu gift from the travelling and generous patrons.

Of course, for many, the thought of flying to the game was far too expensive and completely out of the question. There is a limit to how many suits you can pawn. So, a particularly intrepid band of Celtic followers made their own plans on how best to reach Portugal. A footballing convey of around 100 cars, labelled the 'Celticade', rolled out of Glasgow four days ahead of the game, embarking on the adventurous trek of some 1,700 miles.

Some of the vehicles had seen better days and the standing joke was: "For goodness sake don't get rid of the rust - the car will fall apart." One owner patted his newly painted green-and-white Hillman Imp on the bonnet upon arrival in Lisbon. With a massive sigh of relief, he was heard to say: "Now, Jimmy, the trick is for you to get me home."

They arrived in their thousands via bus, ship and rail as well as air. They trekked through France and Spain before reaching their coveted destination. The rail travellers arrived in various states of bon homie at the Santa Apolonia station and their dishevelled arrival was a matter of disbelief to the citizens. At that stage Lisbon was not the tourists' haunt it is today. The supporters toppled, staggered, struggled and zigzagged their way along the platform. There were unconfirmed reports of some actually walking in a straight line. The incredulous locals took the 'invading' jovial hordes to their hearts.

They may well have been astonished at these green-white-and gold-bedecked legions who arrived from ports dotted around the globe to support their favourites, but they were willing to give the Scots their passionate backing, too. They were urged to do so by none other than the great Eusebio, the Benfica legend who was the Cristiano Ronaldo of his day. He had played against the dull, defensively minded Inter Milan when they had defeated the Portuguese 1-0 in the 1965 European Cup Final. He had been far from impressed by the smothering, spoiling tactics of the Italians and insisted the locals should welcome and embrace Celtic and the club's support. He reassured the locals a triumph for Celtic would be a triumph for football. He was to be proved right in his assessment. So, the citizenry and the visitors dovetailed in harmony from day one.

After negotiating their way to Lisbon, there was now the task for many of those cheery legions of finding a place to park their heads before Thursday's 5.30pm kick-off.

One particular individual hadn't bothered with the irksome task of booking a room for the duration. He was positive his big brother would take care of all his needs. He would be occupying a very special suite reserved for some visiting VIPS at a luxury hotel on the outskirts of the city. Which was just as well because this Glaswegian had spent a heavy percentage of his cash on the flight to Portugal's breathtaking capital and there wasn't too much left in the kitty. But he was confident his brother wouldn't let him down.

There was only one problem. And it came in the formidable shape of a bloke not renowned for his patience or tolerance. Some claimed he could be canterkous; others went as far as curmudgeonly.

His name was Jock Stein.

Ian Auld reckoned his older sibling Bertie would look after arrangements and make certain he had a bed for the night at the official HQ of Celtic Football Club at the five-star Palacio Hotel. Big Jock, of course, would not have welcomed such an intrusion on the eve of the team's most important game in history. The Celtic manager had been meticulous in his preparations for the encounter. Players were ordered inside when he thought they had spent too much time in the sunshine. He would insist: "The sun is your enemy!" They were timed in the swimming pool, when to get in, when to get out, told what to eat and drink and training sessions had been planned with the utmost precision. He had been diligent, thorough and, as some players later agreed, somewhat finicky. Nothing had been left to chance.

It was an accepted fact that interlopers would not be welcome.

Ian Auld didn't take too much notice of the demands of the Celtic boss. Luckily for him, his brother Bertie, with typical Maryhill bravado, agreed with him. On this occasion, anyway.

The masterful midfielder, who dovetailed so awesomely, bewilderingly and consistently with Bobby Murdoch in the team's engine room, takes up the story. "Big Jock patrolled the hotel like a sergeant major. He wanted everything to be perfect. He had the habit of charging into your room without knocking on your door. He would always try to catch you off guard just in case you were getting on the outside of a bottle of gin. As if! The night before the game, Big Jock came into the room I was sharing my good buddy Joe McBride. We were tucked up in our single beds.

"He surveyed the scene. 'Everything okay, you two?' he asked, still peering around. I answered: 'I'm just reading a good book, boss.' Joe said: 'Me, too, gaffer.' Jock took one last look around the room and, satisfied all was in order, closed the door behind him and moved onto another unsuspecting teammate somewhere down the corridor.

"Actually, if Big Jock had bothered to look under my bed he might have got a bit of a surprise - he would have come face to face with Ian!

"My little brother had saved some cash to travel to Portugal to support us, but, being Ian, he hadn't bothered with the little detail of arranging a room in a hotel or elsewhere. With the help of some of my colleagues, I managed to smuggle him into our HQ in Estoril. It was like something out of Colditz - only in reverse. Ian was trying to break IN.

"He ducked and dived to make sure he wasn't spotted by any of the Celtic powers-that-be - and, please remember, Big Jock had spies everywhere. I had little doubt of what I could expect if the manager got wind of my part in the invasion of the team's privacy. A firing squad might have been hastily arranged on the spot!

"No matter how much Big Jock tried to silently creep up on you, we could always hear him coming. He still had that heavy limp that prematurely ended his playing career and you realised immediately he was about to descend upon you. I was playing cards with Ian and Joe the evening he decided to pay an impromptu visit. The alarm bells went off in my head as I heard him approach, stealthily, he hoped, towards our door. 'Quick, Ian, hide!' I practically screamed. 'Where?' he asked, almost as frantically. The wardrobe was too obvious. Big Jock had been known to swing the doors open, look inside, touch a garment and say: 'Nice material.' Of course, he was fooling no one.

"The footsteps got closer. 'Get under the bed. Now!' Ian didn't hesitate as he scrambled out of sight. Looking back, I can see it was a hilarious situation. Didn't seem like it at the time, though. Big Jock had a ferocious temper and I know what I'm talking about because, unfortunately, I was on the receiving end of it a few times. Joe and I grabbed books off the bedside cabinets and threw ourselves under the covers.

"The door swung open, Big Jock looked in, squinted around, said his piece and left without a clue as to the whereabouts of the uninvited 'guest'. I didn't have to worry about getting a good night's sleep - I practically passed out."

Of course, the outrageous tale of the Auld brothers is just one of the many gems that can be mined from such a momentous few days in Celtic's history during a remarkably blissful stay in the Portuguese capital. The accounts are every bit as rich and multihued as the beguiling setting. The visiting support was only too delighted to join in the spontaneity of joy, leap on board the carousel and share many light-hearted moments with their generous Portuguese hosts. They were made welcome in the local tavernas, pubs and tapas bars as the carnival atmosphere lit up the city.

And, of course, they listened to the exaggerated tales from their interesting visitors. They were astounded by one character who wore an outsized green-and-white tammy, huge rosette proudly proclaiming, 'Hail! Hail! The Celts Are Here'. Even in the soaring temperatures the large woolly scarf remained firmly in place around his neck. The locals were in awe of this individual and, in particular, the lengths he had gone to wear the colours of his favourite club. He was even adorned in a green suit. They remarked upon his loyalty to "the famous Glasgow Celtic", as they had learned to call the team.

The character hadn't the heart to tell them he didn't have time to change out of his work clothes before being picked up by his mates in their car to take him on their exhausting journey. Wearing the required dark green uniform of the era, he was, in fact, a bus conductor. Why ruin an illusion?

All sorts of transport was utilised to reach the destination. A week before the game, two extreme optimists were spotted in the Gallowgate in Glasgow, waving thumbs in the time-honoured manner of hitchhikers at passing vehicles. They held a giant placard that spelled simply, 'LISBON'. No one would have bet against them being in position at the Estadio Nacional by kick-off time.

Then there was the individual who worked in the circulation of one of Scotland's biggest-selling national daily newspapers. This chap steadfastly refused even to acknowledge his devotion to a certain club from the east end of Glasgow. No amount of prompting from his colleagues could prise the secret of his allegiance from him. Celtic could win, lose or draw and he would never rise to the bait. Who he supported was his business and no one else's.

His cover was blown on May 25 only minutes after the final chirp from referee Kurt Tschenscher's whistle. He was photographed right there on the pitch alongside triumphant captain Billy McNeill. The world's press paraded that unforgettable image, including the circulation man's own newspaper. By the time he got home from Lisbon, his work-mates confronted with the front page picture. Completely non-plussed he looked at the photograph and remarked: "Aye, looks like me right enough." Then he added: "Can't be, though. I was playing golf with my brother in Troon all week."

And he stuck to that story for years to come - despite the fact he was an only child.

He was one of hundreds who managed to get over the moat that separated the trackside from the terracings. One fan warily asked of one of the local constabulary: "Ah hope ye've no' got any o' them alligators in there."

In broken English, the policeman reassured the supporter of the absence of any such menacing swamp-dwelling species.

"That's just as well," came the retort, "because me and ma mates might get a wee bit peckish roon aboot hauf-time."

One observer looked around the stadium and the pitch just before kick-off, sighed and remarked: "It looks as though the interior decorators have been brought in." Celtic always liked to do things in a certain style.

Four hours or so before the grand occasion, a group of Celtic supporters were sitting in the bar of a hotel psyching themselves up for the most massive game in their club's history. They hardly noticed the quiet, middle-aged couple who sat beside them at a nearby table. The fans were involved in an earnest debate about who would be the team's top man, who was the day's main player who would be the key to piloting Celtic's name into football's Hall of Fame.

"It's got to be Wee Jinky," said one. "Who have Inter Milan got who can match him? Facchetti? He'll be like Bambi on ice, Jinky will torture him."

"Naw," said another. "Boaby's the man. The Italians will pack their defence and midfield and just leave Mazzola up front. But Boaby will do the business in the middle of the park. Looking at the setting, this is Boaby's conditions. Perfect for his range of passing. He'll be the prize guy."

"Aye," added another, "but those conditions will be just as ideal for Wee Bertie. And we all know how crafty and astute he can be, don't we? I doubt if the Italians will ever have come up against anything like him in all their European games."

"Don't forget we'll need Faither to be on his toes in goal," chipped in another. "We can play, dominate, even, but what use is that if your keeper is throwing them over his shoulder at the other end? Don't forget the saves he made against Dukla to get us here. He gets my vote."

The discussion went on for about half-an-hour until one of the supporters decided to bring the couple at the table next to them into the conversation. "What're your names?" he asked. "Alfie and Margaret," came the response.

"Okay, Alfie and Margaret, do you agree with any of our votes? Big Caesar's my choice. He always rises to the occasion, doesn't he? Quite literally at times, too. Remember that winner against Vojvodina at Parkhead? What a goal. Only Caesar can score goals like that. Head meets ball. Bang! In the net and Celtic are in the semi-finals. Lisbon's only three hours away."

Alfie, a strict teetotaller, considered for a moment, sipped his glass of ice-cold water, and said: "There's little doubt Caesar is a leader of men and great at both ends of the pitch, but, sorry, he wouldn't be my choice. Don't get me wrong, though, he will play an enormous part in our success."

"Really?" responded his inquisitor, an eyebrow arching. "Jinky, then? You've got to be a Jinky fan."

"Oh, aye, the Wee Man's one of my favourites," Alfie replied. "In fact, one of the best Scottish footballers I have ever seen, but, no, he wouldn't be my pick, either."

"Lennox? The Buzzbomb?" asked the fan, determined to discover Alfie's main man for the game ahead. "What a player, eh? Inter won't have come up against anyone of his pace in their league."

"There's little doubt he has his qualities and, yes, he will have a huge part to play in proceedings. But I still think there is another guy who will have a major say."

"Wait," said the fan. "Don't tell me, let me guess." He paused for a moment. "I see you're drinking water, so obviously you don't let bevvy interfere with your thought process. Is that right?"

"I have a sweet stout at the bells on Hogmanay," replied Alfie, "and I don't touch another drop for twelve months."

"Right, so you're an observer and no' a drunk like us lot," he swept his arm around the table and smiled. "Wispy? I bet you Willie Wallace is your type of player. Thoughtful, can perform just about everywhere in the team; even did a marking job on that Masopust bloke in Prague. Made sure his contribution to the game was zilch. Wispy, then? Am I right?"

"Wrong," smiled Alfie. "I have to admit, though, he is one of my favourites, too. I'll tell you this; I was delighted when Big Jock bought him from Hearts in December. He was a right nuisance against us. Aye, I would much rather have him with us than against us. But, no, he's not my main threat on this occasion."

"Okay," said the good-natured interrogator, getting a trifle frustrated in his attempts to unlock the thought process of his fellow-fan. "It looks as though we're going to have to go right through the whole team." He paused for a moment, snapped his fingers and grinned. "I know the answer, Alfie. I think you believe the most important guy at the game today isn't a player. It's Big Jock, isn't it?"

Alfie took another swig of his water. "Sorry, my friend, wrong again," he smiled.

"Not Big Jock?" The incredulity in the persistent cross-examiner's tone was getting higher. "Sean Fallon, then?"

"No, it's a player, I promise you," answered Alfie.

"Aye, you look the studious type, right enough. Cairney! It's got to be Jim Craig. Right?"

"I don't think he gets the credit or praise he undoubtedly deserves," said Alfie, turning to his right to wink knowingly at wife Margaret. "That lad is an athlete. He can run all day and gets up and down that wing without complaint. Dovetails brilliantly with Wee Jinky. Maybe doesn't score as many goals as you might want, but sets up plenty. He's a real unsung hero in my book. "

"So, it's Cairney," beamed the questioner. "I thought you looked the sober, intellectual type. I should have guessed you would go for a dentist."

"No, it's not Cairney," replied Alfie, another nod and a wink to Margaret. "Good player though he undoubtedly is."

"Hands up," said the quizmaster. "I've got a game to go to. I've got to be home by Saturday. Go on, then, put us all out of misery. Who gets your vote? Who is going to be Celtic's match winner today?"

Alfie grinned from ear to ear. "I've no doubt who you will be toasting this guy tonight."

"Go on," he was urged. "We've got to know."

"Why it's Big Tommy Gemmell, of course," grinned Alfie, eyes twinkling. "That's the player who will win it for Celtic. Who scored Celtic's first-ever goal in the European Cup? Tommy Gemmell against Zurich. Who was the first player to score three goals in the competition? Tommy Gemmell when he got another two in the second leg in Switzerland. Technically, not a hat trick, of course, but still a notable achievement for a left back. Remember, too, only one of those efforts was from a penalty-kick. Who set up the vital equalising goal in the quarterfinal against Vojvodina while they were leading 1-0 with only half-an-hour so to go? It was Tommy Gemmell who slung over the cross from the left that saw Stevie Chalmers get the equaliser and that paved the way for Caesar's winner."

He paused and beamed again.

"You seem to know an awful lot about our big defender, don't you? Anything else you would like to add?"

"Well, have you forgotten who sent the ball out of defence to land at Wispy's feet for him to lob the Dukla Prague goalkeeper for our second goal at Parkhead? Tommy Gemmell, of course."

"I'm greatly impressed, sir," said the inquisitor. "When you put it like that, it's easy to see why you would go for Big Tam. Aye, good luck with that. We'll all keep an eye on his performance today."

Alfie drained the last of his water and prepared to leave the bar. His wife finished her lemonade and she, too, rose to her feet. "There's a nice little taverna up the road," said Alfie. "Better get the wife a bite to eat before we head for the stadium. Great talking to you, lads, and I hope you are all celebrating tonight. Mark my words, Tommy Gemmell can swing this game for us."

The supporters toasted the couple as they headed for the door. "Certainly knows his Tommy Gemmell," said one admirer.

As Alfie and Margaret made their way across to the eatery, the wife looked admiringly at her husband and laughed: "Do you think we should have told them we're Tommy's mum and dad?"

The street urchins were especially pleased to welcome the garishly attired groups to their city. They would perch around the corners of the bars when the plonk was going down by the tidal wave. The combination of cheap wine and persistent sunshine would often bring on an unscheduled afternoon nap to the imbibing visitor. The unsuspecting, drowsy individual would stir from his unrehearsed stupor to often find his scarf had been removed. The sneak thieves had been at work. The opportunistic and mischievous youths realised the green and white colours of Celtic perfectly matched those of Sporting Lisbon. The garments would then change hands for a few escudos. What a friend gets is no loss, right?

But in the midst of the hurrahs there is always heartache, so please spare a thought for a nineteen-year-old Paisley lad who thought he was in with a chance of getting a place with his work's team on their flight to Lisbon. He believed he was guaranteed a ticket, too. The Celtic-crazy youngster, seen as an emerging talent, recalled: "I knew the team manager had plans to take some of the younger players to Portugal to give them some experience of football at that level.

"You could say I was just a wee bit excited at that prospect. Sadly, it was not to be, though. The travelling squad was announced and my name wasn't on the list. I had left it too late to make travel arrangements or even get a ticket, so the next best thing was to watch it on the television. But I would have given everything to have been there to sample the atmosphere first hand."

Eventually, a youthful Davie Hay got over his disappointment and even played in the European Cup Final for his beloved Celtic three years later in Milan, but that is a completely different story, of course. And it is one that still rankles with a man who went onto become manager of the club.

"My good friend Davie Cattenach was in both squads for Lisbon and Milan," recalls the likeable Hay. "Davie was a handy guy to have around, but, unfortunately for him, didn't play in either final. However, he has always insisted the difference in the club's attitude - from Big Jock through to the players - was night and day. Everything seemed so much more relaxed before the game against Feyenoord in the San Siro. Obviously, I can't talk about Lisbon, but my mate has always said the anticipation and preparation were very different for both finals.

"Yes, I've heard it said we might have been a bit complacent against the Dutch. Possibly, we thought we had done the hard job by beating Leeds United home and away in the semi-final. Against Inter Milan, Celtic were underdogs. Against Feyenoord, we were odds-on favourites and, as we all know, the bookies rarely got it wrong. Whatever the reason, that was without a doubt the worst memory of my playing career. We never got started and were turned over by a team that showed a lot more hunger on the night.

"Yet it all kicked off so well when Big Tommy rammed in the opener in typical fashion, a blistering shot from just outside the box. Rinus Israel equalised for them within two minutes and that shook us a bit. If we had held on to our lead until the interval I'm sure we would have done so much better in the second-half. Mind you, we were only two minutes or so from the end of extra-time and were still level when Ove Kindvall scored their winning goal. Believe me, if we had taken that game to a replay we would have won. No one in the team that night will tell you differently. We were caught with our guard down and Feyenoord, in fairness, were a much better team than we expected.

"Evan Williams was our top performer against the Dutch. When was a Celtic goalkeeper our best player? That just didn't happen because the action was, more often than not, down at the other end of the pitch. There was a strange atmosphere in the ground, too. You could hardly hear our support because of the klaxons that were being used by the Dutch fans. I had never witnessed these things before and they just drowned out our fans. All in all, it was a truly awful experience."

However, turning the clock back three years to Lisbon as the fans headed towards the Estadio Nacional, one carload was treated to a spontaneous rendering of the famous Sam Cooke song from the Fifties, "They Try To Tell Us We're Too Young". It was coming from the coach in front and Hughie Cumming, a veteran of The Jungle, recalled: "The bus was rocking from side to side and most of the windows were open. We could hear the words quite clearly. We were singing along when a pal pointed to one of the warblers on the bus. I had to rub my eyes. It was Jimmy Johnstone. He was giving it pelters and everyone else was joining in. There wasn't long to go until kick-off time and we thought the players would already be at the stadium. But while we were stuck in traffic, I would have paid good money for that concert."

Has time lent enchantment once more to a faulty memory bank? Tommy Gemmell has the answer. "Jinky used to lead off all the sing-songs back then. I think me wee pal was a frustrated Cliff Richard, but, yes, that would have been us. Jinky picked the songs and we just followed the bouncing ball. To be honest, I can't recall if we belted out "They Try To Tell Us We're Too Young" or not, but it would have been a distinct possibility. The fans didn't expect us just to sing Celtic songs, did they? We did that in the tunnel before the game and frightened the hell out of Inter Milan. They looked at us and thought we were a collection of nutcases! And the supporter has got it right - we SHOULD have been at the stadium at that point. Our driver took a couple of wrong turns coming out of Estoril and then we got caught up in the traffic congestion. I believe we made it to the ground just forty-five minutes before the kick-off. It didn't do us any harm, did it? We weren't too worried about being a wee bit late; we figured they wouldn't start without us!"

There is also the story that persists, but no one will support it, of the Celtic team official who had celebrated just a tad too much after the game on the fizzy stuff. The players were in the coach and eager to get back to the hotel before travelling on to the official function where, after a few hours' delay, they would be presented with their medals. One snag - there appeared to be no sign of the driver. "I'll drive," offered the beaming official. Thankfully, before he created any foreign incident, motoring offence or got anywhere near the wheel of the vehicle, the driver materialised and was thrust into his seat with extreme haste by another of the boardroom elite.

The history books show goals from Tommy Gemmell and Stevie Chalmers wiped out a first-half penalty-kick from Sandro Mazzola to earn Celtic's place in the history books. But that was hardly the end of the Lisbon story for many. It was clear that for some fans arrival in the city was the prime objective and the only consideration. Simply put, they hadn't attempted to budget for the journey home.

The British Consulate in the Portuguese capital also hadn't prepared for such an eventuality. Such financial recklessness of a visitor to their city would have been unthinkable. Possibly, there may be the odd tourist every few months who may have misplaced or lost a wallet, but the doors of the building almost came off their hinges as their offices were swamped by around one hundred fans without the means of getting out of Lisbon. Those who may have had the insight to secret some cash upon their person for the trip home would have been sorely tempted to splash out on the local cheap wines and give it yahoo with the rest of their fellow-supporters. Many must have given way to the impulse and lived for the day and the moment.

One Consulate executive, his waxed moustache twirling with every syllable, snorted haughtily: "It is bad enough that these people turn up with no money, but some individuals have no trousers, no kilts, no shirts, no vests and no footwear."

No trousers? No kilts? Sometimes it's best not to know; ignorance, indeed, can be bliss. Eventually something in the region of £4,000 was "loaned" to those in distress to help them continue on the outward-bound journey of the Great Adventure.

The story goes of a Glaswegian wondering through the glass panelled doors of the immaculate Consulate building and weaving merrily towards a rather prim female sitting at the reception desk. Straightening himself up to his full 5ft 4in, he muttered: "Hey, hen, is this no' the place where they gie ye the free money?" Her reply is not known.

Another Consulate worker moaned: "I've filled in enough forms to wallpaper Buckingham Palace."

The legacy of Lisbon, of course, is entrenched in football, on and off the field. The victory for Celtic over Inter Milan released the shackles that had threatened to throttle the beautiful game. Suddenly, coaches were aware that teams could be successful while performing in an enchanting, entrancing, entertaining manner. A bright new era followed.

Away from the action, there are still stories being told about the fabulous fanfare when the Celtic supporters came visiting. Can it be true that the mere mention of "Celtic" and "Jeemy Johnstone" in any bar in the vicinity of Lisbon, years later, ensured an extra drop of whisky in your glass?

However, the most prophetic words must go to the Lisbon Chief of Police. He went on record as saying: "The wonderful Celtic fans can come back any time. We have never had so much enjoyment from anyone."

Sound familiar?

There is little doubt Lisbon was in its own way the perfect dress rehearsal for the Celtic Movement to Seville thirty-six years later.

Written by Alex Gordon, author of Celtic The Awakening published in 2013. Alex is a former Sunday Mail sports editor and chief sports subeditor at the Daily Record and has worked as a columnist for World Soccer Monthly and as Scottish correspondent for France Football and L'Equipe. He has also co-written a number of other football books including A Bhoy Called Bertie with Bertie Auld, The Quite Assassin with Davie Hay and Seeing Red with Chic Charnley

CHAPTER 2

10 SECONDS IN OPORTO

Marcel Proust, born 17 years before Celtic FC, wrote over 3,000 pages in his masterpiece novel, "Remembrance of Things Past", which is, incidentally, the new title of the latest The Rangers Annual. It should be more accurately translated as "In search of Lost Time" and with just over 10 years having passed since our Seville run, it is perhaps time to revisit what is for me the abiding memory in all those matches.

The central point of Proust's 7 volume work is the ability of memory to be invoked involuntarily when it had been previously blocked. In the case of Proust's narrator, a sensitive would-be writer (Proust didn't stretch himself in characterisation) has his memory invoked on partaking of a Madeleine. Now lots of novelists and lyricists are obsessed with describing women, whether it be "Fifty Shades of Grey" or "Forty shades of Green" or even the one particular shade of orange sported by many women in these parts, but Marcel's fancies went in a different direction. He was fonder of cake than women. In fact, his French fancy was a French not so Fancy, as a Madeleine is, in fact, a rather plain sponge cake. Now I don't want to meddle with any middle-aged maudlin obsession with a Madeleine but in the SFTB house, it is a maddening waste to obsess about anything other than the mad mentalness surrounding Celtic and its pursuit of medallions.

So my Madeleine moment concerns 11 seconds in Oporto and the memory it encapsulates and invokes for me of our Seville run. But first we must set the scene.

We are in the Estadio Do Besso on the 24th April 2003. We are far into the 78th minute of the 2nd leg of a UEFA Cup Semi-Final. The first leg in Glasgow, a fortnight earlier had seen Celtic obtain a 1:1 draw with Boavista, a relative minnow in Portuguese terms who had won their first ever top league title in season 2000/01, having only been 2nd on 2 previous occasions in their history. Their European achievements were similarly modest having been in European competition on 18 previous occasions. They usually managed to get knocked out of the UEFA Cup or Cup-Winners Cup at 1st or 2nd round stages. However they made the quarter final stages of the UEFA Cup in 1994, the 3rd round in 96/97, and in 2001/2 finished 2nd in their Champions league Group, behind Liverpool but ahead of Dortmund and Kiev. The top 2 teams qualified that year for a second group stage where Boavista finished their Euro run in 3rd place, behind Manchester United and Bayern but ahead of Nantes. They lost 3 of their matches but beat Nantes and drew with Bayern at home and drew in France too. Obviously, these were minnows-that-used-to-be and only a parochial Scottish Press would fail to spot that they could no longer be dismissed as a Pub team. Celtic had, in fact played them previously in the CWC in 75/76 when we won 3:1 at Parkhead following a goalless away leg before we exited Europe yet again to an East German Pub team with an unpronounceable name.

Boavista were the outsiders from the group of 4 remaining teams: Boavista, Celtic, Lazio and Porto. To get to this semi-final stage they had beaten Maccabi Tel Aviv (4:2 on aggregate), Anorthosis Famagusta (3:1on aggregate), PSG (2:2 on away goals), Hertha Berlin (3:3 on away goals), and Malaga (1:1 on pens). They were also motivated strongly by the prospect of staging a Porto Derby as the final of the UEFA Cup as their city rivals were taking a home lead of 4:1 into the 2nd leg of their tie with Lazio in Rome that same night.

In the first leg, Boavista had opened the scoring at Celtic Park after 48 minutes when Joes Valgaeren had slotted an own goal past Rab Douglas. Even though Henrik had equalised a minute later, he missed a penalty 15 minutes from the end, the 3rd good penalty shout we had that night.

Boavista's away goal in a 1:1 draw meant that a win or goalless draw would see them through whilst Celtic needed to win or score more than once in a draw to ensure victory without a penalty shoot out on an away pitch. The approach of the Boavista Coach, Jaime Pacheco, already inclined to emphasise defensive aspects of the game, seemed to have been further hardened in this approach by the first leg score. They were cautiously defensive hoping to benefit from Celtic being forced on to a gung ho attack style to allow them breakaway opportunities, such as they had benefited from in the first leg. Celtic, under Martin O'Neill's instructions had resisted such temptation and the coolness and experience of senior players such as Sutton (a 34th minute sub off the bench for Paul Lambert), Hartson, Larsson, Petrov, Lennon and Thompson allowed them to avoid panicky football up to this point. However Celtic had shown few signs of penetration with an 8th minute header, two foot wide, from Henrik as close as we had come. Boavista were no better and their only chance had come in the 58th minute when Rab Douglas paid homage to Packie Bonner by sailing out to punch the ball to an opposition player. However Elpidio Silva's resultant header was deflected wide by Johan Mjallby.

However, as we now enter the 78th minute of the second leg, it is not long before such cool control will be pressurised by the gnawing awareness that the team is less than 10 minutes away from missing out on a chance of our first European final for 33 years and an opportunity for redemption for a club starved of any level of European success between 1980 when we just fell short of beating Real Madrid in the European Cup Quarter final and 2001/02 when we regained European credibility in gaining 9 points at Champions League Group stage before exiting the UEFA Cup to Valencia on penalties at the 3rd round stage.

So the 78th minute had been entered and a rare Boavista excursion upfield breaks down harmlessly and a yellow shirted Celt brings the ball out of our defensive third. This was when time started to slow down for auld Setting Free The Bears, his senses became heightened, time was being distilled and the football equivalent of a Madeleine moment stretched over the next 11 seconds.

77 mins. 48 secs. : Johan Mjallby, erstwhile stunt double for Dolph

Lundgren, former Swedish tennis prospect, and the hardest man in Christendom, is driving out of the Celtic half towards the half way line. A group of Boavista players wearing their checked tablecloth strip, which has replaced their founding club's All-Black outfit, retreat in orderly fashion to form a stronger banked defensive line in front of the rampaging Norseman. Johann is not immediately pressed on the ball and starts to see visions of a Gary Caldwell moment (he can see the future; it is a Norse trait) with a game winning imaginative pass. However the reality strikes him as he looks up and sees all the Celtic forward players are closely man marked, often by more than one player. Johann calculates the odds faster than Raymond Babbitt. His mathematical prowess, in fact, makes Raymond Babbitt look as puzzled as Kirk Broadfoot digesting the workings of an egg timer.

77 mins. 49 secs. : His mind made up by the marking and the lack of pressure on the ball, Johann drives on to cross the half way line. We are now in the usual mundane territory where 90% of the "action" of this game has taken place. There is still no evident danger and Boavista players are either tightly marking their man or retreating to their coached positions like a training ground drill for defending against an unthreatening defender. The nearest Boavista defender is almost 10 yards away. It's almost as if their coach and players have forgotten about Johann's midfield experience in playing for AIK, Sweden and for Celtic, occasionally, under Venglos and Barnes, until Martin O'Neill determined he was invaluable as a Centre Back.

77 mins. 50 secs. : Johann is almost 40 yards from goal. He has still not been pressed. One Boavista midfielder has detached from the retreating group of 3 but he is more interested in placing himself ahead of and inside of Johann to force him up the wing and deny him a direct charge into the penalty box. Johann's initiative seems to be about to be thwarted but two intelligent Celts, Larsson and Sutton both decide that maybe the giant Swede needs a little assistance.

Henrik is first to act, breaking backwards from goal towards Johann and dragging two defenders with him. He creates a 3 yard gap - enough to receive a pass without the defender immediately tackling, fouling or bumping him and, as he is now 5 yards from Johann, he breaks off his retreat and turns towards goal in a position to be influential. Chris, also, has started to head towards the right hand side of the penalty box to complement the movement. He too drags his defender with him but, since he is not as nippy as Henrik, he has not created a gap and is still tightly marked. Nonetheless, what Chris lacks in speed of movement is more than made up by his speed of thought, strength and all-round streetwise nature in how to ride a challenge.

77 mins. 51 secs. : Johann decides it is time to pass the baton. Even a Norseman on a Berserker drive forward is cool enough to recognise that Henrik and Chris are better bets for unlocking a well organised defence but, as he makes his short 5 yard pass into Henrik's path, either his adrenaline causes him to over hit it slightly beyond Henrik's control, or he has overcome the normal restrictions of perspective in vision, to see that Chris has established a one yard gap between himself and his marker. Whichever is true, and I would not bet against the latter explanation, the ball rolls away from Henrik and the, by now, four Boavista defenders closing in on him. It speeds towards Chris 5 yards outside the penalty box with a Boavista defender closing the gap to nothing as the ball arrives. Is time speeding up or slowing down? The action is frantic but the thought processes are ice cool and the breath of spectators is still and apprehensive.

77 mins. 52 secs. : Chris has been here before. He has carried out more than 10,000 hours in building his craft. He is in his 13th season as a pro footballer. A maverick character with an abrasive and acerbic side and a scathing sense of humour. He struggles to hide the resentment towards the ill-educated opinion that has wiped out his record of continuous achievement at Norwich, Blackburn and in European football with a Scottish club, and has filed him as a failure because of an ill starred year long spell at Chelsea who had paid £10 million for him and got 4 goals in return, two of them in a single European qualifying tie. He failed to add to his one England cap earned as a Blackburn player because of this ignorance and snobbishness.

As the ball arrives, Chris is aware that his man marker has closed the gap and is intent on fouling him or molesting him sufficiently to disrupt any accuracy in control or lay off. Chris has already calculated this approach and is working like a Martial Arts Ninja to turn his opponents attack to his advantage. He wants to achieve two things. Firstly, if he can, to turn the ball into the path of the onrushing Larsson, whose spin and turn has earned him a half yard gap on the inside of the markers to his left who should be guarding the precious area towards the centre of the penalty area and, secondly, to make sure that the ref sees the foul that Chris is sure is coming and, if unsuccessful in the pass, will award a foul around 30 yards out towards the right hand side of the penalty box, giving Alan Thompson or Henrik a direct shot at goal or allow for an opportunity to provide Bobo, Johann, BBJ or himself with a chance to inflict aerial damage and a nervy conclusion to the match.

Chris angles his body, stiffens his sinews and prepares to lean back and stick a foot forward to lay off the ball to his right into Henrik's path. As the ball arrives, he is immediately fouled by a cynical defender who has belatedly recognised the danger and wants to give Chris no opportunity to continue this move. Chris crumples to the ground and looks to the ref who is in a perfect position to witness this foul play. It seems that, even Chris has not expected the pass to be made, but, as he looks up to petition the ref he also sees the ball has popped out exactly where he has intended, sitting up and begging for Henrik 5 yards away, chased by 4 Boavista players with 3 Celts behind them. Henrik is able to continue the move and the Russian referee, Mr. Ivanov, is cool enough to allow this advantage to develop and he keeps his mouth dry on the whistle.

77 mins. 53 secs. : Henrik advances in no time to take clean possession of the ball. One of the two Centre backs who were previously marking Hartson has sensed the danger and split to the right side of the D to form a barrier to a long range Henrik shot. There is still a chance for Henrik to attempt a first time shot from 30 yards with a 4 yard gap to this defender but Henrik is in no mood for a Hail Mary effort and knows there are more misses than happy endings with such efforts. As a professional he is much cooler than the watching spectators, some of whom are uttering their 200th profanity of the night at this unwillingness to be speculative.

Henrik is faced with one direct defensive opponent and two more to his immediate right, cutting off the chance to enter the box on the right hand side. he must go towards the centre where both Boavista defenders and the goalkeeper lie ahead. Henrik, in contrast has only one ally ahead of him, Big John Hartson. Fortunately John is not just a lumbering presence and an aerial threat, he also understands football and knows that even the miracle worker Henrik, needs help. John too has a football brain and decides that a run in behind Henrik's immediate opponent will discomfit him and will drag his own marker away from the central space that Henrik will be free to attack. John gets the head down and sprints. Yes, I can call that nothing other than a sprint.

77 mins. 54 secs. : John has reached the half way point in the D on the 18 yard line. Henrik is only a yard to his right. The Centre back in direct opposition to Larsson has now closed to within a yard and is spreading himself to block or intercept the slip pass. Two other retreating Boavista midfielders have inserted themselves as barriers to Henke's right but John is still ahead of them all being chase by one marker. Henke feints inside with his body but his right foot releases a slip pass against this shown angle to by pass three defenders and leave John in behind with one defender to face. Henrik's pass is so delicate that his marking Centre back almost intercepts but the deceptive feint delayed his leg stretch long enough to make it fractionally late.

77 mins. 55 secs. : The ball is reaching John 15 yards from goal. He has a yard space ahead of his inside marker. Henrik thinks John will collect and attempt to return it to him so he continues his drive through the empty centre. Though John has made space ahead of his immediate defender, he is no match for one of the two retreating midfielder who, in matching Henrik's run and defending the right side of the box have built up a greater speed than BBJ and reach the ball fractionally ahead of him. Fortunately for Celtic, at that speed and wishing to avoid competing with BBJ for the ball, the defender cannot be cool and composed with his clearance. He reaches the ball a yard into the penalty area. He goes to ground to slide behind the ball and hook it out of the penalty area but he connects with the ball before his forward hook has time to take effect. The result is that the ball vectors to the side, in the opposite direction from his approach run and moves forward by less than a foot - straight into the path of Henrik Larsson, 17 yards and dead centre from the goal. This is a great goal scoring chance.

77 mins. 56 secs. : Henrik is free in perfect position, His body is open and his right foot drawn back ready to shoot. the goalkeeper Ricardo has been sleeping and has only managed to get a yard off his line. Big John's move has taken 3 Boavista players away and left two of them on the ground. The nearest defenders to Henrik, 3 yards to his right and slightly behind, is the Centre back who missed the slip pass. The right back who has detached himself from marking Celtic's number 39 is a good 4 yards to Henrik's left, surely unable to influence matters.

The stage is set for an explosive shot from an elusive attacker who has outwitted a packed defence and is now favourite to score. But before I can visualise it, Henrik's right foot has not propelled into a shot. Instead he has cushioned it awkwardly while pirouetting on both feet, and brought the ball even closer to goal. In doing so he has managed to reach level with the penalty spot, 12 yards out but instead of a right foot shot with a drawn back foot, he now faces a left foot shot from a standing foot. The keeper has reached a yard from his 6 yard box, narrowing the angle, and, though Henrik has isolated the 4 defenders to his right by this action, the charging right back is now close enough to launch into a block before Henrik can draw his left foot back to add power to the shot. Time has slowed through my anguish to allow me to double to the number of profanities aimed at this Celtic deity.

The clock still reads 77 minutes and 56 seconds as an awkward scooped powderpuff shot leaves Henrik's left boot. The right back has reached there anticipating it would be 77 minutes and 57 seconds before he was needed.

77 mins. 57 secs. : The second hand advances before the ball reaches the keeper 4 yards away. The right back lies on his back in front of Henrik. In leaning back to scoop his shot Henke has fallen away to his left and is about to fall. Two other Boavista defenders are charging back to clear the ball if the keeper can stop it or slow it down. The odds are very much in the balance. The keeper, seeing the ball go to Henrik's left foot has automatically adjusted to expect a shot to go to his left hand side. However the scoop and the awkward stance seems to have sliced the ball to the right. It rises in a drunken parabola. Ricardo sees that, in adjusting to his left, his right hand will not now reach the ball on his right while it is in front of him. He springs backwards with a mighty leap attempting to paw the ball away from behind him. I have slowed down this moment hundreds of times and each time it looks like Ricardo is the favourite to reach the ball, but anyone diving backwards will find it difficult to retain height and reach as it is an action rarely performed, outwith a mosh pit, for good anatomical reasons. Ricardo manages to lay a glove on the ball, and is criticised by an English co-commentator for his "chocolate wrists", but the scoop and slice have created just enough upward and leftward movement, off Henke's boot, to render his attempted stop ineffective. The English co-commentator attributes the blame rather than award the achievement to Henrik, who, of course, had not, according to this jingoistic Colonel Blimp, yet proved himself in the EPL.

Ricardo is still in mid air falling down to earth as the ball reaches the goal line and I am just about to emulate Ricardo in adopting some peculiar and unlikely aerial shape in my own living room. Though I am a few years away from turning 50 at this point, the expensive light fitting hanging above my sofa in the SFTB living room is in real danger of damage, as am I from it.

77 mins. 58 secs. : The ball hits the ground a yard behind the line. Ricardo is on his back hoping to see the ball has sliced enough to hit the post or go wide. Henrik is on all fours ready to sprint to the left hand corner flag in familiar celebration. The Boavista number 3 has his head in his hands, perhaps the most aware player of the import of the situation. A small band of Celtic fans is going wild in the stadium. A decibel roar loud enough to short several power supplies is heard across Scotland and Ireland and in small pockets across the globe. There is an instinctive understanding of the importance of this goal but it is a visceral understanding. This is no time for rational appraisal. this is a time to go legitimately mad.

77 mins. 59 secs. to Infinity: Time has no meaning after a goal has been scored by your team. You enter the realms of celebration madness. Henrik leads the charge to madness and the corner flag. He passes Celtic's number 39 (cosmologically significant as this was Henrik's 40th strike of that season), Jamie Smith, who has no compass bearings for such a moment and is unlikely ever to face them again unless Colorado Rapids benefits from a rich owner. Chris Sutton joins this pair in a hug celebration, which, though joyous, seems understated when you see what the fans are doing. On the sidelines, Martin O'Neill relives his GAA career by leaping even higher than his personal best. The sidelines are a shambling mix of aimless direction change and roaring. Boavista players hurriedly retrieve the ball from the net, Ricardo seems close to tears. He is far from the first or last keeper to have been or be Larssoned

After Infinity: The game lasts for a further 11 minutes plus 4 minutes and 22 seconds of injury time. It is frantic and fraught but just as undistinguished as the period before Henrik's goal. In total, there were 94 minutes and 11 seconds of undistinguished action but it was illuminated, like a dog whose defecation conceals a minute Faberge egg, by a small amount of precious and timeless beauty.

Celtic marched on to Seville and a date with Boavista's more glamorous and theatrical sister, Porto but that can wait. For now, there will be a lot more than 11 seconds of running, shouting, singing, partying, and maybe a few tears of remembrance of times past.

I think I just heard the sound of an article whose wheels have turned full circle. I'm away to dip a Jaffa cake in my tea.

Written by Setting Free the Bears, a regular and distinguished contributor to Celtic Quick News and a feature writer for CQN Magazine.

CHAPTER 3
SEVILLE – CELTIC!

Seville: the ancient Roman City originally called Hispalis. The Capital of Andalucía in Southern Spain.

Seville: a municipal population of about 703,000 as of 2011, and metropolitan population of about 1.5 million, making it the fourth-largest city in Spain and the 30th most populous municipality in the European Union. Its Old Town, the third largest in Europe with an area of 4 km², contains three UNESCO World Heritage Sites: the Alcázar palace complex, the Cathedral and the General Archive of the Indies.

Seville: known as Ishbiliya after the Muslim conquest in 712.

Seville: One of the economic centres of the Spanish Empire, after the discovery of the Americas, as its port monopolised the trans-oceanic trade and the Casa de Contratación (House of Trade) wielded its power, opening a Golden Age of arts and literature.

Seville: From where Ferdinand Magellan departed in 1519 for the first circumnavigation of the Earth.

Seville: A city which saw the horrors of the Spanish Civil War, and many glories, triumphs and tragedies in its 2,200 year History.

Seville: Invaded and populated by the Romans, The Phoenicians, The Moors, and The Castilians.

Seville: a town with all that history, all that culture, all those tales to tell and all those influences but where just one word is guaranteed to bring a smile to the face of any local:

CELTIC!

Any discussion about modern European Football and cup competition will eventually throw up the link between the Catalan capital and the team founded by a Marist brother from the east end of Glasgow.

What makes the link between the two all the more remarkable is that the connection was made over only a handful of days in May 2003 which culminated in the Glasgow club coming to Spain and losing a football match. The victors on the day were F.C. Porto who, under the guidance of an audacious young manager called Jose Mourinho, would go on to lift the big Prize of the Champions League, or in old money, the European Cup, the following year.

It was a Golden period for F.C.Porto, yet it was the losing side that would stamp their name, if not in the history books, then in the annals of endless folklore, because in truth there was no real story in Seville were it not for the Celtic supporters.

As a result of those few days in Spain, the major players in the sport, the European and World bodies who govern the game, would depart from all previous convention and practice by honouring, commending and, to be frank, standing in awe of the football supporter—or to be more precise—The Celtic supporter!

They say there were 80,000 there. And the rest! They say it is or was the biggest travelling support in the history of Sport. It remains the biggest travelling support to trek across Europe to support a football team.

CNN reported that on the day before the game 3% of the earth's flying population were all headed for Seville and were sporting a Celtic scarf – a statistic that no sector of industry could ignore and which would change the policy of many airlines as a result.

They say that the Celtic support was worth 600 Million Euros to the Spanish economy—they didn't count the money spent by the thousands of us who crossed the border from Portugal to support the hoops—the Portuguese just got a wee spin off.

There are literally thousands of stories surrounding the trips to and from the Spanish City.

Long lost friends who somehow bumped into one another after years apart: People who turned up on the spur of the moment yet who managed to find friends and family among the mayhem—like homing pigeons who somehow mysteriously know their way home.

People who missed flights, arrived by car, left their desks at the last moment, lied to their bosses about where they were going, met a girlfriend or boyfriend to be at the airport, had a ticket, didn't have a ticket and couldn't care less!

Seville was a town where football came to learn the value of "The Green Pound" and as a result many a civic authority would take an interest in an approaching UEFA draw in the hope that the word "Celtic" would be matched with their local heroes.

However, the most important thing about Seville in my eyes is that Seville is the town where Glasgow Celtic Football Club rediscovered itself, its value and its wonder.

Blessed with a team that could hold its own in ANY competition, Celtic would come to the heat of Seville and face a team that were to be the Kings of Europe within the twelve month.

Twice they would fall behind, and twice they would fight back through the talismanic head of the King of Kings, The sporting hero of Sweden, the once dreadlocked and now balding Rastafarian Larsson.

Whilst Deco and Derlei of Porto would rightly be praised for lovely football in the course of the final - though their memory may be tarnished by play acting and gamesmanship - any examination of the 2003 UEFA Cup Final shows that the Swedish born son of a Cape Verde Father was in a class of his own in his chosen position. He may have been on the losing side, but

Larsson was chosen as the UEFA Man of the Match and deservedly so.

Over and above showing a determination to play and win which was draining just to watch, Larsson would score a goal, which should be the object of study by anyone with serious ambitions to play professional football in the striker position.

As Didier Agathe crossed a high loping ball towards the Porto back post, a study of Larsson's movement and guile shows the perfect striker's motion and execution of a football move.

The manipulation and manoeuvring of the defender, the seemingly impossible leap and never ending hang in the air, is only bettered by the vision and ability which enabled him to head the ball spinning back across the goal and into the net via the inside of the far post.

In essence, Larsson defeated two central defenders; a fullback and a goalkeeper by using one elongated twisting leaping motion, which culminated in his placing the ball into the one exact spot where it could not be saved.

In sheer striking terms it was perfect—with no one in the world being able to say that they would have executed that piece of football any better. This was Celtic's King of Kings scoring the strikers goal of goals.

However, despite Larsson's heroics, the team from Glasgow would lose the match.

Yet, the club from Glasgow would win everything – everything from respect, to admiration, to awe and wonder—from the city, UEFA, FIFA, Governments, F.C.Porto, international broadcasters, airlines and everyone else.

If football and Europe had needed reminding just what Celtic Football Club brings to any major event then Seville was it. Equally, for different generations of Celtic fan, Seville afforded them the opportunity to see, be part of, and feel the experience of the Celtic support acting on instinct, en masse and with one purpose—to support—with a smile and a song or three.

Following the 2012 defeat of Barcelona in a Champion's League group stage match at Celtic park, one Spanish magazine described what they saw as " The Greatest Home advantage" in European Football--- in an attempt to describe the atmosphere created by the Celtic support at Celtic Park.

Those May days in the heat of Seville saw the Celtic support conquer a European city whilst at all times remaining guests, visitors, customers, party goers and most of all Celtic supporters. They brought that atmosphere and spirit from Kerrydale Street and unleashed it on the unsuspecting and bemused Andalusian. They came, they saw, they sang, they drank (plenty!), they spent, they laughed and they conquered—with sheer weight of numbers, force of spirit and their Celtic personality.

This was a festival, a carnival, a party, an audience, a crowd, a family and a club all rolled into one. This was the Celtic support in all its glory for the entire world to see.

There were no strangers, just members of a family that you had not yet met and who were all there with the one purpose, one goal, one intention and one vision—and that was to be part of the family that is Celtic Football Club.

Yes, players took to the field and management managed from the sidelines, but the spirit of Celtic stood in the stands, the fan zones, the pubs, the parks, the airports, the hotels, the bus stations, train stations, petrol stations—everywhere—except the Police stations.

Celtic—a name that was meant to be all inclusive from the beginning, which said that everyone and anybody was welcome, and which has meant and always will mean that those who support this club are not and never will consider themselves THE people but A People—a body of support—a brotherhood or family or a club in which we are all members.

As each member of that family rolled into town by whatever means, the cumulative glow and presence increased with powerful effect. If smiling and singing were a currency, then this Green and White brigade were the richest of the rich—so rich that media moguls and TV crews from all over the world could not ignore the remarkable gathering—and all for a football team who had not as yet kicked a football.

I often think of Seville and want to shout:

" See! – See what we can do when we all act together? —As one body, as one support, as one club, as one movement, as one spirit?"

I am not sure that the "Celtic" effect is truly understood or realised by those involved with the "business" of football or even the "Business" of Celtic Football Club or PLC.

There is little that the Celtic support cannot achieve when acting as one. Whether it be raising money for charity, being the twelfth man in a stadium, being an economic force to be reckoned with, or just being the world's biggest infectious party--- all of which was shown in Seville.

For me, "Seville" is no longer a city or a town—it is a feeling—an emotion—an experience—a spirit - when I for one felt as if I was a king of kings!

Many will wonder will it ever happen again.

I genuinely don't know.

All I do know is—that if there is going to be a show—then the Glasgow Celtic will be there.

BRTH

CHAPTER 4
THE ROAD AND THE SMILES TO SEVILLE

As you go through the pages of this book you will find many short accounts of individual stories about how people got to Seville, how they got back home and what they did when they were there or en route.

There are tales of misfortune, ingenuity, sheer luck, utter bravado, potential disaster, unbelievable kindness, astonishing disbelief and just about every other human condition and frailty. As you are about to see, however, what runs through all of these conditions and circumstances is a unique bond and great humour.

The Seville story is one which is drawn from every section of society as those wearing green and white hoops on the day included everyone from the long term unemployed and unemployable to Peers of the Realm, Members of Parliament, High Court judges, the captains of industry, famous actors, international stars from the music business, all the professions and everyone in between. There were all ages and people who had come from damn nearly every country in the world just to be there. The Celtic ladies were in Seville. There were mums pushing prams, wives, girlfriends, grannies and one or two great grannies. There were old men and young men – and old men who thought they were young men. There were kids, children, teenagers- all brought up in and invited to this gathering of gatherings. All of these people stood side-by-side, cheek-by-cheek, and come the night, many would sleep on the pavement...side by side and in the open air.

Think about that. Thousands of people, from all sections of society and from every background, were blissfully homeless in a foreign land. Not because of war, an earthquake, famine or political uprising, but because they had consciously taken the decision to follow a football team and because something from within told them that they just could not miss out on the occasion no matter what conditions they had to endure or how far they had to depart from their normal comfort zone.

Surely, whatever it was that caused such a voluntary mass migration had to be astonishing?

Back home in Glasgow some described the city as a ghost town, yet it is often forgotten that the dear green place was still populated by tens of thousands more who would have given an arm and a leg to have been among the roasted and homeless in Seville on the night of the final. Some tried to emulate the feeling and the atmosphere – Baird's Bar in the Gallowgate even created its own sandy beach in an attempt to create a true Andalusian atmosphere --- though the absence of a truly scorching sun would ensure that the valiant attempt would never come close to the reality.

However what was important was neither the sun nor the sand but the atmosphere, the spirit and the common purpose of all of these people in coming to support Celtic. But where did that spirit come from, how did it get there and how did it arise in the first place?

Well, I can only really tell my story, and along the way drag in examples of what other people saw and felt at the time in the hope that by the end of this book all of these examples add up to as complete a picture of the feeling of Seville as we ordinary, everyday supporters can muster - leaving the reader with a feel, a taste and a hunger for what was … and what will hopefully come again.

Some say the whole Seville adventure started with defeat in Basel and the unexpected exit from the Champions League at the hands of the Swiss champions and their iconic midfielder Hakin Yakin who was having the season of his life. Had Chris Sutton's late effort on the Basel goal been more accurate by a single inch then there would have been no Seville and Celtic would have been in the Champions League.

Maybe it was destiny that he missed.

However, I don't think the road to Seville started that night in Switzerland – the same country where the road to Lisbon started.

For me the road to Seville starts with Lisbon and the 1967 European Cup Final where Celtic defeated the previously all-conquering Inter Milan of Helennio Herrera --- and yes you will read about the Celtic supporters' trip to Lisbon in this book too!

That final in Lisbon saw at least a couple of footballing firsts in that not only were Celtic the first non-Latin side to walk off with the cup with the big ears, they were the first European side to have a mass fan base and support which would cross a continent to see the team in action. More importantly, that travelling support set the benchmark for all further sojourns into Europe by the supporters of any other club. Lisbon saw a party, a celebration, and a mass infection of goodwill that spread from the visitor to the native and which lived long in the memory.

As Alex Gordon has described earlier in this book, the people of Lisbon in the main wanted to support Celtic in the final due to the fact that they did not fancy Inter and their football, so when it came to picking one of the two sides in the final they had an automatic leaning towards the rather unknown and unfancied Glaswegians.

However, that was the view of the Lisbon folk who followed football. There were plenty more who were ambivalent towards the whole event and who could not care less which side won or lost... and then came the Celtic supporters!

Lisbon was not prepared for the invasion of Green and White hoops, just as Milan and later Seville would not be prepared for what happens when Celtic reach a European Final. It is often forgotten by us Celtic fans that in 1967 Portugal was in a state of political flux with the Portuguese Colonial war raging from 1961 onwards and that eventually in 1974 the longstanding Portuguese political regime was overthrown by a bloodless military coup. The Portuguese Government which was in situ in 1967 has been described as "authoritarian and oppressive", conservative and very right wing, and so Lisbon in May '67 does not sound like a natural party town…and it wasn't.

When UEFA decided that Lisbon would host the 1967 final in the park like atmosphere of the Estadio Nacional, they did not envisage that thousands of Scots and Irish would travel to see a football match. To be fair they did not envisage thousands of Germans or Italians or Dutch or whoever would travel to the final because the travelling football army had never been seen or even imagined. The Portuguese, the people of Lisbon, UEFA and everyone else thought that come the day of the final, while there might be a few fans from the clubs playing there, the majority of the crowd in the picturesque three sided stadium would be locals. How wrong they were!

However, the Celtic fans changed that and as Alex has described they piled into Lisbon by plane, by car and by any other means possible.

Personally, I had a ringside seat in the building of the Lisbon atmosphere and in our house there was a feeling - a sense of euphoria - surrounding Lisbon that must have been unique and which formed a platform of belief that has never left me.

My father and mother had a travel business and following the 3-1 home win against Ducla Prague, they decided to gamble on Celtic – and more importantly the Celtic supporters --- by chartering as many planes as they could get their hands on for the days surrounding 25th May 1967. They wanted to fly as many Celtic fans to Lisbon as they could, as they believed, from their own longstanding experience as Celtic supporters, that Celtic fans would travel to virtually anywhere to support their team. Further, they believed that they would travel by the thousand to see their heroes in a European Final.

When the heat of Lisbon had subsided and the team had marched off with the trophy, the last of their 19 flights eventually took off from Lisbon airport returning many inebriated fans to their homeland – including the legendary fan who woke up as the plane was landing and declared " Awe Naw --- my car is in Lisbon!"

In the weeks after the final, our house rang with the stories my folks were able to tell of the thousands of fans that they had flown, many of whom had never been on a plane before and had never travelled abroad before. The stories were hilarious and heart-warming – even to a small boy.

Over the next 9 years I would hear countless stories of the Celtic support abroad as each European draw would result in more planes, more fans and more supporters' stories. I grew up thinking that it was perfectly natural for Celtic fans to jump on a plane and fly to wherever just to support the team. I also thought it was absolutely normal to hear that supporters had gotten themselves into the most unbelievable situations abroad and returned with the most mental of stories.

I grew up believing that a visit to Pittodrie or Dumfries was just a wee local match and that an "away" game meant places like Nantes, Lisbon, Copenhagen, Amsterdam, Budapest, Malta, Basel, Milan, Saint Etienne, Florence, Dublin, Athens, Buenos Aries and at a push even Leeds. Further, really away games were those games played in those exceptionally strange places where you could not fly such as the Eastern Bloc (Prague, Belgrade, Novi Sad etc) and those places where nobody wanted to go to even though they could actually get there --- like Helsinki and even Iceland which, in those days were considered too bloody cold or inhospitable for a proper Celtic party!

For as long as Celtic remained among the elite of football in Europe I heard tale after tale of fans in Europe which were just astonishing, funny and brilliant - and so when the Celtic star faded in European terms, I would look back on those halcyon days and, possibly more than any other, I would long for their return just for the fans' stories and the unmistakable feeling of all for one and one for all that I knew the Celtic support would bring to any destination.

I also grew up in the midst of the business of travel and the realisation that if you want to get from A to B there will always be a way and that there will always be a route or a connecting flight --- from somewhere. That of course is far truer today than it was in the '60's,'70's and even '80's.

Many airlines – some of which are now defunct --- took thousands of Celtic fans across the globe in the course of those early years – Aer Lingus, British European Airways, Donaldson Airways, Invicta Airlines, Britannia Air, Lloyd International, Laker Airlines, Martin Air, Stirling Air, Dan Air, Iberia Airlines, British Eagle, British Caledonian, Pan Am and many more all saw "business" in Celtic fans.Both Ryanair and Easyjet are Johnny come lately merchants in my eyes.

However, when I was asked to stop and consider where my real journey to Seville started I have to move forward a few years to the evening of the 18th of June 1982.

On that evening I found myself in the town of Ericeira some 22 miles northwest of the Estadio Nacional on the Lisbon coast. I had organised a holiday for a fairly large group of friends (I think there were 28 of us in total over a three week period). The World Cup was in full flow and in the afternoon we had watched Scotland annoy the Brazil of Socrates, Zico, Falcao and Eder by taking a 1-0 lead by way of a magnificent 25 yard toe poke from big Dave Narey from Dundee United.

Of course, that goal just spurred the bearded doctor and his team-mates into action and they delivered a footballing lesson of the type that was to cement their reputation as the greatest and classiest football team to win precisely nothing! The Brazilian football was a joy to watch.

Understandably, a travelling group of twenty plus roaming around a smallish holiday town gets noticed and each night, as we strolled through the town centre, various restaurants would try and entice us in to eat in their establishment. So it was on the night of that Scotland-Brazil game, and we just walked into one such establishment mob handed and sat down to eat.

I can see the place in my mind's eye with its light brown tables, which we had to push together so we could all be one big party. Portuguese food is spectacular and I recall the fish dishes in particular as being absolutely excellent. We tended to eschew the nightclubs that were available and had developed a habit of making a meal last for hours with gallons of Vinho Verde, crates of beer and more than a splash of a wicked illicit Portuguese spirit called Madronia which made your hair stick straight up!

So there we are in this restaurant, eating and drinking and talking about how good Brazil had been. Many of us were Celtic fans and had various Celtic connections. There were relatives of Matt Lynch and Peter Goldie who had worn the hoops, and others with long familial connections to Celtic.

As I recall, I was sitting at the table when I got a shout from some friends to come to the bar where they had engaged in conversation with the owner of the restaurant – Luis – who was originally from Lisbon. At the bar, Luis introduced himself and quickly handed me an official postcard complete with a place for a stamp and a message although this particular card was blank and had never been sent.

The Picture on the card was the Estadio Nacional on the afternoon of 25th May 1967 at the precise moment when Stevie Chalmers turned the ball into the Inter Milan Net for the winner. Luis had been in Lisbon that day and he had kept this postcard as a memento of the day and had held it for 15 years as his own wee homage not so much to Celtic as the Celtic fans.

Here for the first time, I was told about the experience of the local when Celtic came to town. This man described the partying in the streets, the singing, the laughing, the dancing, the joking, and the crying of the thousands of fans in the capitol. He said that the Celtic fans "lifted" Lisbon, made the local people forget the oppressive regime for a day or two and were an inspiration with their infectious enthusiasm and spirit. He said it was something he never forgot.

For some bizarre reason, he had another postcard – this time of a young Davie Hay and strangely one of Davie's relatives was among our number which resulted in yet another round of drinks and toasts.

Eventually, Luis brought us the bill for our food and drinks and immediately I told him that with all due respect we were not ready to leave yet and so we were not ready for the bill. With no fuss whatsoever, he simply explained that he wanted us to pay for the meal and whatever we had drank to that point. There was no question of us being asked to leave and that anything else we wished—tea, coffee, alcohol, more food, or whatever --- was on the house because we were Celtic fans!

In the early(ish) hours of the morning when I eventually went to my bed the reaction of this man to learning that we were Celtic fans was going round and round in my head. Nothing was too good for us and nothing was too much trouble. Here was someone who had had no connection to Celtic Football Club whatsoever yet who had carried the feeling of the 25th May 1967 and the spirit of the Celtic fans in Lisbon around with him ever since. I swore that if we ever reached another final I would move heaven and earth just to be there to see for myself just how the Celtic fans mixed with the locals and how those locals would respond to what Luis had described as the infectious Celtic carnival, which simply lifted a whole city.

I was in Milan on the 6th May 1970 and cried like a 9 year old when we lost in extra time. Yet, once again I heard fantastic tales of the Celtic fans in the Italian city. However, that meeting with Luis in 1982 made me determined to see and be part of "Celtic" if they ever reached another European Final because I believed that no matter when or where it happened, the Celtic fans would once again invade the final with their unique spirit and sense of fun.

I was to wait a few decades but the result was Seville ……… and the Celtic fans and the people of Seville did not disappoint. I sometimes wonder if Luis came down from the Lisbon coast just for the craic?

I am willing to bet that he did ……… in spirit if not in body!

BRTH

CHAPTER 5
A STRANGE WAY TO GET TO SEVILLE

Within minutes of the final whistle of the home leg against FK Sūduva Marijampolė of Lithuania, I found myself with a beer glass in hand and a grin the size of the famed Cheshire cat standing deep in the bowels of the lounges within the North Stand at Celtic Park. With a blistering display Martin O'Neill's bhoys had dispatched Sudova by 8 goals to 1 and guaranteed a place in the next round of the UEFA Cup. The team had played really well and in particular there had been two great goals from Henrik Larsson and Stan Petrov.

After the disappointment of Basel, such a comprehensive victory against the little known Lithuanians was just what the doctor ordered and there was a degree of utter exuberance in the lounge as we all grinned our way through our drinks.

However, even beyond that I felt a degree of inexplicable optimism that went way beyond the game and the result.

"Where is the Final of this competition being held?" I asked.

The assembled group of my sister Anne Marie and her husband Geoff, my cousin Paul and his partner Maureen, second cousin William and I can't remember who else, looked at me askance but eventually came up with the answer between them.

"Seville" someone said.

"Seville?" I repeated. "OK – check the price of airline tickets now because there is every chance that this team will get to the final!"

Of course no one really took my idea too seriously, and I was not absolutely predicting that we would get there, but the feeling of euphoria in the stadium after this performance, the location of the final itself and the quality of the team we had at the time all bode well for substantial progress in UEFA's second tier competition.

Further, with an eye always on travel I took the view that booking some flights now might turn out to be a shrewd investment as when it comes to any European Final the costs of flying were bound to go up once the teams playing were known.

When I went home that night, I looked at the other results in the round and looking through the remaining teams I honestly felt that there was no-one that this Celtic team need fear. Of course, there would be Champions League teams dropping in, but in truth we had a team that was the match of anyone who fell out of the Champions League after the group stage.

It is amazing to think that in 2003 Scotland had four teams all playing in that 1st round proper of the UEFA Cup. As well as ourselves, Rangers would take on Viktoria Žižkov of the Czech Republic and eventually lose on away goals. Aberdeen were held to a no scoring draw by Hertha Berlin at Pittodrie and were unfortunate to lose by a single goal in Berlin, and amazingly Livingstone went out at the first round stage by the amazing aggregate score of 8-6 in favour of Strum Graz of Austria.

My notion of Celtic going to Seville was no way dented when we were drawn against Blackburn Rovers in the next round. The spice of being matched against a team managed by Graham Souness was huge, and Blackburn were going really well in the English Premier League lying in sixth position with an array of experienced European players in Damien Duff, Andy Cole, Dwight York, Brad Freidal, David Thompson and the ex

Rangers player Tuguy.

However, it should be remembered that the Celtic team of 2003 were no mean players themselves and in that season the wage bill for the club would match that of Bayern Munich. We had big players, and big time players and I thought we could progress against a normally middle of the road EPL team.

I wasn't able to attend the first leg at Celtic Park as I was in London on business and my plane arrived back in Glasgow too late to get me to the kick off in time. So, I listened to the commentary on the radio for some reason preferring BBC 5 Live to Radio Scotland, and had to endure Alan Green repeatedly telling me that my team were being well and truly outplayed by the English outfit. Somehow I don't think that we're Alan's favourites.

Big Rab Douglas in goal made some great saves that night—and many of the Celtic team will tell you that the form of Douglas in that season was a key factor in them getting to Seville.

I was listening to the radio when Henrik scored a messy goal with only 5 minutes to go. The noise through the speakers was deafening and my own shouts were enough to get me arrested in the car. Then came the final whistle, the men against boys comment from the Blackburn camp, and the commentators unmistakeable belief that Celtic would get pumped at Ewood Park!

If I remember correctly, Mark Lawrenson described Celtic as awful and at times embarrassing in comparison to Blackburn.

Two weeks later, I was in London again when Celtic travelled south for the second leg. This time my plane would not touch down until just about full time and I will be honest and say that as I sat in the departure lounge at London City Airport I did not want to know what the score was. I wanted to avoid the game completely and only find out what had happened once I was back in the security blanket of Glasgow.

Accordingly when the plane touched down I consciously avoided putting my phone back on, walked down the steps of the aircraft, through the terminal building and straight out to my car. I threw my briefcase in the back seat, put my key in the ignition, and braced myself in the knowledge that as soon as I turned the key the radio would come on and whatever had happened in Blackburn could no longer be avoided. I knew that the game had finished and that I would not be facing commentary but more likely post-match interviews.

When the radio did come on I immediately heard the tones of a rather angry sounding Henrik Larsson, speaking in that gravelly voice of his, saying that people should have more respect and they should not speak until the tie was over. Souness had been dismissive of Celtic after the first leg and had said that he was not impressed by a single Celtic player – so—did this mean that Celtic had won? I wasn't sure.

Then the interviewer said something like "…and when Chris Sutton scored the second did you know the tie was over?" - I didn't wait for Henrik's answer. I was too busy sitting in the car singing Hail Hail the Celts are here at the top of my voice and speeding for the exit so I could get home to the highlights and the pub!

Seville was still on and the arrogant Souness had been put to the Celtic sword! Oh how sweet. Even in 2013, in the course of an interview with the Lancashire Telegraph reflecting on the end of his time at Blackburn, Souness couldn't bring himself to admit that his Blackburn side had been out-fought and out-thought in the second leg. Or that they just did not cope with Sutton dropping to midfield at the expense of Paul Lambert, and their defence having to cope with Larsson and Hartson at their peak.

Revealing the same dismissive tone that Martin O'Neill had used to fire up the Celtic players before taking the field at Ewood Park, Souness commented "We should have won the first leg at their place in front of 60,000 people. Unfortunately the little Swedish lad, Henrik Larsson, got a goal early on at Ewood and then the momentum was with them."

It was funny how often the "little Swedish lad" would grab a goal and switch the momentum of a game, yet to this day Souness makes it sound like a fluke!

I was at Celtic Park on the 28th November to see Celtic take on a Celta Vigo side which included, Alexander Mostovoy, the Brazilian Henrique Guedes da Silva Catanha; who had an excellent scoring record of more than one every two games; Silvinho who had until recently played for Arsenal, and Gustavo Lopez. On the bench they had the ever dangerous Benni McCarthy and Edu. For their part, Celtic once again deployed Larsson, Sutton and Hartson in the one team and Stan Petrov had to play with a phantom of the Opera style mask following a cheek injury sustained against Livingstone the week before. The first half was open but goalless and the little Swedish lad popped up to score the only goal of the game in the 52nd minute when he headed home a Steve Guppy cross which had been knocked on by Bobo Balde.

Vigo had proven to be awkward opponents. They were well organised, had not given much away and most of all they had shown that they were prepared to attack at pace, even at Celtic Park.

The chat in the lounges after was all about how tough any Spanish opposition was at this level and there was a fair degree of doubt about whether or not we would remain in Europe after Christmas. Yes we had beaten a top class Spanish side at home, but would it be enough to see us through to the next round? Spain was a tough place to go and get a result—would we go and defend or would we try and sneak another goal?

There was no talk whatsoever about going to Seville.

For the second leg, I was at home firmly parked in front of the TV hoping beyond hope that we could defeat the men from Galicia. This time the tricky McCarthy would be on from the start and he was to be partnered by the skilful Jesuli who, by coincidence, was a native of Seville.

After the first leg, the Celta manager had been none too complimentary about the Celtic side and as the Spaniards were giving a serious challenge at the top of their domestic league there was no doubt that this was going to be a tough tie. It was made ever harder half way through the first half when a Jesuli shot was deflected passed an otherwise excellent Rab Douglas by Ulrik Laursen.

We were now all square. It wasn't looking good.

I had gone out of the room for a minute when I heard my young son suddenly shout "GOAL!" and so I had to dash back into the living room to see a long-flighted ball being knocked down by Chris Sutton to Big Bad John who absolutely brushed his marker aside to smack the ball low into the net. The Spanish now needed to score twice!

That became once on the 53rd minute when McCarthy enhanced his striker's reputation by putting Vigo in front – but by a mixture of skill, luck and the prayers being said on my couch, and your couch, Celtic survived and progressed on the away goals rule.

However, the tie against Celta Vigo was to have another significance. Some fans who had travelled to Galicia complained that they had been badly treated by the Spanish police. There were allegations that the Police had drawn their batons and had set about the Celtic fans for no reason. Further, a flight returning to Glasgow had to be diverted to Cardiff as a result of some on board disagreements between Celtic fans and airline staff which is discussed elsewhere in this book by Bhoys who were on that flight. Celtic football club announced an enquiry into what had happened in Vigo and on the journey home, but all the signs were that Spain may well not be a country that the Celtic fans would enjoy visiting again in the near future.

After Christmas, Celtic would face the formidable German side VfB Stuttgart or to give them their full name Verein für Bewegungsspiele Stuttgart 1893 E. V who played their home games at the Gottlieb-Daimler-Stadion although it has since been renamed the Mecedes Benz Arena.

Now, we were getting into serious European territory in terms of pedigree and quality. Where Celta Vigo had conquered the rather unknown Viking of Norway before meeting Celtic, Stuttgart had dispatched teams of the quality and reputation of Club Brugge and Ferencváros to earn the right to face Celtic. The German side boasted players who would go on to become household names throughout Europe - Alexander Hleb would later join Arsenal for £15 Million, Kevin Kurányi was a top marksman at International level with a prolific goal scoring record throughout his career, Krasimir

Balakov would play 236 times for Stuttgart and was the key component in a midfield described by the locals as the magic triangle - and they had a solid fullback in Andreas Hinkel.

At Celtic Park, the match was presided over by the iconic Per Luigi Collina and the atmosphere fair bristled as the teams took to the field.

Celtic had to play without the talismanic Larsson who had suffered a double fracture of the jaw, and instead Martin O'Neill chose to call on the services of the diminutive but clever Shaun Maloney.

When Kurányi headed home a Balakov cross on the 27th minute the buzzing Celtic crowd were silenced as it looked as if their team was in trouble. Most had thought that it was essential not to concede an away goal and so being one down did not bode well.

However, once again the mood in the lounges at full time was buoyant, as not only had Celtic equalised but had gone on to win by two clear goals and ran out 3-1 winners with goals from Lambert, Maloney and Petrov.

Larsson was still missing for the return leg, but John Hartson returned having been suspended from the first leg.

I was at home for the second leg but had stupidly agreed to go and visit a friend who needed some help with something on the night of the game. The lady concerned had a son who had severe autism problems and she had asked me to come and give her some help and advice about his care—and of course I had agreed on the date without realising its significance in footballing terms.

However, I would be able to watch the first fifteen minutes of the game before walking from my house to the pre-arranged meeting at my friend's house. Accordingly before I left the house I had seen Celtic go two up with goals from Thompson and Sutton, and as I walked up the road I was cock a hoop that we were winning 5-1 on aggregate—surely we would not concede 5 goals while I was out?

During the meeting I was as helpful as I could and as the lady concerned knew I was a Celtic fan, she asked me if I wanted to turn the television on so that the match could be on in the background. I declined this offer until we had more or less concluded our business. When I saw that the score was now two each I knew I could not sit in someone else's house and watch this game—if Stuttgart scored again I would have started to eat the furniture whilst if Celtic scored again absolutely anything was possible!

Accordingly with ten minutes to go, I took my leave and headed for home knowing that by the time I got in the door it would be all over. I was greeted with the news that the final score had been 3-2 to Felix Magath's men but the score on the night really didn't matter – yet again Celtic were through— and yes Seville was still on!

I had been keeping an eye on the plane fares to Seville around the date of the final and had even been looking at hotels and the likes to see what was on offer.

Not only that, I had been careful to make sure that as each away leg approached I was applying for away tickets at every stage as some of the members of my group (although not me personally) were going to the away games. I wanted to make sure that if we did achieve the unthinkable and made it to Seville I had a real chance of getting my hands on match tickets.

Now all the pub talk was about who was next up for Celtic and that just one more win made Seville a real possibility. The speculation increased once everyone started to look at who was left in the competition which had now reached the Quarter Final stage.

The other seven clubs left were: Porto, Liverpool, Boavista, Panathanaikos, Lazio, Besitkas and Malaga.

Whilst there was some good European pedigree there, there were teams that you would definitely fancy your chances against among that lot—after all Blackburn, Stuttgart and Celta Vigo were no mugs and from possibly the best three leagues in Europe so if you can beat them, then surely some of these clubs must be ripe for the taking?

Among the group that were left the big three to perhaps avoid were

Liverpool, Porto and possibly Lazio with the rest being looked upon as lesser threats.

In the end, Celtic would face Liverpool in a tie that would bring with it all the history and baggage that the press could force on the footballing public.

It was the second "Battle of Britain" of the year.

Souness was once again rolled out for his expert assessment of his old club's chances against the team that had comprehensively knocked his Blackburn side out of the competition (Souness, Souness what's the score?) – sounding a little bitter, not surprisingly he ventured the opinion that Liverpool would be far too strong for Celtic.

History was revisited with everything from Bobby Lennox's incorrectly chopped off goal from 1964 to Liverpool's first match after the Hillsborough disaster and the link between the two clubs at that time being examined in great detail.

The last big game between the two clubs had seen Celtic draw with the "Spice Boys" Liverpool team that contained the likes of Owen, Fowler, Ince and McManaman. We had come from behind that night with goals from Jackie McNamara and a confidently taken penalty that Simon Donnelly dispatched into the top left hand corner of the Liverpool net. Liverpool only equalised in the dying moments after a long mazy run by McManaman who older and wiser Celtic players would have stopped—legally or otherwise --- before he had left his own half and gotten anywhere near the Celtic goal.

It had been a great night at Celtic Park, made all the more moving by parents and representatives of the families caught up in the Dunblane tragedy taking to the field at half time to thank the Celtic support for the many thousands of pounds they had raised for the relief fund. You'll Never Walk Alone was never so heartfelt and poignant.

However all that was in the past and now we had a similar but different Liverpool team to face—and to my mind we had an altogether different Celtic team.

Of the clubs left in the competition, Liverpool clearly had the greatest European pedigree but they were far from unbeatable. If this was the best that there was left in the competition then I really believed that we were absolutely bound for Seville.

With players like Dudek, Carragher, Hypia, Gerrard, Riise, Hamann, Owen and Heskey Liverpool were what one would term as a "right good side" and had finished as runners –up to Arsenal in the EPL a couple of years before. Their manager, Gerard Houllier, knew all about European competition and was well liked and respected—there was no chance of Houllier making the same public gaffs as the arrogant Souness.

In the previous rounds, Liverpool had beaten both Vitesse and Auxerre home and away however this Liverpool team were not invincible and Celtic had faced and beaten tougher teams before this. When I was asked by my work colleagues in London how I thought we would fare against the Scousers I said confidently that we would win.

Liverpool had dropped into this competition when they were beaten to second spot in the group stages of the Champions League by Basel who had knocked Celtic out in the qualifiers. Basel were a good side, and Hakin Yakin cited the game against Liverpool at Anfield in that year's Champions League Group stages as the greatest of his career. However, Celtic had not played well against the Swiss and several months later looked a far more accomplished side. Whatsmore, this Celtic side had a few old heads in it and I could not see them allowing someone from the opposition to wander through them like Steve McManaman had done years before. No—this Celtic side would use all their guile and craft to prevent anyone travelling that far with the ball.

Besides, if the fans were beginning to dream of Seville, then the players could surely taste it if they got past Liverpool.

For me, personally, however the Liverpool games saw the start of some of the most bizarre and inexplicable decisions that I have ever made in my life. I was quite happy to take in the occasion at Celtic Park on 13th March. The atmosphere before the game was absolutely sensational with both sets of fans singing like a chorus from heaven, and I was out of my seat jumping with joy when Henrik put us in front early on with a Shuggy Edvaldson type knee in from three yards.

However, Liverpool equalised through Emile Heskey and of course that most curious of individuals El-Hadji Diouf did his best to ruin the occasion when he spat at completely innocent Celtic fans seated at the front of the South stand.

The big question in the lounges below the North Stand was could we score without reply at Anfield?

The away goal dampened some of the enthusiasm for planning any Seville trip although there were many who opined that we were far from out. The BBC described the events at Celtic Park as being on a knife-edge with Emile Heskey's goal just edging Liverpool in front. What was clear from listening to the car radio on the way home was that it was now accepted by the doyennes of BBC Radio 5 Live that this Celtic team were a good side and had played far better than in the home tie against Blackburn – but they all took the view that Liverpool at Anfield would be too strong.

Personally, I faced a different problem.

My line of work at the time called for regular trips to London as I was working as a solicitor / legal consultant to a London restaurant chain and I was due to attend one of the regular meetings on or about the night of the away leg in Liverpool. No-one in London would insist that I spend the day in the office instead of going to Anfield and all of them, to a man, were now supporting Celtic especially as I had a habit of bringing them down Celtic scarves, T- shirts, DVDs and the like.

However, by this time I had developed a rather strange phobia or superstition. For one reason or another, I had been unable to attend or watch any of the second legs in this competition, and the only one I had sat down to watch was the match against Celta Vigo – and when I went out of the room for a moment in the middle of that game we had scored! Beyond that, I had not been present at, seen, or been available for any of the second legs.

I have never avoided walking under ladders, or thrown salt over my shoulder, or sat with fingers crossed but for whatever reason I now felt compelled to miss Liverpool altogether because I had suddenly become superstitious!

Accordingly, I arranged my meeting for the day of the game and travelled down to London that morning. All the chat was about whether Celtic could win and everyone presumed that I would be heading off back up the road by mid-afternoon to watch the match – some were surprised that I was there at all. That surprise became even greater when I revealed that I had actually obtained tickets for Anfield and that my pals were away to the game without me. Eventually when I informed them that my return flight was sometime after 8 pm I can assure you that there was a degree of complete and utter bewilderment.

That is how it came to be that I was at Heathrow when Celtic kicked off against Liverpool at Anfield. I took some quite extreme steps to avoid any of the lounges that had a TV on where there could be even a report of the match in progress, so by the time I boarded a delayed flight I had no idea what the score was.

Just as in the case of the Blackburn game, I arrived at Glasgow, did not switch my phone on and headed straight for my car. Once again I put the keys in the ignition, turned, and allowed the radio to burst into life only to find the absolutely screaming tones of a commentator (to this day I cannot remember who) describing Big Bad John's screamer to make it two nothing!

I couldn't believe it!

I turned my phone on and found that it was going into meltdown with calls and messages most of which said only one word—SEVILLE!--- over and over again!

I had already told my office that if we got past Liverpool then Seville was on and that travel arrangements would have to be made because at the semi-final stage you have to gamble – you have to take a punt and roll the green and white dice.

I already knew that Seville itself did not have the biggest allocation of hotel beds and I felt that if Celtic got there the place would be crowded out no matter who the opponents were. Accordingly, I said that if we defeated Liverpool there would have to be some serious research done and some arrangements made because you dare not leave it to the period between the semi-final and the final.

As I sat there in the car taking in that Liverpool had been outplayed by a brilliantly organised and disciplined Celtic side (those old heads kicking in), I read and heard numerous messages from all sorts of people saying "Ok count me in for Seville – no matter what the arrangements!"

Now we had some momentum for the mad notion of going to Andalucía and suddenly the curiosity of looking at flight schedules and accommodation took on a whole new meaning and seriousness.

Of course, it wasn't only my staff and my pals who were now on the Seville bandwagon, everyone was and all the chat in my local pub and other places was about just where you might be staying and how you would get there—and we hadn't even qualified yet!

BRTH

CHAPTER 6
JUST AFTER EASTER WE BEAT BOAVISTA

Of course before getting to the final Celtic had to face one further hurdle—and that hurdle came in the form of Portuguese side Boavista who had rather surprisingly defeated Malaga in their quarter-final after a penalty shoot out.

In the other half of the draw the big guns of Porto and Lazio were paired together and so Celtic knew that should they overcome the less famous Portuguese side then they would face a big European name in the final.

Nobody knew too much about Boavista – including where they played!

Suddenly, it dawned on a few folk that there could be an all Porto final with the more fancied Porto playing their near neighbours Boavista in Seville – and while that would be a good Portuguese and European story it was not one that was in the Celtic script.

Surely, after defeating the likes of Celta Vigo, Stuttgart and Liverpool Celtic were not going to fall to this little heard of Portuguese outfit?

Yet, Boavista had gotten this far, and a little research showed that they were the most successful Portuguese team outside the big 3 of Benfica, Sporting Lisbon and Porto—so they would be no pushovers.

However, most of the Celtic fans were expectant by the time the first leg of the semi-final was played at Celtic Park on the 10th April. Despite the fact that there was a full month between the second leg of the semi-final and the final itself, many fans were ready to commit to the trip to Seville before the game, and even more like myself were prepared to press the travel button immediately on full time provided Celtic delivered the right result at home.

In my house, a win by two clear goals meant that you gambled and stuck your money where your heart was. Two clear goals took you to Seville with the expectation that Celtic would make it through the second leg with the lead intact.

One clear goal was less of a certainty – I swithered and swayed at what I would do at one nil to the good guys – essentially I would wait and see.

As for any other result? Well that was just never considered!

As I sat in the North Stand that night I kicked and headed every ball along with my fellow Celtic fans.

It was a strange match. Boavista were nowhere near as good as many of the teams that had visited Paradise that season—including some of the Scottish ones. The first half passed without a goal and was as infuriating a 45 minutes of football as you will ever see with Celtic not really being that good and Boavista being worse. At half time in the lounges downstairs we consoled ourselves with the fact that we had not conceded a goal and that surely we would get a breakthrough in the second half? Besides, we trusted in blessed Martin to sort things out!

Four minutes of the second half passed and whether it was nerves, fate or whatever, the "auld heids" of this Celtic team could not break them down and when Joos Valgaeren deflected a sort of nothing ball into his own net I could scarcely believe that this mediocre bunch were in front!

I remember sitting with my hands under my thighs in my seat because I was in danger of smacking everyone around me with my involuntarily flailing arms which seemed to have developed a life of their own and had taken up good old fashioned semaphore with every move of the ball.

Then the King of Kings drew us level within a minute! That was more like it! That was my Celtic! Now we would go at them!

And go at them we did but to no great avail until we won a penalty. Up steps the King again. Put a team behind after they have had a lead and their heads will drop—consequently those who have come from behind will run quicker and jump higher especially when there is a final at the end of the rainbow. Score now and the odds of a third were good.

This was it – here we go – get in there—BUT HENRIK MISSED!

Of all the times to miss a penalty! Of all the players to miss a penalty!

The crowd were as edgy as hell. Neil Lennon got pelters for a long back pass to Robert Douglas in goal. Martin O'Neill rounded on the crowd behind the dugout for getting on to Lennon and had to be sort of carried away by John Robertson.

None of this was good for the heart—or any other part of the anatomy!

Suddenly full time was upon us and the match ended in a draw—Boavista were leading on away goals! We had to go there and win – bloody Hell - what did you do about Seville now?

In the lounges we quickly discovered that Porto had beaten Lazio 4-1 in the first leg of the other semi-final, and so barring a miracle from the Italians, one Portuguese team was definitely in the final. I remember thinking that is not a good result for us—that will only inspire this Boavista mob to get over the line at home.

We were still in with a chance—a good chance - but the Seville travel plans were put on hold. Instead, applications were made for tickets for the second leg and as usual our group got some with the result that my sister Anne Marie and her husband Geoff decided they were going to the second leg—just in case we never got to Seville.

Back in my office, all we could talk about was the what ifs and possibilities, but in the interim business and life had to go on and towards the end of the month I had to go to my monthly meeting in London.

Without any hesitation, I made sure that that meeting would take place on the day of the return leg and I once again made sure that my return flight to Glasgow would be in the air while the game was going on. I was now as superstitious as hell.

I know fine well that a competent manager in charge of a team of highly trained, highly professional and experienced footballers is what can win a game, and that there is no recorded instance of an idiotic football fan winning or influencing any type of match from 33,000 feet up in the sky, but every single second leg had gone our way when I had been "elsewhere" or just plain unable to watch or listen – and there was no way on this earth that anyone was going to change my routine.

With my wee sister and some other friends in Portugal for the second leg, I headed for London and my meeting. In the interim, I was still planning routes to Seville – package holidays, flights only, two-day trips, out of the way accommodation—anything you could think of.

That day in London was of no significance at all and as usual I was asked if we could win in Porto? Surely this team would come out and attack and give us a bit of room? Surely we could not be as ineffective as we had been at home?

Thank God I never had to watch that match—either in person or on a television. I would have been a basket case.

Instead, I adopted the usual routine from Heathrow and if I remember correctly I flew home with British Midland. I had made sure that I had turned my phone off when I entered the aircraft, and throughout the flight I chewed every finger, crossed and uncrossed my legs, drank several coffees and generally fidgeted something awful. Had there been a criminal profiler on board who was studying me I am sure that they would have reached the conclusion that I was a suicide bomber!

Eventually the Captain announced to the crew that we were 10 minutes from landing!

God I felt sick! Ten Minutes away from finding out. Ten minutes of being strapped into a seat as the aircraft banked and swerved in the wind above the Campsies and then over Clydebank. Ten minutes that seemed like an eternity. I knew I couldn't adopt the usual routine of leaving the phone off until I got to the car – that would have killed me! Also I wondered how many others on this flight were in the same state of flux as me waiting on finding out the result? I looked around and everyone else seemed pretty normal. They were tired after a long day, but no one seemed to look the way I felt which was as if I had swallowed a washing machine which was now in full spin cycle inside my stomach.

Then the wheels bumped down and the reverse thrusters came on slowing the plane down as it sped down the runway. The Captain's voice came over the tannoy "Welcome to Glasgow ladies and gentleman, where the local time is…" – who cares about the time—what was the score? Are you going to give us the score ya glorified bus driver?

No he wasn't going to give us the score but he did give us the temperature and told us it was raining slightly—I could see that it was raining slightly—the man was clearly an idiot!

I had decided that before the plane had reached a stop I was going to switch my phone on. I had also decided that I did not need to receive any phone call or receive any text message to know the score. I knew that if we had not made it the phone would remain silent – I also knew that if the phone burst into life then that meant we were through.

We were still moving when I pressed the power button on the phone and the light came on. It took a couple of seconds for the device to find a signal and then another couple of seconds for all the bars and usual stuff to come on. I was staring at that phone so hard—I had it up to my nose and was damn nearly climbing inside it.

And then it beeped – and I just looked at it. I was slightly uncertain – I could almost not dare to open the message and then it beeped again— and then again – and again. Suddenly all over the plane other people's phones were getting messages. I couldn't see their faces I was still in my seat. I was sure the woman next to me was convinced I was some kind of certifiable head-case.

Eventually, taking a deep breath, I opened the first message. Until then I still wasn't absolutely sure if we had won – I thought we had—but I wasn't sure.

The message was from a friend of mine and it didn't mention the match directly at all.

All it said was:

YOU HAD BETTER BOOK A VILLA--- WE ARE GOING TO SEVILLE!

BRTH

CHAPTER 7
TEARS FOR SEVILLE

I never got to the other messages until I got into my car as the reaction to this one messages was instantaneous and involuntary.

TEARS!

Smiles and tears all at once – we were going to Seville. MY Celtic, OUR Celtic, we were in a European Final and my first thought was that it was going to be one hell of a party—a HUGE Celtic party.

I had been looking at all sorts of ways to get to the Andalusian capital in the event of us progressing and knew that as soon as the final whistle went all the flights through carriers like Ryanair and Easyjet would be gone and so there had to be another method of sorting out the travel arrangements.

Fortunately, while I was driving home from the airport others were already on the job and had been from the moment the final whistle had blown. One of my pals called and said that his wife had been on tele-text and had found a package deal flying from Gatwick to Faro in the Algarve with a full week's worth of accommodation in an apartment complex complete with pool and everything else you could want plus a hire car – and all for under £250! It was booked in seconds – and five of us were now officially on our way to Seville - all we had to do was get to Gatwick.

As for staying in Seville itself, over the next few days that was sorted too.

My sister and her husband plus some others all booked onto a 3 day package staying in a hotel on the outskirts of the town which meant we now had a number of rooms in the city and if necessary we would just bunk up in the hotel en masse on the night of the game – in essence we were sorted just as soon after the final whistle as possible.

That was the route, Glasgow- Gatwick, Gatwick –Faro, and finally Faro to Seville. A week's holiday with the Cup Final in the middle – I sported a smile that would have put the Cheshire cat to shame!

Little did I know it then, but the fates would conspire to ensure that my smile was completely misplaced – I would never make it to Gatwick and would look on helplessly and in despair while everyone else flew off on this most anticipated of journeys.

In the 27 days between the victory against Boavista and the final itself, it seemed to me as if the entire world was asking the one question - Are you going to Seville?

Whether I met people in person, spoke to them on the phone or opened up an e-mail, everyone seemed to want to know if I was headed for Seville and just as quickly they would tell me if they were or if they weren't. Initially, some said they were not sure if they would go or not, with many saying that they would wait and see if they could get tickets for the match.

However, within a week there was a complete sea change on that particular issue and more and more people were saying that they were going tickets or no tickets! What had started out as the notion of going to see Celtic in a European Final rapidly turned into something else entirely—as it soon became evident that the majority of Celtic supporters going to Spain would never get into the ground at all. In essence the people travelling were not so much going to support Celtic and instead were going to BE Celtic.

Further, the trip to Seville would see a football support the likes of which had never been seen before. Not just in numbers but also in how that support was made up and where it came from.

Whereas Lisbon had been a first in terms of sheer numbers and people movement, it was a predominantly male only trip. By the time Celtic went to Seville in 2003 the world had spun on its axis and whilst there would certainly be more men than women, a huge number of female fans travelled to Spain sporting the hoops.

Not only that, the age demographic of the travelling fans spanned all generations. Many fans went with fathers or mothers or in whole family groups. Many, like me, booked a full package holiday, which meant that three generations of the one family were in attendance in or around Seville on the day of the game. Grandparents, parents and children were all to be seen on the Spanish Costas in the week leading up to the match – the Celtic invasion of Spain in particular was to be absolutely massive with all ages, generations, lifestyles and both sexes represented in huge numbers.

In addition, the mass movement of the fans brought together people from completely differing backgrounds.

Football – and Celtic football club in particular—was once the stronghold of the working class or the manual labourer. However, in Seville the only thing that mattered was whether you were wearing Green and White – not what job you did, what kind of house you lived in or anything like that.

Again, in contrast to Lisbon, Seville would see High Court Judges, Sheriffs, International Company Directors, International entertainers and celebrities, Doctors, Surgeons, University Professors and lecturers, Accountants and Surveyors and every type of professional class all descend on the Spanish mainland wearing the green and white hoops and carrying a beer to quench their thirst in the oppressive heat.

In every single way, the supporters of Celtic football club in Seville crossed every social and cultural divide. If ever there was a support that was truly "all inclusive" then this was it.

Further, they came from every corner of the world and by every means possible. Celtic Supporters Clubs from all around the globe got themselves organised and made their plans to get to Spain.

Fans came from the United States, Australia, Bermuda and the Caribbean,

Canada, throughout mainland Europe, Iceland, Scandinavia, Asia, Africa, South America and just about anywhere else you could think of. Those that never made it – like the Celtic supporters from New Zealand, made their own arrangements to watch the Final and Mike Maher writes about their exploits in a later chapter in this book.

Not only that, the final brought a truly unique situation about, with many football fans who supported another club entirely turning up in Seville to support Celtic. Many would have said that Celtic were their second team, others simply went along with a friend who was a Celtic fan. Supporters from Scotland who perhaps supported Dundee United or Aberdeen but who were lucky enough to get tickets donned the Green and White hoops and shouted on the Bhoys with gusto.

500 fans from St Pauli in Germany – a club long associated with Celtic— crossed mainland Europe in Green and White, while all sorts of others just jumped on the bandwagon of this biggest ever Celtic party.

Interestingly, many Celtic fans went with the intention of proclaiming their dual affiliation to Celtic and Scotland – Seville would be awash with hoops and kilts!

However, all of that was in the future.

In the first few days after the semi-finals the talk was all about travel arrangements and ticket for the match. As the lack of a match ticket diminished in importance in determining whether someone would travel or not, so the party atmosphere just grew and grew and gathered a momentum all of its own.

Throughout the European campaign, Celtic fans increasingly found their identity with the result that the singing and chanting about even having the chance of getting to Seville was something to celebrate.

On Sunday 27th April, the weekend after Celtic secured their passage to Seville, the European euphoria reached new heights when Celtic were the visitors at Ibrox. What became known as "Beachball Sunday" saw the Celtic support rubbing our European success into their blue noses.

The Celtic fans turned up en masse at Ibrox with the intention of out singing, out supporting and out mickey-taking their Glasgow rivals – and they did such a good job of it that they only succeeded in cranking up the Seville mood to unprecedented levels.

For a start the sight of thousands of Celtic supporters turning up at Ibrox in sombreros was just astonishing. Their constant chanting that the Rangers fans would be "watching the Bill, while we're in Seville" was enough to make the Celtic hordes smile from ear to ear. However, it was the hundreds of beach balls which flew on to the pitch that brought the biggest TV coverage. National television picked up on the party atmosphere showing the Ibrox pitch festooned with multi-coloured inflatable beach balls. Referee Kenny Clark was shown asking the Police and the Ibrox backroom staff for help in clearing the goal mouth area in front of the Celtic fans which looked like a beach ball showroom. Various policemen, ball boys and stewards set about getting rid of the offending spheres by bursting them with pen knives whilst the Celtic fans sang louder and louder. No sooner had the beach balls been burst and removed, when another lot suddenly flew onto the pitch making the whole scene even more hilarious.

Later, Rangers Captain Barry Ferguson would say that he was sure that he could see his father in law in the stands and amongst those who were littering the park with the offending inflatables.

However, it was not just the beach balls, the singing and the sombreros that were captured on television. One enterprising Celtic fan had presumably relieved his local chemist of a 5ft high Ambre Solaire bottle to waive at the Rangers fans. Clearly "Sevillitis" had taken hold of the green and white population. Not only that, but the mood got even better when Celtic came away as 2-1 victors.

As a result of the mass coverage of Beach Ball Sunday, the enquiries about going to Seville for the final soared. It became clear that there would be literally thousands of Celtic fans travelling – and all consideration of the opposition in Seville was virtually abandoned. Sure Porto and their fans would be there--- but who cared about them? This was about Celtic.

However, while most of us were scurrying about making arrangements to get to Seville, some were resigned to the fact that they just would not be going at all – even though they were desperate to make the trip.

One such person was Marie Clark. Marie was desperate to go to Seville but knew she would just have to sit and watch the whole thing on television at home. Marie herself could have gotten to Seville but she would have had to have travelled with her daughter Clare who was at school at the time and there was no way that she was taking Clare out of school during term time. Eventually, Clare would leave school without ever having missed a day of primary or secondary education – her attendance rate was 100% perfect and the trip to Seville would have ruined that. However, another factor was that Marie did not want to risk running the wrath of Clare's Grandfather John – though he would surely be otherwise engaged in the Celtic dugout?

As we shall see, various others didn't get to Seville despite the best laid plans of mice and men.

One such tale belongs to a fellow Glasgow businessman, who like me, had more or less made his travel arrangements not long after the final whistle of the second leg against Boavista. For him, the weeks in between the Semi-Final and the Final were to be an emotional roller coaster—which I suspect he has not recovered from to this day!

Here he describes how he came to miss the final and he's remaining anonymous to save the guy who let him down from embarrassment. Let bygones be bygones and all that…

"A few weeks before the big day I received a call from a mate who owns a big house in Spain. The conversation went along the lines of - are we going? The answer was obvious, so plans were set out – fly over on the Sunday before the game, play some golf, drive to Seville on the morning of the game take in the atmosphere, go to the game, he would get a hotel around Seville then drive back the next day. He would take care of the arrangements. Sorted!

In the weeks leading up to the game I was really busy with work commitments – I had spent 3 of the 4 weeks before Seville in the States, mainly bragging to Ex-Pat Celts that I was going to the Final.

When I arrived back in Glasgow airport on the Thursday before the match I was amazed to meet a couple of guys I know decked out in the hoops who were already on their way out to Seville. They invited me to join them and offered me tickets for the game. I thanked them but declined the offer explaining that my mate had booked flights and had tickets for us but that I would call them when I got there. The Excitement was building ever higher.

After I left them, I called my mate from home to find out the details of the travel arrangements. There was no answer but I honestly just though "never mind - he is a busy man and I will get him soon enough."

On the Friday I called again – still no answer and no call back and to be honest I thought this was strange, but let it go.

Later in the day I called again and after a long delay I finally got a ringing tone – not ring ring but the long beep of an international ring. I still wasn't panicking and thought he must be away on business and due back soon. Later on I called again - still no answer.

Finally, on Friday evening contact was made. Phew I was glad to hear him at the end of the line and I asked – OK – what are the arrangements?

There was a pregnant pause and an "Ahem" – "I am here already" was the response.

I was furious—absolutely furious and you can imagine my language - especially having declined a couple of tickets I was not a happy bhoy. My wife and kids did their best to console me but the reality was that I was not going make it to the biggest game of my life - excluding Lisbon when I was 4.

Alternative plans were put in place to make the best of it.

I told my 2 boys that I was not going to Spain and we were going to have a Seville party instead. My youngest was so happy, jumping up and down and I actually felt guilty about not taking in the game with him in the first place. He was 8 at the time, and he was and still is a 100% Celtic fanatic. He has had a season ticket since he was born when the new stadium was being built. I bought him one so that we could all sit together.

Then, out of the blue, on the day before the game I received a call from a very good friend of mine who is a box holder at Porto – and at one time he also had a brief time on the Porto board. He asked me where I was staying and wanted to meet that evening for dinner and to chat about the game. He has been to Glasgow many times to visit his brother-in-law who was Russell Latapy and who played for the dark side, but he always came with me to the Celtic games.

When he found out that I was not going to Seville he could not believe it and immediately offered me a ticket to sit with him in the Porto Directors box and invited me to stay at their team hotel. While he was on the phone I was trying to imagine me in the Hoops mixing with the Porto officials.

Despite his kind and very tempting offer, in the end I declined as I was now committed to watching the game with my two sons.

That day Glasgow was empty – the Kingston Bridge was like a Sunday – where had all the people gone?

In the evening of the game we had a Barbeque, my wife painted the faces of the kids in the street, my eldest had his first beer and we made the most of the evening – even the light rain could not dampen our spirits. The only rule was that there was no burgers for any kids who did not have a green face. So a couple of the local Rangers supporters' kids sold out and took the green face for a burger. Probably causing family riots when they went home.

We watched the game, shouted, sang, and I took a call from a mate who is a Rangers die hard with 20 minutes to go. He started by telling me what happened in "The Bill" that night but really phoned to let me know that we were the only team going to win and it was not Porto, and to go easy on him.

Then it was all over, Bobo was off and the 3rd Porto goal ended it for us. Some of the kids were crying but my youngest was proud to be a Celt and told me that it was great that we watched it together. At that point I knew that not being there was a blessing.

I still bump into my old pal who let me down with the ticket and my youngest, who is now 19, calls him "the Seville guy."

BRTH

CHAPTER 8
EXTRA SPECIAL ARRANGEMENTS FOR SEVILLE

Of course during the weeks leading up to Seville some people had to make extra special arrangements. These were the people who knew instinctively that they would not be allowed any time away from their work place to attend a Celtic match in Spain. Some were not allowed to go because of the sheer nature of their job.

Policemen, teachers, firemen, paramedics, doctors and various others including priests could not necessarily get the appropriate time off, and so following the traditions established in both Lisbon and Milan, special arrangements had to be made in such cases.

Some people prepared for an anticipated absence around the 21st May. For some reason quite a few folk had to attend funerals of the wife's aunt or a godparent or whoever on that date. Strangely enough many of these relatives apparently lived in places like Dorset or somewhere equally far away and so requiring at least one overnight stay.

Of course, towards the end of the month when it was suggested that some of the mourners were in fact in Seville, this was steadfastly denied amid claims that the parties concerned had watched the game in some pub or other. Just as in Lisbon, there are many to this day who swear that they were never there—although they can describe the interior of Flaherty's Bar supposedly from a previous or subsequent visit which no one can remember!

Some other people were very enterprising in finding a convenient "excuse" for being in Seville. In 1967 a considerable number of priests had attended the final and many had flown with my father and mother's travel company. Imagine how surprised my Father was to receive a letter from Archbishop Scanlan after the Lisbon final asking if the priests who had travelled had managed to get to Fatima for the day?

Similarly, there would be a few enterprising Scottish clergy in or around Andalusia on the 21st May. One group of fans travelling up from Malaga stopped their bus to give two priests a lift, with the padres immediately offering a blessing for the coach and its occupants – the prayer started with "Hail Hail the Celts are here!"

However, perhaps the greatest piece of divine inspiration, if not intervention, came in the form of Father Stephen Dunn from Glasgow. It would be fair to say that Father Dunn is a bit of a character and is known to his former fellow school pupils and many more simply by his long held nickname --- Dancer Dunn!

Now lest anyone get the wrong impression, Dancer was so called because of the involuntary gyrations he performed at school whenever he got the belt – a not infrequent occurrence to be fair.

Anyway, for whatever reason, by sheer coincidence, divine providence or extremely clever planning, Father Dunn was booked in to celebrate Mass in the main Cathedral in Seville at precisely twelve noon on the day of the final. Ya Dancer – as someone might have said.

However, if the good Lord was with Stephen Dunn, he was fast deserting this particular sinner!

My flights and accommodation were secured, all my group had finalised their own arrangements and I was confident that we would all have match tickets. As the news coverage of the mass emigration to Seville cranked up I watched in astonishment and admiration as we were treated to the tales of the mad and mental journeys that were being taken by the Celtic faithful.

There were guys who were hitchhiking from Norway or Sweden. The revamped Volkswagen Camper coming from Orkney. The guys who were driving all the way there in the green and white Volkswagen beetle nicknamed Jinky and all the others who seemed to be travelling by plane, train, car, boat, bus, foot or any other available method.

With each report and each madcap tale my anticipation and excitement was increasing.

However there was a blot on the landscape that I could have never foreseen.

In the early weeks of May 2003 I was due to complete a land purchase for one of my clients who just happened to be the son of a former Rangers player. The property concerned was a former hospital site, which was being sold by the NHS with the purchase being funded by a finance house called Pearl Holdings which in turn was funded by Lloyds Bank. Everything was going great in that the rather complex missives with the NHS solicitors had all been signed, the price agreed, the date of entry agreed and all the conditions met—all that was needed now was the money and the whole deal could be done and dusted the week before I was due to go to Seville.

My bag for my weeks holiday was packed, all the air tickets and accommodation vouchers were checked and double checked, and as a result of our group always applying for away tickets for every competition possible, I had secured 12 treasured tickets for the UEFA Cup Final – Not only were we all going to Seville but we were all going to the match!

The Hospital deal was due to complete on the 5th of May and I anticipated on getting that done and more or less easing off on the work front and getting into full Seville party mode.

Except that come the 5th of May there was no sign of the loan money from Pearl Holdings. All the work had been done with the solicitors and so there was no reason for there being any delay but such things happen and I presumed that we would get things sorted the following day. I called the lawyers for the NHS and explained there had been a delay with the bank red tape and we would get things sorted the following day no problem.

The following day, came and went, and even the day after that with still no sign of the money. The Scottish solicitors for Pearl were most helpful and explained that they were all set to go and that the delay was something to do with there being a problem at the company's head office in Manchester. Naturally, I was a bit concerned about this and spent a considerable amount of time running between the Pearl solicitors and the lawyers for the NHS who understandably were getting a bit anxious as they had been due to be paid 3 days before.

We were now at Thursday 8th May and I was due to fly out to Faro with my pals on Saturday the 17th so there was still plenty of time to sort this out. Then on the Friday I was given an explanation for the delay. The solicitors for Pearl in Manchester had fallen out with their bosses or partners and had been suspended, and in turn the solicitors firm concerned had suspended all Pearl transactions pending the resolution of this dispute. The transaction was on hold meantime.

This was now a real problem and I could feel that something was not quite right here! I had a plane to catch to you know where and I immediately foresaw that there was a real chance of me not going to Seville after all.

Accordingly, I was determined that the whole thing would be resolved on Monday 12th May.

As soon as I got to work that morning I started on a mammoth series of phone calls to try and trace down what was going on.

However, as the day progressed things got slowly worse as it became plain that the chain of events at the Pearl Holdings / Lloyds Bank end was so complex that a number of transactions were being delayed at their end…For some reason or other which I could not quite fathom.

SEVILLE
THE CELTIC MOVEMENT

"The Celtic support in Seville was magnificent" - *NEIL LENNON*

CQN BOOKS

SEVILLE – THE CELTIC MOVEMENT

SEVILLE – THE CELTIC MOVEMENT

SEVILLE – THE CELTIC MOVEMENT

L Monaghan

L Monaghan

SEVILLE – THE CELTIC MOVEMENT

SEVILLE – THE CELTIC MOVEMENT

SEVILLE – THE CELTIC MOVEMENT

SEVILLE – THE CELTIC MOVEMENT

SEVILLE – THE CELTIC MOVEMENT

SEVILLE – THE CELTIC MOVEMENT

SEVILLE – THE CELTIC MOVEMENT

SEVILLE – THE CELTIC MOVEMENT

SEVILLE – THE CELTIC MOVEMENT

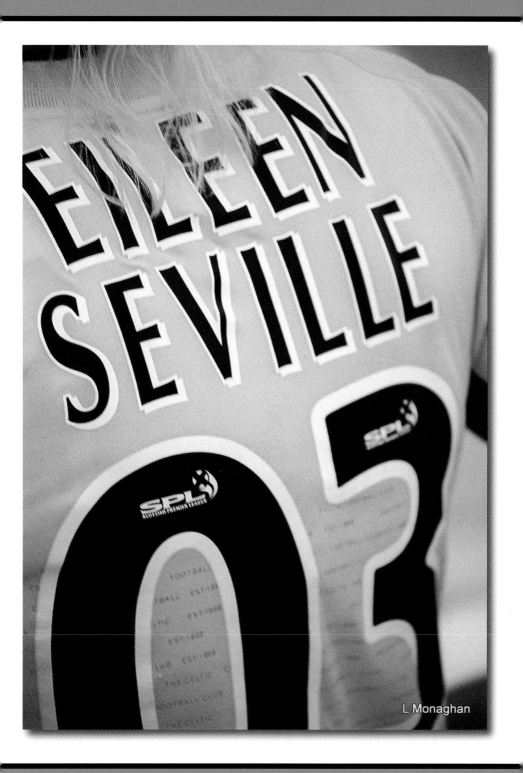

L Monaghan

L Monagha

SEVILLE – THE CELTIC MOVEMENT

L Monaghan

VISIT WWW.CELTICQUICKNEWS.CO.UK

L Monaghan

SEVILLE – THE CELTIC MOVEMENT

The two female solicitors in Glasgow who worked for Pearl were very helpful and extremely apologetic but they were helpless really as the problem lay in Manchester. As it became clear that there was nothing more that I could do to make sure everything fell into place and that going to Seville for me was completely dependent on others I slowly started losing the plot.

Each Monday night I met with some of my pals in the pub, and that night we were making final arrangements for Saturday and were even discussing where to go in Seville and the Algarve and so on.

"Guys, I may have a problem!"

"What do you mean? A problem!"

"There is a situation at work which I have no control over and unless it gets resolved I might not be able to go!"

"Whit?"

"You heard—I might not be able to go!"

This was a cue for various expletives.

I explained the position as best I could but remained positive and said that hopefully things would work out.

However, that conversation in the pub inspired me to take a new tack in trying to deal with the problem the following day. Yet again I started on a series of phone calls to try and break the log jam with everyone in my office - and there were 25 or so of us - all now conscious of the fact that I was having a real problem with this. Worse still, a good few from the office were heading out to Seville themselves including my sister, who was my business partner, so it was not as if I could just leave this for someone else to resolve.

That day I started all my phone calls as professionally as I could but when I received no satisfaction I came clean about my primary motive.

"Look, I am trying to get to Seville for the UEFA Cup Final! I am due to be on a plane on Saturday 17th and unless this is sorted within the next two days I am in dire danger of missing out on the experience of a lifetime" – the fact that this was the third European Final Celtic had played in during my lifetime was lost on most folk as the pleading in my voice became ever more desperate.

By this time, the news cameras were all setting up in Seville itself as the party atmosphere was cranking up ever higher with the result that loads of folk decided just to travel at the last minute with a desperate scramble to find some sort of way of getting there. The newspapers were predicting a big Celtic support with some saying that as many as 50,000 would be there.

I saw it differently—I thought there would be more than that—how many more I wasn't sure but definitely more than 50,000. I was just worried that I would not be among them as that looked increasingly likely.

Late on the Tuesday afternoon, my pleading achieved some sort of result as suddenly I was told that one of the solicitors in Manchester was on the phone for me.

"Hello, this is Mr So and So, I believe you are awaiting a transfer of funds from our clients Pearl Holdings?"

"Yes."

"Well sorry about the delay, but we are trying to sort things at our end and we will be with you just as soon as possible."

"Eh - that's great but I am due to be going to Seville on Saturday and I really need this to happen before then."

"Ah—I take it you are a Celtic fan then?"

"Yes – of course, and I am desperate to be at that match."

"Have you got tickets? The world and their granny seem to be going there!"

"Yes I have tickets. There are twelve of us in total going, but I need you to produce the money or I can't go."

"Right, leave this with me. I know what you are going through, I am a

Manchester United fan and there is no way you want to miss that Final. We will get back to you!"

I was somewhat relieved and started to ring round the clients, the NHS and anyone else involved whilst all the time answering texts from my friends:

"Is it sorted yet?" "Are you coming?"

"No" and "Yes" were the hopeful replies.

In the afternoon my phone went again. This time it was a different solicitor from Manchester.

"Hi, you spoke to my colleague earlier on today about a Pearl Holdings Transaction?" said an unfamiliar male voice.

"Yes " I said hopefully.

" Well, we are hoping to complete this tomorrow now, sorry for the delay."

I could have punched the air with joy.

"Do your Scottish agents know?"

"Yes, we have briefed them, hopefully they will have the money tomorrow – Oh and good luck in Seville!"

"Oh, Thanks – are you a Celtic fan by any chance?"

"Sort of – I am more of a Liverpool fan but Celtic are my Scottish team."

" And your colleague is a Manchester United fan?"

"Yes he is – but no-one is perfect – and we both have a soft spot for Celtic – hope you win!"

…and with that he was gone.

Once again I started on a round of phone calls, first to the client and then to the NHS where I got a bit of a shock when I spoke to the solicitor in charge of the transaction.

"That's good that this will be sorted tomorrow, but you will have to deal with my colleague Graham as I am taking a few days off!"

" Eh excuse me for being nosey, but would you be by any chance going to Seville?"

"Where?"

"Seville! Capital of Andalusia! UEFA Cup Final?"

"Eh—No! I am not!" – and my enquiry was dismissed somewhat abruptly and surprisingly – which to be honest made me wonder.

I came in to the office on Wednesday, full of the joys of spring. We were going to get this bit of business out of the way today and I would be free to relax and mentally attune to my forthcoming trip. The night before the TV had been full of stories about Celtic fans travelling by car to Spain.

Included in that number was my cousin Paul and his partner Maureen who were not keen on flying. They decided to take a prolonged road trip holiday through Europe and of course planned to be in Seville for the Final.

The airports were starting to fill up with fans heading off for the sun.

My first task that morning was to phone the Scottish solicitors to ask them to let me know just as soon as the money arrived. In the course of some friendly chat I discovered that my colleague at the end of the phone was a Rangers fan and that her favourite player at the time was Chris Burke.

The office was increasingly in party mode with at least half the office chat about Celtic and Seville – the other half was about how I was now living a manic lifestyle. Over the past week I had barely slept. I kept waking up in the middle of the night and wondering about this bloody money and if it would come through on time and I was rapidly working myself up into a state of full-blown mania!

Those who were not going to Seville were praying for the money to come through just to get rid of me!

There was no sign of the money by lunchtime and I was by now climbing the walls and more or less gnawing the edge of my desk. Then came the call that I had dreaded. It was the Liverpool fan on the phone from Manchester to say that there had been yet another delay but that they were hopeful that the money would appear tomorrow—Thursday.

I went home that night absolutely frazzled. I was shattered as deep down I knew that there was a problem at the back of all this which I was not being told about and I was powerless to influence other than by keeping everyone at the ready and by begging as if my life depended on it.

Sleep was virtually impossible other than for a couple of snatched hours at a time.

Thursday morning.

The usual round of phone calls started as soon as I got in with everyone I called sounding positive. We were good to go.

Every news bulletin now contained some kind of story about mad Celtic supporters heading to Seville, which didn't help as I started to wear a hole in the office carpet with my constant walking up and down waiting for the money. Our office was in the West End of Glasgow and even a trip out to Byres Road did not relieve the tension as I kept bumping into people I knew and all of them asked the same question:

"Are you going to Seville?"

"Yes I said—leaving on Saturday for a week!" I replied – though each time I answered I could feel and hear my stomach lurch.

About half past two on that Thursday afternoon my phone went again and our receptionist told me that there was a Mr Luqman on the phone:

Shaid Luqman was Mr Pearl Holdings. Within a year he would be named young entrepreneur of the year and would feature on the Sunday Times rich list which told of his £230 Million Pounds worth of personal wealth and how he had his own private jet. Perhaps he too was going to Seville and was offering to meet me for a few drinks—but I didn't think so.

Before I even spoke to Luqman I had a sinking feeling in my stomach. Why would the main man be on the phone to me? Why not have his solicitors call me as before? This was not the kind of thing that normally happened and for professional reasons I was not happy speaking to someone else's client. However, he had called me and I was desperate for good news if he had any.

Instead of good news, Luqman was on the phone to personally convey his apologies for the worst news possible. Not only was the money not coming that day, it would now not be coming until the following week. He explained that in actual fact, the money concerned -- £1 Million—had gone missing.

I was apoplectic at this. Just how could £1 Million disappear or go missing? It all seemed very fishy to me.

He apologised profusely again and assured me that he would do everything he could to personally speed things up – and then he ended the conversation by saying " Oh—and I hope Celtic win in Seville!"

I could have killed him!

By saying that the money would not be through until Monday Luqman had more or less guaranteed that I would not be getting the flight to Gatwick on Saturday.

I was not going to Seville!

I told the staff, I told my family, I told my friends – all of which took hours and all of which was horrible.

Thursday night was awful and I was absolutely beside myself with disappointment.

However, Friday morning saw me more resilient and plan B started to form in my head. Basically, if the money arrived on the Monday I could somehow get out to Seville and meet up with my pals albeit somewhat late.

Accordingly, I set about teeing everything up for the Monday although I was not wholly confident that things would pan out – however you had to try.

First of all I gritted my teeth and called Luqman who took my call at the second attempt. There was no change in the position or the anticipated timescale. There was no chance of the transaction happening today and Monday was it. He even asked me when I was going to Seville and when I said I was due to be going on Saturday there was an awkward pause at the end of the phone when he realised that I could not go with this outstanding.

The so and so never even offered me his jet!

Next on the phone was Pearl's lawyers in Glasgow and the Rangers supporter at the end of the line could not have been more sympathetic or helpful. She would check every hour or so with her clients to see if there was any movement. At the first sign of any good news she would let me know.

Lastly, I placed a call to Graham, the substitute solicitor at the NHS in Edinburgh just to tell him that all the signs were that we could have all of this sorted on Monday—after all his clients had been waiting for payment now for a fortnight or so.

"Eh—Monday is a holiday here!"

"WHAT?"

"Monday – It's a holiday—we're closed!"

"You can't be!" I virtually screamed down the phone.

"Well we are" he replied " But don't worry about it, if you get the money you can just transfer it to us on Tuesday—we will be cool with that" he said in a somewhat laid back fashion.

"You don't understand" I said "I am not concerned about the bloody transaction, I am trying to get to Seville. I am due to be on a plane tomorrow, which I am now having to miss, and I can't go until this is completed. As you know, your office and mine have to sign some documents more or less simultaneously to get this over the line so I need to be here and I want it done ASAP so I can get to Seville – but you are closed on Monday and to be honest Tuesday will be too late!"

There was a stunned silence at the end of the phone for a brief few seconds.

Then, Graham the NHS solicitor revealed that he was a Hibbee and continued on " Ok we can't have that. Are you sure that the money will be here on Monday?"

"That is what I have been told from the horse's mouth!"

"Right—I will come in on Monday just to receive it. Here - take my private number as the switch board will be off. We can't have you missing the Final!"

I swear to God I could have kissed him!

Friday came and went with no change and so on Saturday 17th May I drove my friends to Glasgow Airport with all their bags, handed them their Cup Final tickets and waved them goodbye as they headed off for a week in the sun with the UEFA Cup Final party in the middle.

I was as sick as a parrot. Absolutely gutted. I couldn't eat, couldn't sleep and had absolutely no confidence that this transaction would complete on the Monday.

However you had to have faith and the rest of the weekend was spent trying to avoid the pictures of Celtic supporters on the TV and checking all sorts of different routes to get to Seville just on the off chance that the missing money would come through.

By the time everyone came into the office on the Monday morning, they arrived to the site of me occupying a blank desk on which I had stuck literarily hundreds of yellow post it notes with each one specifying a route to Seville starting that afternoon.

1:15pm Glasgow – Prague. Prague - Seville arrive 8:15pm tonight.

1:50pm Glasgow – Heathrow. Heathrow- Paris. Paris –Seville arrive 8:40pm tonight.

2:00pm Glasgow – Dublin. Dublin – Lisbon. Lisbon -- Seville arrive 9:45pm tonight.

And on it went covering departures for the next 24 hours.

By noon, there was no sign of any movement. I checked in with the Hibbee in Edinburgh who confirmed that he was ready and waiting and calls to the Rangers fan in Glasgow and the Manchester United and Liverpool fans in Manchester confirmed that they were all ready but nothing was happening as yet.

In the interim I was fielding calls from all over. My friends in Portugal were calling for updates to see if I was coming. My cousin on the road trip was texting to see what was happening. My sister and others in the office had cleared their desks and were starting to head to the airports for their flights out—and I could give them no progress.

BRTH

CHAPTER 9
SEVILLE – YOU LUCKY BHOYS!

Others were more fortunate even although the odd stroke of good luck can lead to the most awkward of situations.

One such situation arose when one fan unexpectedly won a last minute trip to the match through the Sunday Mail. He was already going to Seville and so this surprise win allowed someone else to go as well but that proved to have its own complications. The story is taken up by a friend:

"My work mate Owen and I had booked up to go and we were taking his younger brother James who suffers Down Syndrome. We could not wait for the adventure. Then, on the Friday before the match Owen got a call at the office to tell him he had won the Sunday Mail VIP Trip for Two to Seville. He explained to them that he was booked up and could his wife and young son take the VIP trip. The paper explained that this wasn't possible as Owen had won the competition and he had to travel with a relative.

We quickly reached a compromise and arranged that I was to travel with his wife and 6 year old son and Owen and James took the VIP trip.

Everything worked out perfectly. We were staying in Jerez and Owen and James were in Seville. We were bussed up on the morning of the game and arrived at their luxury hotel to the "German" treatment of our towels already being on the sun loungers! It was fantastic in every way but one!

The decidedly tricky bit was that everywhere we went I kept bumping into people who knew my wife and Owen. So the sight of me travelling with Owen's wife and son, and staying with Owen's wife in the hotel drew more than a few questions and odd looks. It started at Prestwick on the way out, when I found out my near neighbours were on the same flight, and continued thereafter!!"

By this time, the full rush was on with thousands now leaving constantly for Seville. The car cavalcades had gone, the ferries to San Sebastien had gone and virtually all of those going by train had gone. That morning's Fred McAuley show on BBC Radio Scotland was co-hosted by Richard Gordon live from Seville and so even travelling in the car you could not escape the constant reporting of the huge party that was beginning to gather in Seville.

Looking back Richard Gordon told me that "Seville was terrific. The sheer number of Celtic fans was extraordinary – they just seemed to come from everywhere and be everywhere. We did one programme from Flaherty's Bar which was very lively but I was astonished when we turned into that square and just saw these thousands and thousands of Celtic fans – happy, smiling Celtic fans—It was really funny and the atmosphere was fantastic. There were a few of us from Radio Scotland and we had an official interpreter who was Mikel Arteta's sister! What she made of it I don't know. The great thing about her being there was that she was actually able to be a proper interpreter—unlike a member of the BBC staff called Dave who had gone out to the final because he could speak Spanish…. Allegedly!

"His attempt at the Spanish language were perhaps not all that fluent and so it was just as well that we had a proper interpreter at our disposal. By the way 10 years on and that guy is still with the BBC and everyone now refers to him as "Spanish Dave" due to his non-fluent Spanish on the Seville trip!"

In the days before the game, many Celtic fans were to be found in and around many other Spanish towns and cities. Thousands had gone to

Madrid and were making their way to Seville by way of the express train, which runs between the two cities. For three days—from the Sunday before the game onwards – that train became more or less the old fashioned "Celtic Special."

One group of fans on that train on the Monday had started their journey with a 14 hour Ferry trip to Aberdeen from where the flew to Heathrow and then onto Madrid where they were walking about the street when they heard the mass cry "C'Mon The Hoops!" and so found that Madrid was awash with Celtic fans.

Other fans were flying into Malaga, Jerez, Gibraltar, Barcelona, Gerona and virtually anywhere else that a commercial jet could land.

Parties were springing up all over the place, which was a surprise to some especially after the incidents following the Celta Vigo game where there had been complaints about the Police being heavy handed.

One fan, Dave McCann who travelled to the game with his son Stuart, described the scene in Torremolinos.

"When we got to Torremolinos there were loads of Celtic fans there and it seemed as if they all marched into the main square at once. Initially there were Police there with guard dogs and helmets and for about half an hour it looked as if the Police were edgy.

However once they saw and appreciated the good humoured mood of all these football fans in Green and White, they muzzled the dogs and posed for photographs with us. Some even began to kick a football around with us. The friendly atmosphere was amazing."

Meanwhile, I was still in Glasgow in an ever more deserted office and still waiting on the magic phone call which would tell me Shaid Luqman and his team had found the missing £1 Million, which would let me head off for Seville.

As the clock reached 1pm I started to tear off the yellow sticky notes I had put out on the desk that morning, with each sticky note that went into the bin representing a flight that had departed without me on board. As the afternoon wore on, the bin got fuller…and fuller…and fuller!

Despite numerous phone calls throughout the afternoon by 3:30pm (the cut off time for chaps bank transfers in those days) I knew that the money was not coming. The number of yellow stickies remaining on the desk could more or less all be pulled off and thrown in the bin. No wired money, meant no travel --- I was not going to Seville!

That evening I took numerous calls from friends who were all in and around the vicinity of Southern Spain. There was nowhere you could escape reports of the massive party that was taking place without me. On the TV and radio there were extended bulletins showing the Celtic fans partying all around Spain. The newspapers were full of pictures and reports. Friends were phoning and describing the atmosphere – even though they were trying to be downbeat when they realised I was not coming. They just could not help themselves in describing the numbers and the atmosphere.

However as the late afternoon turned into evening and then night the number of calls got fewer and fewer. Some people sent me texts saying that they would not call to ask for progress again as it was clear I was stuck, and that to keep asking was akin to torturing me even though the enquiry was well intended. Not unnaturally, when my friends went out into the night to join in the party, the last thing on their mind was to keep calling me back in Glasgow.

That night I put my head on my pillow and simply went to sleep knowing that there was nothing that I could do. My clients were really apologetic and did everything they could to console me and swore that when things did happen they would do what they could to make things up to me. The various other people involved in the transaction all made the right noises, but like me, there was nothing they could do.

The following day I went to the office still harbouring some forlorn hope that a miracle would occur and that this money would come and that somehow or other I would be able to get to the Final. The calls from my pals and my sister had dried up entirely. The desk I had set out with all the possible routes now stood with only a few yellow notes left to go and as the hands swept round the clock fewer and fewer remained. Of course there were loads of charter flights going out the day before the Final and even on the morning of the Final but I had checked and all of these were full and so the chances of getting on one at the last minute were apparently nil.

Accordingly the very last chance to realistically get there was rapidly approaching.

Lunchtime came and went with no movement at all and once again I gazed at the clock knowing that half past three represented one deadline for sure as there would be no bank transfers after then. Not only that, if you hadn't made any travel arrangements by that time then in truth you were going nowhere.

Then, at around 3:05pm the phone went and at the end of it was the Scottish solicitor for Pearl—the one who was a Rangers fan. I had no idea what she was going to say, and what she did say I could have never forseen:

"Hiya, has the money arrived yet?" I asked.

"No—not exactly!"

"Sorry?—What does not exactly mean?"

"Well the money is still missing so to speak, but the guys in Manchester have found some other money – about £440,000!

They are also certain now that they will have the balance tomorrow!"

"OK" I said somewhat stunned.

"We were wondering if £440,000 would be enough to let you do a deal with the health board just now and on that basis you could finalise something and maybe get off to your football match?"

My mind went into over drive as I was certain that some kind of deal could be reached here but it would have to be done quickly.

In the space of the next fifteen minutes I called the Hibs fan at the Health Board, agreed something with him, which I then relayed back to Pearl's solicitors and told them to transfer the money NOW!

At precisely 4:00pm we received a call from the bank to say that the money had arrived and that was my cue to quickly change my clothes, call a taxi and run out of the office. However, before I left I had one very important conversation to have, otherwise I was wasting my time going anywhere and that conversation was with my secretary Sheena.

"Sheena, book me on the first plane to London Heathrow. I am pretty sure there is a British Midland that leaves at 5:10pm. If I run to the airport in a taxi I can just about get there in time to check in. I don't care how much it costs but I have to be in London just as quickly as possible. Once you have booked it call me in the taxi and let me know that it is done so that I definitely know where to go as the airport will be jam packed and it will take forever to get through security and all that stuff so I need to go now!"

And with that I disappeared out the door.

I was going to Seville – or at least I thought I was—pretty sure I was, though I was not absolutely certain.

Just after the taxi cleared the Clyde Tunnel my phone went and it was Sheena who informed me that I was now flying to London with British Midland within the hour – an hour in which I had to check in and clear security, something which I thought would not be easy so I had to rush.

Not only that, this flight would only take me to Heathrow so while I was going through the security at Glasgow airport I asked Sheena to see if there was a flight from Heathrow directly into Seville.

I ran to the British Midland desk and checked myself in. I had a bag to check in—I had been carrying it about for several days in my car and once relieved of the bag I ran up to the departure lounges through a security line that snaked ever so slowly forwards. Something was holding it up and I would only find out what it was once I got near the front of the queue—sombreros!

Damn nearly every second person had a sombrero, which had to go through the security scanner. Many of the offending hats were too big to fit through the machine and so the security staff were bending them in two only for the hats to spring open again. So now they were cello taping up the brims of the hats just to get them through the scanners. It was hilarious—but took up precious time!

Later I heard of other fans who delayed the checking in process for flights for precisely the opposite reason—they had no bags or baggage of any kind, which lead to the check in assistants being slightly suspicious and then just astounded!

"Any bags to check in sir?"

"No"

"Any hand luggage?"

"No!"

"Nothing at all?" Said the assistant worryingly as the man concerned was going to Spain for three days.

The passenger reached into his pocket and produced a solitary item of clothing…

"Just spare hoops!"

I got through security just about in time to run onto my flight, but before boarding I took another call from Sheena who told me there were no flights to Seville from Heathrow.

"OK but there will be a flight to Amsterdam—get me on that! I will explain later" and with that I took my seat and swiftly fell asleep.

Before I did so, however, I noticed that the flight was half full of fans in full Celtic outfits (complete with sombreros) heading for Seville via Heathrow. Many of the sombreros wouldn't fit into the overhead baggage compartments or under the seats so all these folk had to sit through the entire flight with these daft hats on their heads while the business types looked on!

Next thing I knew we were landing at Terminal One. Once down the steps of the aircraft and inside the terminal building I switched my phone back on only to find a message from Sheena to say she had booked me on another British Midland flight to Amsterdam leaving at 8:30pm from terminal one. It was due to arrive at 10:30pm local time in Amsterdam.

I collected my bag and just as I did so Sheena called.

"Did you get my message?"

"Yes Amsterdam at half past eight?"

"Go to the ticket desk at International Departures and collect the ticket from there, then you can check in."

"Thanks—that's great! Ok I need you to do me one more thing and then I am sorted!"

"Let me guess—you want me to book you a flight from Amsterdam to Seville?"

"No—I need you to find me an hotel bed for the night in one of the airport Hotels as I have to be in the airport building really early in the morning and it is not an airport I am particularly familiar with so I need time to get my bearings."

"Ok—but what about the flight to Seville—don't you need to get on that?"

"Oh I am already booked on that! That was the first thing I did as soon as the news came that the money was coming through!"

"But—what if there had been no flights to Amsterdam tonight—what would you have done then?"

"Well it was always likely that there would be Amsterdam flights tonight…"

"Well the one you are on is the last one so you are bloody lucky!"

"If there were no flights then I would have had to resort to Plan B!"

"And what was plan B?"

"Hire car from Heathrow, drive to the channel, get across tonight and be in Amsterdam in the morning! But I don't need to do that now because I am on a flight!"

Ten minutes later she was back on the phone confirming that I was now booked into a hotel and I was ever so grateful for all her help.

"Is that me finished for the night?"

"Yes and thanks very much for all your help."

"OK – say hello to Anne Marie (my sister) and everyone else for me."

"Will do."

"And can I point something out?"

"Yes."

"You are completely and utterly - MENTAL!!"

In the international departures lounge there was a good number of Celtic fans all waiting for flights to somewhere. The notice board showed no direct flights to Seville so they must all have been heading to Madrid, or Malaga or Barcelona or somewhere.

There was a big crowd attracting quite a bit of attention with their never ending rendition of "You'll be watching the Bill, while we're in Seville" which drew smiles from a lot of passers-by.

Soon enough, I was taking off and just on midnight I climbed into my bed in my hotel—all set to be up again in just 5 hours.

I put my television on just in time to catch the news from CNN. Their business section came on, and suddenly the screen was full of Celtic fans and the presenter was reporting that 3% of all of the world's air travellers over a 24 hour period ending noon tomorrow will have been travelling to follow a football team called Glasgow Celtic who were playing in the UEFA Cup Final in Seville. The programme reported that the fans were flying from every part of the globe and that virtually every major airline was able to report that they were carrying some Celtic fans on at least part of the journey.

Further, it was estimated that from the UK, the Celtic fans accounted for 20% of all air traffic – concluding that these were statistics that the travel industry just could not ignore and that such figures would change the way that the industry dealt with football fans in future.

This was the biggest travelling support in the history of sport!

When the news item finished I switched channels and caught the end of a football show being presented by an elderly chap in a three-piece suit. There was some footage of a recent Dutch game and a commentary, which I didn't understand a word of. Then the suited man began to talk about the UEFA Cup Final clearly mentioning Celtic and Porto in Seville. There was a bit of modern footage of both teams before the man spoke some more and then suddenly cutting away to a video clip of Tommy Gemmell and Stevie Chalmers scoring in Lisbon. When the producers cut back to the presenter, he was opening what looked like a bottle of Champagne, and with some light music in the background he filled a glass, raised it, looked at the camera and simply said "Celtic" as he downed the champers just as the credits rolled.

I was astonished - everyone was a Celtic fan - even in Holland!

The following morning, I was in a taxi to Schiphol bright and early as I was none too sure how to find where the flight to Seville checked in.

When it had become apparent that there was a chance of me actually getting to Seville I had consulted my yellow stickies that were left on the desk and noticed an early morning flight to Seville from the Dutch capitol. All I knew from a very quick look on the internet was that the flight was operated by someone called Basic Air which sounded dodgy as hell but the flight was scheduled. Not only that but Basic Air had some connection to "Transylvania Airlines" which conjured up all sorts of images in my head.

However, I felt that this flight offered the best chance of me getting to the match and so with absolutely no idea about just how I was going to get to Amsterdam in time for take off, I rolled those Green and White dice and gambled by booking a one way seat to Seville.

What I was concerned about now was that Basic Air and Transylvania Airlines might be some tiny outfit who operated out of a cupboard somewhere in this vast airport and that I would never find their desk or staff.

However, I needn't have worried as all you had to do was follow the substantial line of Celtic fans in the airport who, sure enough, were all lined up before a desk that was checking in "Seville".

When I got to the front of the queue I started to laugh inwardly as I realised that in my haste to book this flight the previous day, I had failed to notice that "Basic Air" were no more than ticket handlers, and that where I had quickly read that the flight was operated by Transylvania Airlines, in fact the aircraft belonged to a company called Transavia – who just happened to be one of the biggest air carriers in Europe! Not only that—but all of their fleet of large commercial jets were Green and White!

Down at the departure gate I was astonished to see how many Celtic fans were on this flight, and when I bumped into someone I knew but hadn't seen in years I started to get a flavour of just how special this entire occasion was.

BRTH

CHAPTER 10
WELCOME TO SEVILLE!

The atmosphere really took off as we were coming into Seville just at 9:00am. As soon as the wheels hit the ground, it seemed as if the whole plane just burst into song! " Hail…Hail…The Celts are here…what the hell do we care, what the hell do we care! HAIL…HAIL…The Celts are here…"

And on it went.

Even the Captain got in on the act as he welcomed everyone to Seville, told us the local time, gave us the weather forecast and signed off by saying " On behalf of myself and the crew, and everyone else working for Transavia Airlines, we would like to wish Glasgow Celtic and their supporters every success in the UEFA Cup Final later today. Enjoy your stay in Seville and we hope to see you on a victorious journey home!"

Everyone really was a Celtic fan and more importantly…I was in Seville when at times I had been convinced that I would never get there. Then it dawned on me that no one else in my wee group had the faintest notion that I was there.

At that point my phone rang and I found my skin and blister on the end of it. She asked if the £1 Million had arrived and I truthfully answered, telling her it hadn't arrived. She then asked where I was and when I said at the airport she immediately concluded that I had gone out to Glasgow Airport just to take in the atmosphere of all the Celtic fans leaving for Seville and I did not disabuse her of that notion. When she hung up she simply said well hopefully the money would come through and when it did I should just go out to the pub and get drunk and that she thought it was a real shame that I wasn't there!

All of my friends and various others who were scattered around Spain had agreed to meet on the morning of the final at the hotel where she was staying. Everyone agreed that this was a sensible plan rather than try to find one another in and around the sea of Celtic fans in Seville. Accordingly within minutes of hanging up the phone, I was in a taxi heading for that hotel for what I was certain was going to be an amazing party culminating in all of us going to the game together. I was absolutely thrilled to bits to be there.

When I got to the hotel it was obvious that loads of fans were staying there and fortunately I didn't see anyone I knew as I walked through the lobby. It was still only about half past nine in the morning but I felt it was around lunchtime.

I found a seat, dumped my bag, and called my sister again.

"Hello!"

"Hello, what's happened now?"

"Well, there is good news and there is bad news."

"Christ! What?"

"Well some of the money has come through, so we have sorted the deal with the NHS and the rest can wait till next week!"

"Well that is good but at the same time it is a real bummer because if it had happened just that wee bit earlier you could have got here!"

"Yes I know but c'est la vie!"

"So what are you going to do now? Where will you go to watch the game?"

"I was thinking of just going to get drunk, and no doubt I will find someone to watch the game with --- somewhere."

"Yes quite right. We are just getting ready to go down for breakfast here, and then we will head out. Go and get yourself sorted and get down to

Tennents or somewhere and have a day out!"

"Are you all going for breakfast then?"

"Yes?"

Maybe, it was the way I asked that question. Maybe it was the way I had answered the previous question. Maybe it was just something in my voice or something she overheard in the background noise but suddenly she said:

"Wait a minute…You're here aren't you? You are bloody well here?"

"Eh…yes!"

"Where precisely are you? What has happened? How did you get here?"

"I flew in from Amsterdam this morning."

"Amsterdam? What the hell were you doing in Amsterdam? No don't tell me…Anyway when you say "here" precisely where is "here" in your case?"

"I am sitting in reception…"

"What reception?"

"The reception of your hotel…you know like downstairs from your room… and I am getting awfully thirsty!"

The phone went dead, and within minutes there I was reunited with at least some of our party, having breakfast and the first of many large beers amidst lots of laughter and tears as I told the tale of how I got to Seville in the end.

However, the day was only just beginning and there were some adventures to have yet. My friends arrived from the Algarve. They had not expected to find me there and so there were more celebrations. Others arrived bit by bit and the party got into full flow.

BRTH

CHAPTER 11
SEVILLE - ANY SPARE TICKETS?

Throughout the city of Seville the Celtic fans would party that day...and they would party like there was no tomorrow. They continued to arrive by every means possible. Later there was said to be a cavalcade of mopeds and Vespas, which travelled up the coast. The motorways were awash with cars, vans, buses and even lorries carrying Celtic fans into the Andalusian capital.

Meanwhile, with more and more fans arriving in the city swelling the numbers even more, one question was heard more than any other: "Any spare tickets?"

One fan with no such worries about tickets arrived in Seville that morning in the most luxurious of fashions, with his day all mapped out and planned to the nth degree. However, throughout the course of the day he was to marvel at the ingenuity and sheer brass neck of the average Celtic fan. It would seem that Celtic fans could talk their way into and out of anywhere and any situation.

"I grew up listening to tales of how fans got to and returned from Lisbon. That was a different age, and foreign travel of any kind was an adventure for working class folks.

Forty years may have made the world of difference to the ability of fans to travel efficiently, but it hasn't dulled the entrepreneurial and innovative nature of the Celtic fans.

My journey started in non-typical Bhoy's fashion from the private jet Terminal at Barcelona airport. The concierge service of Amex had fixed up a Gulfstream Jet for me and some others followed by drinks at Seville's best hotel and lunch at the best restaurant in the City. There was a chauffeur driven Mercedes S Class at our disposal for the entire trip, and a celebration dinner, tentatively arranged before flying back to Barcelona that evening. This was going to be Seville with style!

American Express could not have been more efficient in their organisation, but even they hadn't reckoned with the determination and the ability of fellow Tims to completely hijack the party and their carefully planned arrangements.

The flight from Barcelona was perfect, and the S class was parked, air con in full on mode, only yards from our landing point. Just as well as Barcelona was 28 degrees and Seville 42.

So far so good!

Our driver didn't speak a word of English, but he had Amex's concierge service on speed dial to interpret if he didn't understand our pigeon Spanish.

We headed straight to Hotel Alfonso XIII, where UEFA and every celeb in town was billeted. Thinking ourselves pretty smart that we had reserved a booth and some ice cold drinks, we ran headfirst into problem number one. When we arrived at the hotel, there was a line of security who decided they had heard just about every story possible from those in the hoops wanting in. They had already been faced with Rod Stewart's best pal, Henrik's cousin , Martins brother and everyone else. You name it - they had heard every excuse. One guy was even trying to convince security he was Dermott Desmondo (yes that is the name he used) and that he was the owner of the club!

As we stood there I thought "we have a reservation" was just not going to cut it here.

Anyway Amex did their job and after a fraught 15 minutes wait we were in. The first person we met inside was Eddie Jordan and it's no myth that where an F1 personality goes, Jessica Alba lookalikes are a plenty! He was surrounded by absolutely gorgeous women!

Anyway security negotiated and quickly washed and refreshed, we headed to lunch. We were assured by Amex the restaurant we were going to was the best and most exclusive in the City, with great food and a terrific ambience. We were also told it was incredibly difficult to get a table, and that Amex had had to leverage their relationship just to get us in.

I never knew so many Celtic fans had personal concierge service at Amex, as when we got there dozens of Celtic fans in hoops were in the lobby insisting they had reservations. When we eventually got to the reception desk, the maître D told us that our party were already inside and were seated at the table! That was news to us, as we hadn't arranged to meet anyone! This was problem number two.

A quick call to Amex saved the day again, and they told us that some resourceful hoops fans, had blagged their way in by looking at the reservation list and claimed they were us!

On to the game and as everyone will know public transport was really deficient and we were lucky that our driver got us right to the edge of the security cordon, and an arrangement was made for him to be there to collect us after the game.

With the game over, and the celebration dinner cancelled, we trudged back towards our driver. We shouldn't have been surprised, but were, to find three sets of hoops in the back of the car and telling a bemused driver that...

"...the big man said to take us into town and come back for him!"

Apparently their bus for The Sooside was leaving in 30 minutes and wouldn't wait for them!

If Big Bobo had been as fly as these guys, then we would probably have had our celebration dinner after all!"

Other fans I know had mixed fortunes on both the ticket and the accommodation front. Some were let down badly while others struck incredibly lucky. One lucky guy was Drew Pollock from Guernsey whose brother Gerry was one of my pals who had gone to the Algarve and driven up to Seville. Lots of fans have amazing stories about how they got tickets and who the tickets were sourced through but Drew's was quite unique.

Like everyone else he had been scrambling about for tickets using every contact he had when eventually he got word through a friend of a friend that he could get some tickets that had been given away as complimentaries… to Greg Rusedski the tennis player!

In contrast, John McTaggart from Aberdour was to have an entirely different experience, but one that lead to a bizarre chance encounter with someone he did not know and had never met:

"As soon as it looked as if we might get to Seville I asked a Spanish acquaintance who lived in the city to get me tickets for the game and to reserve a nice hotel to stay in. If we never got there then the hotel rooms could be released and I was sure I could sell the tickets on. The guy I spoke to duly did that and confirmed that he had booked both the hotel and the tickets. Of course at that time, this guy had no idea that the entire world would descend on Seville and that tickets for the match and hotel rooms were going to be in such huge demand.

Surprise surprise, when he realised just how valuable his little package was he totally blanked me and left me in the lurch with neither hotel rooms or tickets for the match. I was bloody furious.

However, there I was, sitting in the bar in this rather posh hotel where I wasn't staying, on the night before the game. I was with some others and we were formulating a plan as to what we would do in these unforeseen and unfortunate circumstances, when it became clear that there was this bloke who was selling tickets for the match. He had a book of tickets and was selling them to anyone who was willing to pay the price.

As I say it was a rather swish hotel and there were plenty of takers with the appropriate money. I was tempted, but at the end of the day decided that I wasn't paying and opted instead to just watch the game and enjoy the party at one of the fan zones. But your man with the tickets did a good steady trade selling to Celtic fans and Porto fans alike.

I was in the fan zone the following day when suddenly the face of the ticket seller from the night before appeared on the big screen. I recognised him immediately but still had no idea who he was and was quite bemused as to why this guy's face would be up on screen. Then I realised he was sitting on the Porto bench, I think his name was Jose something or other!"

Meanwhile Richard Gordon was taking his seat for what was meant to be another exclusive event…The pre match press conference where press passes were obligatory. Except that the world's press seemed to have decided to wear Green and White shirts!

"I have no idea how these guys got in there but there were loads of them all sitting there at the presser. What they had said to get by security I will never know but there they were. However, the most amazing thing was that they were not just content to sit there and take in the press conference—they wanted to ask questions as well. Eventually the main press corps gave up because the fans just asked question after question – it was hilarious."

While all these events were going on, I was happily tucking into some food and a few beers – I even managed to get an impromptu haircut from someone using scissors that were borrowed from reception.

Then we hit a problem—or what I saw as a problem. A female member of our party had been meant to travel to Seville with her dad, but at the last minute he was not able to come and so she was there on her own. She and her dad did not have tickets for the match and so the intention had been for the pair of them to go to one of the fan parks and watch the game on the big screen. Now that her dad was not there she said that she would come into town with us and then go to the fan park on her own.

While the atmosphere in Seville was great I was not too keen on this idea. I didn't like the idea of all of us spending the day together only for one of us not to get into the game – especially when it was a woman who would be left on her own. That is not meant to sound sexist or anything like that—it was just a situation I thought we could avoid.

Whether it was the effect of a few pints that early in the day, or the release of tension as a result of all the hassle surrounding getting there, or just my sheer and unbridled joy at being part of this Seville thing I announced that she could have my ticket!

This was met with some strange looks and some protestations on the part of the lady concerned. However, I was insistent and went on to explain my reasoning. " Look, we are all here together and everyone is going to the game, including me. All I have to do is get another ticket and there is a far greater chance of me getting a ticket by making a few phone calls than anyone else. So - let's agree this just now, everyone takes a ticket and for the moment we are one ticket short so I will go without one and will set about getting a replacement. If I don't get one, I don't get one…but I am pretty sure I will!"

As everyone knows the tickets were like gold dust and throughout the city there were tens of thousands looking for tickets. However, I was supremely confident of getting one, which was why I was able to give away one ticket in the knowledge that I could get another.

With my friends still in the bar mulling over these events, I excused myself and found a quiet corner to make a phone call.

Some years before I had done some legal work for one of London's best known ticket touts. This guy had more or less taken over the gap in the market left by the legendary Stan Flashman- London's best known ticket man of the 70's and early 80's. Stories about Flashman were legendary as he seemed able to produce tickets for just about everything and anything - at a price. The only time I had heard of him being bested was by a member of the Tartan Army who had approached him somewhere on Wembley Way looking for five tickets to the England Scotland International which was due to start within the hour. Stan advised the rather large Scot that he did indeed have five tickets but he was asking for a price that was way above face value—which the large and somewhat outraged Scot was just not willing to pay.

The two had reached an impasse when suddenly the large Scot unleashed a mighty right hook which sent "Stan the man" sprawling to the floor at which point the Tartan Army member picked up the 5 tickets and threw down a reasonable price for them and legged it. Flashman got to his feet, picked up the money, dusted himself down and urgently approached a nearby Policeman who could not have failed to witness the whole event.

"Did you see that? Get after that man - he assaulted me and robbed me— go and arrest him!"

The big copper just stared straight ahead wearing a slight grin – " Sorry sir, I didn't see what happened there at all and have no idea what you are talking about?"

Stan was apparently furious.

Anyway, I had done some work for Tony who had taken over his mantle as the ticket man, and I knew fine well that Tony would somehow somewhere have tickets for this Final at his disposal—even at this late hour. Tony was also very friendly with someone I knew back in Glasgow with whom I also had a very strong working relationship so I dialled the Glasgow number first.

"Hello"

"Hello yourself, I thought you were in Seville?"

"I am! But I have a problem – I need one ticket for one of our group—in fact I need a ticket for me!"

"Where are you?"

"In a hotel about 5 miles from the city centre!"

"I will call you back!"

I informed my friends I had made my call and that I was to wait a call back. I am not sure that they believed I would ever get a call back but sure enough the phone rang ten minutes later.

"Right - get yourself to the Alfonso the Thirteenth Hotel, go to reception and ask for the envelope that has been left in your name—the ticket is inside!"

And that was that...

One of our number had decided not to have a drink until the afternoon and so he jumped into a hire car and together we sped off across Seville following directions we had been given at reception. It took us fully half an hour to travel just the few miles and for the first time I was able to see how jam-packed the city actually was.

All the way my driver kept saying "I don't believe this...I don't believe this... What if this is a wild goose chase, what will you do then?"

I was confident however and soon enough we arrived at this rather posh looking hotel and by this time all hint of security had been abandoned as there were literally thousands of Celtic fans there.

I jumped out of the car, went to reception, flashed my passport and said that I believed an envelope had been left for me in the hotel safe. The man at the desk took a note of my name and disappeared into a room somewhere. A few moments later he was back clutching a small envelope and inside was a match ticket. We were all going to the game.

The journey back to our own hotel passed in a flash and soon enough we were back with our group and the singing and the drinking really got under way.

BRTH

CHAPTER 12

FLAHERTY'S BAR, SEVILLE

After some lunch, we decided it was time to head into town and somewhat optimistically we decided to head for Flaherty's Bar in the main square opposite the Cathedral travelling in a series of taxis. Amazingly, we all got there at just about the same time.

What a sight! I don't think I have ever seen as many Celtic fans.

The place was just a sea of Green and White with wave after wave of songs – " C'mon the hoops, Cmon the hoops...oh oh oh oh oh...oh, oh oh,oh oh… " The entire square just echoed with fans chanting and singing… It went on and on…

However, the heat was bordering on the unbearable so we decided to try and get into Flaherty's and again our luck held. Once inside we met up with yet more friends and acquaintances including Drew Pollock who received his match tickets from Greg Rusedski!

We were having a huge singsong when suddenly I felt a tap on my shoulder. I turned round and found myself staring at the chest of a rather large, dark haired Irishman.

"Excuse me, but can you tell me your name?" he said smiling.

"Sorry?"

"Can you tell me your name?"

I was perplexed by this and asked him why he wanted to know.

"It's like this" he said, "there is a bet riding on this, and if you are who I am told you are then I lose £20!"

"Sorry but I don't understand this?"

"Look what is your name?"

So I told him my name.

"Can you prove that?"

I showed him my passport and said " Right, who are you and why do you want to know who I am?"

"Yesterday afternoon I was sitting at my desk when one of my work colleagues said—and I quote---" Screw it, let's just go to Seville!" I took some persuading but not much and within an hour, I changed into the clothes that you see me in now and we were booked on a plane to Malaga. We arrived last night fairly late on, hired a car and drove up here early this morning.

On the way up in the car, we were discussing the fact that we had no tickets and were not likely to be getting any tickets, when my colleague mentioned your name and said that there was a remote chance you might be able to get some tickets. However, before we even faced the tickets issue I asked my colleague just how he expected to find one Celtic fan in and amongst the tens of thousands that are in Seville and he said that as sure as eggs were eggs you would be in this pub and you would be singing! To be honest, I simply did not believe that was possible and so I bet him £20 and a round of drinks that we could not and would not find you. Now, we have walked in here, bought a drink and right away my colleague pointed over at you and said "Told you—there is our man over there!" I thought he was joshing and so to prove the whole thing and make sure this is not some kind of fix, here I am asking you what your name is.

That is my story!"

I just looked at the fella all the while thinking that he was far bigger than me.

"Where do you work?" I asked.

"At the European Commission in Brussels" he replied.

I burst out laughing. "In that case you are here with a long streak of nonsense and a total head-case called Frank Mather! Am I right or am I wrong?"

Sure enough I was right and from out of nowhere came the sight of the bold Frank, who I had not seen in years and I am not sure I have seen since.

Frank used to send letters to the Kremlin from the Smiddy Bar in Partick nominating people for the award of "Hero of the Soviet Union" – his two favourite nominees had been Andy Ritchie and Jocky Wilson. When the Kremlin never replied he denounced the Communist Party for its complete lack of manners!

"I knew you'd be in here," he said and added without waiting for any kind of reply "I don't suppose you'd have any chance of getting us a ticket?"

I didn't bother telling him that had he called me a couple of hours before there was every chance of getting them tickets and they seemed quite content to just get drunk and go to the fan zone.

After a few hours, the occasional libation and more than a few songs we decided that we had better start to make our way towards the stadium. I genuinely thought that we could maybe get a taxi out there and perhaps stop at a bar next to the ground!

Fat chance. As everyone now knows the walk to the stadium in the baking heat was a killer and there were thousands upon thousands making that walk in virtually unbearable temperatures. For some it was almost a journey too far and for others it was a journey that would end with considerable worries about those cherished tickets.

One person making that walk was Jeanette Findlay of the Celtic Trust who tells her story in her own inimitable style:

"I got my tickets round about the February of that year from the UEFA website. Myself and a friend were sitting at our respective PCs having got through to the site (it had crashed a few times the day before) and we were speaking on the phone and debating how many tickets to get. We could have had 6 each but we decided to play it safe and take 6 from which I would take 2 (for me and my 5 year old son) – that was my first mistake, I should have had more faith!

In the end my da (then aged 75) and my brother decided they were coming. I felt bad that they didn't have a ticket and the wean did, but they were adamant that if a ticket didn't come they would watch it somewhere. I did have an idea that the Spanish would not expect a small child to have his own ticket and had suggested that my da would come along with me and see if we could get in – the fall-back position being that he would head off to watch it somewhere if we couldn't.

So on the morning before the game I collected Caomhín from school at lunchtime (didn't give him the whole day off, it's a harsh regime in our house) and he was waved off by his P1 class to his first (!) European Final. Our hotel was in Jerez and we arrived the evening before. On the morning of the game the bus came at 10am to take us into Seville. That was my second mistake!

We should have stayed by the pool and got the train in late in the afternoon. I had completely underestimated the heat and we spent the day in Seville with my brother getting drunker, my da and my wee fella getting hotter and more tired and me getting increasingly anxious that they were both going to collapse with heatstroke.

We did, on a number of occasions that day, try to pull drunk, sleeping people into the shade! I was really worried that I was going to have to go home to the rest of the family and tell them I had killed my da and the wean! My brother wasn't bothering his backside as he 'soaked up the atmosphere' as they say!

My da decided the stadium was too far away for him to take a chance so around 6pm he and my brother headed out to find somewhere to watch the game and me and the wee man headed to the stadium.

There was supposed to have been transport from the city centre, but as we all know, that didn't happen. I was assured by many people that it was in walking distance so I turned down the offer of an incredibly expensive horse-drawn carriage arrangement and me and the wean began to walk – that was my third mistake! We walked, and we walked and we walked.

The wee man held my hand and didn't complain once. In fact that was more worrying; he was like one of those weans in a refugee camp in Africa who are too exhausted to even speak. My feet were ripped to shreds by my daft sandals and I simply could not carry him. We kept getting told we were near but the stadium never came into site. Then came the killer; the wee man looked up at me and said 'Mammy, could I please sit down just for a wee minute?

I am nearly greeting even now when I think of that. We sat by the roadside and I desperately tried to think what to do. I had given up on trying to get there and was going to give our tickets away.

Then a taxi stopped with two guys in it (from Dundee it transpired) and one of them shouted out; we have two seats if anyone wants a lift. Two guys ran and got in and I then did something that I have never done before and never since; I abandoned all dignity and self-respect and I ran over and begged them to take us instead – such is a mother's love! The two guys, to their credit, jumped straight back out and gave us their space in the taxi. I could hardly speak I was so grateful.

Anyway, the guys from Dundee (Lochee I think) dropped us off at the stadium and we began to make our way to our turnstile. Just at that an Irish guy in his 30s fell into step beside us. We chatted a bit and I noticed he seemed nervous. Eventually he spat it out; he had a dodgy ticket and he reckoned if he approached the turnstile in a 'family' group he would be subject to less scrutiny.

So I says, 'Look, you are welcome to walk along with us and take your chance but if you get stopped, me and my wee fella will just head in because we don't know you'.

So that was agreed and on we went. Yer man was panicking more and more as we approached the turnstile and when he realised it was electronic he nearly turned and ran. I calmed him down and in we went. I lifted the wean and went to put the first ticket in the waist high turnstile but it was a bit bent (I had had it for some time you understand!) and it wouldn't go in, so the steward reaches across the turnstile and looks at our two tickets and then just opens a wee gate and waves the three of us in!

The Spanish obviously don't expect weans to have their own tickets – in fact I saw a new-born baby in there that night! So the Irish fella was all grateful and I wished him the best and bade him farewell! I expect he still tells that tale.

The rest, as they say, is history! The postscript to this tale is that I wanted to thank the Dundee guys but I had only taken first names, so when I got back I phoned someone from the Lochee No 1 who sat beside me at Celtic Park at that time. I asked what was the local paper that everybody read in Dundee and he said the Dundee Courier. I wrote to the readers page and passed on my deepest gratitude to these bhoys; the paper contacted me and asked for a photo of me and the wean in Seville and they published it along with the tale of the gallant Dundee Tims!

Seville? My favourite Celtic memory? Not in a million years, give me the Boavista game every time – it was all in front of us...and I went there on my ownsome!

Someone else on that walk who faced a completely different but equally bizarre ticket issue was Dave McCann:

"I attended most of the away games in the lead up to the final (except Boavista) the rule was if you attended the away games you got a ticket for Seville. I had 3 season tickets at the time and ended with 3 Seville tickets, of which, only two were needed. I therefore had one of the most sought after commodities in the western hemisphere...(despite the 30€ ticket price).

Now, you will remember that a lot of Celtic fans who went week in week out couldn't get a ticket and a lot of glory hunters had managed to, people with money could pay bonkers amounts to get one and forgeries were everywhere. I decided that the extra ticket I had would only go to a Celtic fan who went every week was in Seville and had no ticket.

I booked to go to Seville with Rickie Ferns (a well kent Celtic fan who ran a company called Hail Hail Promotions). The trip was a flight out of Glasgow a couple of nights in Torremolinos and a bus to Seville and flight back. The bus party was interesting and included ex- Celtic player Tommy Coyne and a certain Peter Lawell (pre Celtic employment). The trip went well and when in Spain I started contacting all my Celtic mates to find a deserving recipient for my extra ticket, but incredibly they all had tickets and were sorted. When we arrived in Seville Simon Donnelly got on our bus and asked if anyone had a spare ticket, a few guys knew I did but I kept my head down and said nothing (he didn't meet the "go every week hail rain or shine" criteria...)

As we approached the stadium I still had this spare ticket, so I went on a walk around and came across a guy who sat near me in the South Stand. Three of them had travelled with two tickets, had a draw and he lost out, and so as he met all the criteria he became the recipient of my precious spare ticket. He was a very happy man.

I then made my way round to the barrier with my son (who was 12). You will remember when you approached the gates you put in your barcode and a big tick or a cross appeared. My son went in first, and as it was packed I told him to stand to the side when he got inside until I got in. He presented his ticket, got a tick and in he went. My turn next, I presented my ticket got a tick and as I went to go in an old guy (and I mean an old guy) took a commando dive through the gates rolled and tried to run in. He was quickly captured by the Police, given the customary Spanish smack and thrown out!

However... by the time the commotion was over the gates had shut and when I represented my ticket I got a cross as it thought I was already in! (5 minutes previously I had 3 tickets between 2 of us and now my 12 year old son was in the stadium getting moved along in the crowd and I was stuck outside with a copper wanting to burst my head)...

God was, however, watching over me. Each gate had Celtic stewards on them, and the guy on our gate had seen what happened and persuaded the Police they should leave my head alone and let me in...

Richard Gordon and the BBC crew were also caught up in that long march to the ground, however he had a handicap that most of us didn't have.

"Our Hotel was at the Real Betis ground and my bedroom looked directly into the stadium. We had been co-hosting the Fred McAuley show throughout the week and we had some outside broadcast kit with us, which we needed to take to the ground for the game. We headed off in a taxi and under normal circumstances the journey would not have taken too long but on the day of the game the approach to the stadium was just a sea of people. The taxi crawled to a standstill and eventually the driver explained that he could simply go no further. So I had no option but to get out carrying what looked like two heavy suitcases of equipment. They were bloody heavy and we had about two miles to go and the heat was terrible - I have never felt heat like it. Every now and then I just had to stop even just to get into the shade. Of course every time we stopped I was asked the inevitable question: "Any tickets big man?" - The walk to the ground was back breaking - absolute torture. How the players actually played in that heat I will never know."

BRTH

HEARTACHE IN SEVILLE

Meanwhile back in Glasgow some said the city was like a ghost town while others told an altogether different story.

It was reported in the papers that Bairds Bar imported some sand in an attempt to recreate the Seville atmosphere, but perhaps an even more extreme recreation came about at the McVitties biscuit factory in Tollcross. There the story goes that the week before the final the nightshift Celtic supporters got a barrel of biscuit mix and spread it across part of the car park to look like sand. The fans concerned also brought in a couple of deckchairs, kiddies paddling pool, beach balls, towels, sunglasses and so on and 15 minutes before their shift ended they changed into beachwear went into the car park and started using the stuff they had brought in with them.

Steve Harley of Cockney Rebel had been booked to perform a concert at Glasgow's Renfrew Ferry on the night of the Final and would later complain that it was the smallest crowd he had ever played to in Glasgow in 25 years of performing! It would seem that a big part of his Glasgow audience were Celtic fans and they were all of watching the Final as opposed to listening to Steve. In a later concert he recounted this experience and said that he didn't mind the Celtic fans not being there and watching their team instead. However, he was somewhat surprised when his wife—a West of Scotland native - made it quite plain that she too would not be at the concert and instead would be watching the TV and cheering on the hoops!

Another Celtic fan remained in Glasgow and went for a business lunch with a colleague from Leeds. In the course of the day he was to find out something about the Glasgow traffic wardens that he did not know:

"On the day of the game I had a business lunch in Gamba with an associate from Leeds. We drove up parked outside no problem - the place was a ghost town. I had no change and asked the head waiter to change a tenner to let me park and he replied – "don't worry mate the traffic wardens won't book anyone today - all the Tims are in Seville!"… My English associate finally understood Glasgow.

Back in Seville when our group finally reached the ground I found that my one solitary ticket was in a different section to everyone else and so at the gates I waved them all goodbye and arranged to see them at full time.

When I got in I found that my seat was an excellent one right on the halfway line and that I was entirely surrounded by Celtic supporters. Amazingly I bumped into the brother in law of mad Frank from the European Commission who was astonished to find that his errant in law was anywhere near Seville!

Away to my right was the amazing sight of the massed Celtic fans with their huge banners and displays. What a sight that was! It made me so proud to be a Celtic supporter.

However, despite my seat providing me with a great view of the game, the seat was also a bit of a disaster as it was directly facing into the setting but still incredibly hot sun and within a few minutes of sitting down I was absolutely baking.

Away from the exhilaration of my friends and having had only a few hours sleep after an amazingly emotional roller coaster of a week and having had a fair amount to drink during the day I began to flag and wilt. Then the teams came out and all the fanfare of the occasion got under way and after a while we were playing football.

For most of the first half I thought Celtic looked nervy and were not at their best. Porto played well and looked dangerous with Deco and Derlei being prominent and of course just before half time they scored. The joy of the Porto fans was there for all to see in contrast to the silent despair and dread felt by our own supporters.

I hated seeing that. All that jubilation and joy turned to looks of angst and worry.

I know it is ludicrous and I know it is only a football game but when you have travelled so far in both miles and emotions, seeing a football crowd down is not a comfortable site. After all this was the Celtic crowd, the very people that I had come to Seville to be part of and experience being part of and now during half time they were like the mourners at a wake.

I walked up to the back of the stand to get into the shade as I was now absolutely boiling.

Maybe it was the lack of sleep, maybe it was the drink, or maybe my secretary was right and that I was just plain mental, but as I stood there a completely illogical and insane thought took hold of my brain. Of course I should have had the sense to walk round the interior of the ground and find my friends—I could have done that—but didn't. Had I done that then things would have been different.

Inside my head however my insane superstitions had returned and I specifically recall battling with my illogical reasoning - a sure sign of temporary madness.

I had missed the second leg of every single game on the way to this Final, and on each occasion Celtic had prevailed when it looked as if they might not. I was debating this in my head as the teams emerged for the second half. I thought of some of my friends—at least one of whom was not known to be the best loser in the world - and wondered how they would feel if we did not win?

Of course the answer was fine but in my head at that moment I was thinking that it would not be good if we lost—and kept coming back to the fact that in all the previous games or ties we won in the second half if I was not watching!

This feeling became so strong that I began to make my way down the steps heading towards the exit. The game was flowing in front of me and Celtic seemed to be holding their own. I turned into the stadium, away from the pitch and headed into the bowels of the ground making my way towards the exit and just as I pushed through the barriers to walk out of the stadium a roar went up that could only have come from one group of fans in the entire world.

Unknown to me Henrik Larsson had risen, twisted, turned and nodded Didier Agathe's cross into the Porto net. Unbelievably my superstition had worked – with me outside Celtic had scored and drawn level!

I daren't go back in, that would have jinxed the whole thing and so kept on going till I reached a bench on the concourse outside the stadium where I sat down, eventually lay down, and listened to the match ebbing and flowing inside.

After my oh so on off trip and having had all those potential routes to get to this game and having given my ticket away and the mad dash across town to get a replacement, here I was now quite deliberately sitting outside in the absolutely mad belief that the key factor in determining whether Celtic would win or lose the UEFA Cup Final was not the players skill or the ability of Porto—but whether yours truly was watching or not—and if it took me missing the rest of the game for Celtic to win then here I would sit!

Inside the ground, for a period of time at least the Celtic fans were able to celebrate and engage in a completely different type of madness.

Paul Hamill takes up his story, which has more than a smack of magic about it.

"I was only 10 when I was in Seville and before leaving I decided to write my details on a beach ball and take it with me to the stadium. I inflated it at the ground and flung it away inside the ground thinking no more about it.

Around a year after the Seville game, I returned home from school to find that I was the recipient of a parcel from Switzerland.

I opened up the parcel and it was full of Swiss CSC stuff and other Swiss items. A letter was also enclosed to explain why this parcel had been sent.

A Swiss Celtic fan had found the ball and decided to return it as I was part of the "Celtic family". His name was Achim and obviously he didn't make many games but tried to come over as often as he could. My dad and he kept in touch after he sent me the parcel and the next time he was over we took him to the Scotland v Switzerland game at Hampden. So here we are, standing outside Hampden waiting on this stranger turning up when up comes a bearded man with a ponytail, a kilt (Celtic Tartan of course) carrying a half and half Celtic / Switzerland flag. (He went down a treat at the national ground!)

After that we never really kept in contact with him. However, years later in Milan (2007) we were walking down to the stadium and a man running to the game bumped into us and fell. We helped him up and as he got up and apologised we noticed he looked a bit familiar - it was the bearded man with a ponytail, a kilt, carrying a half and half Celtic / Switzerland flag. It was Achim!

Seville was great but what started with my wee beach ball sums up what it's like following Celtic and being part of the Celtic Family – you just never know who or what will happen next!

BRTH

CHAPTER 14
SEVILLE THE AFTERMATH

Of course what happened next in Seville was that we lost and that the vast majority of fans were stranded in the city centre that night. Despite the loss and the initial disappointment, the Celtic fans mixed with the victorious Porto fans and behaved impeccably.

This was no surprise as it had happened 30 years before in Milan where Feyenoord and Celtic fans were effectively trapped in a strike-ridden airport immediately after the 1970 European Cup Final. Despite there being fears of trouble between the two groups there was not so much as a broken window! Apparently the only thing that was broken was wind!

Now in Seville there was great fun and laughter amidst the logistical nightmare of trying to get home - at least by the way you had planned!

With no taxis or other transport we could not even get to the hotel where my sister was staying and eventually had to have a sleep on the street. Others were packed 10 and 12 to a room in various hotels and hostels.

The stories about fans getting to Seville are good, but the ones about getting back are even better and show the Celtic support at their most intuitive, generous and funny!

Two boys from Dumfries had travelled to Seville on the day of the game and were due to fly home the following day. They didn't want to take their bags to the game and as they didn't have a hotel they were looking for somewhere to store the bags overnight. Suddenly they came upon the idea of leaving the bags in a shop and so an agreement was made with a local shoe shop where the shopkeeper said they would be happy to store the bags in the window so that the boys would remember which shop to come back to.

That was a great plan…except that the boys concerned forgot to check whether or not the shop was due to open on the day after the game! It remained firmly shut and so the two concerned missed their flight, had to spend an extra night in Seville, and pay for another flight home!

Much luckier was Wul Gray who has the generosity of an elderly Celtic fan to thank for getting him home on time.

"I went to Seville with my mate Jim. We flew to Malaga and got a taxi with 2 strangers to Seville without knowing that Seville was so far away. Once we got there we met Jim's son and daughter in law and watched the game in one of the squares.

En-route to the square we agreed to meet at a certain place if we got split up as we were leaving to go home immediately after the game.

Just before the game finished, Jim went to the toilet and got lost, I waited for ages on him but he never came back so I made my way to the meeting place but he never appeared there either.

I met loads of people from home but they were all staying there for a few days and I could not stay with them. It was essential that I find Jim as I didn't have enough money for a taxi to Malaga on my own.

I decided to go to the train station only to be told that there were no more trains to Malaga that night and so I was now truly stranded.

By chance I met an old man who asked me if I knew where the train station was. "It's no good mate they are all off—all the trains have gone!"

The old man laughed and explained that he wasn't looking to get a train, but just needed to find the station as that is where he had parked his car while he and his wife went to the game.

We spoke for a few minutes about what had happened to me and then he said if I could get him to the station he would drive me to Malaga as they were staying twenty minutes outside Malaga for the rest of the week!

I was delighted and accepted the lift and we got to the airport just as the last call went out for my flight. I rushed on board and guess who was there? None other than my mate Jim.

I owe that old man and his wife so much for their help."

However, the record for missing your trip home and getting home on the cheap has to be held by the Celtic fan who had travelled to Spain by bus and who missed the bus that was meant to take him home all the way to Glasgow. He was now stranded in Seville with no way home.

He explained his predicament to a fellow fan who promptly gave him a National Express bus ticket which would take him all the way from Seville to London. When the stranded fan tried to pay for the ticket, his newly found friend refused to accept any money whatsoever and wished him Bon Voyage!

When the fan concerned got to London, different Celtic fans bought him a ticket home to Glasgow and once again they refused to accept any money and once again said goodbye wishing him all the best. The result was that our man travelled from Seville to Anniesland cross for the princely sum of £1.07 – possibly a world or at least European Record!

After the game, Richard Gordon was gutted that Celtic hadn't won. "As soon as we came off air there was a sense of real deflation—a real let down. I am an Aberdeen fan, and I won't pretend that there was not a wee part of me that thought about Aberdeen still being the only Scottish team to win two European trophies, but I was genuinely gutted for Celtic and their fans...and on the night I was one of those fans and was cheering them on.

We left the ground and got back to our hotel and to be honest we had a wee drink to commiserate and then we just drank some more and it turned into a very funny, very good spirited party. The Celtic fans had been amazing all week and now we were just having the biggest of laughs! There was a guy in our company, and I don't know how it came about, but one of his pals claimed that he had the biggest testicles in the world!

We were in mixed company and the conversation just grew extremely silly and extremely funny with all of us in fits of laughter and with tears rolling down our cheeks - not tears of sorrow but tears of real laugher and fun. At one point the dramatically endowed gentleman was asked to prove that he was a genital world record holder which he duly did in the most bizarre fashion creating even more laughter. At some point a photograph was taken of this unique man and his record-breaking testicles – I won't bother with the details but it is one of the silliest and funniest nights I have ever had…And that is the thing about Seville… it was the atmosphere that was brilliant even to the bitter end. That is what I will always remember."

For me, my Seville experience was far from over as after the match I was heading to the Algarve with my pals to enjoy what was left of a week's holiday. We said our goodbyes to my sister and others and five of us headed to our apartment in Villamoura. That night we had a few drinks and I was introduced to the 5 litre cask of red wine that my friend Gerry Pollock had purchased. I am not saying that it was rough stuff but it had been nicknamed Gutrot and upon first tasting it seemed absolutely disgusting and virtually undrinkable. The potency and potential danger of this substance was demonstrated when a glass of the offending wine was spilt on a brilliant white Formica table on the balcony of the apartment. Much to our horror, the red wine burnt right into and through the Formica leaving an indelible stain and mark! There was a brief discussion about what this same substance was doing to our insides but we finished the bottle none the less.

The Algarve was full of Celtic fans who had had the same idea as us. They were holidaying there after the game and everywhere we went you could hear "C'mon the hoops!"

Two days after the game we went for a day out to Albufeira where Gerry had a particular score to settle. He had been in the town when Celtic played the second leg against Boavista and after the game he had wondered into a wee bar which was run by a die hard Porto fan who did not hesitate to tell him that Porto was the greatest team and that they would beat Celtic in the Final. Gerry had told him " I'll be back—win lose or draw!" and he wanted to be as good as his word.

We had been out all day and had had an absolutely fabulous day drinking and laughing and chatting to anyone we happened to meet when eventually we made our way to this wee bar. Inside, it was honestly like someone's living room and it was almost entirely filled by a busload of Irish old age pensioners who were on some kind of trip. We reduced the average age of the place by about twenty years easily. However, if we were expecting a hard time from the Porto supporting owner then we were to be sorely disappointed.

The owner was behind the bar alright and he was wearing training shoes, white football socks, white football shorts, and that famous green and white hooped shirt. His pub stereo seemed to have been taken over by the Wolfe Tones and our owner had clearly been his own best customer for the best part of the day. The OAPs had sort of put up with his eccentricity but were not really engaging with him and later we found out that they had presumed he was some kind of mad Celtic fan. Every now and then he would shout "Celtic! Celtic!" and later on in the evening he got so drunk he literally laid his head down on the bar and went to sleep leaving the pub to fend for itself! Once in a while he would raise his head and shout "Celtic" before promptly passing out on the bar once more!

Eventually, the staff from the Bluebell Bar, which was about 50 yards down the road, came in and lifted him out from behind the bar like a sack of potatoes. The atmosphere in the pub was brilliant and we had a right old singsong with all these old folk who started to get up and dance to songs like "If your Irish, come into the parlour" while your man the pub owner slept and the people from down the road pulled the pints and served the drinks on a voluntary basis!

That was the essence of Seville – even though we were in Portugal if that makes sense. The whole experience was one where the Celtic fans travelled as one and had fun on a huge basis that did not discriminate on the grounds of age, sex, social standing or group or even which team you supported.

It was in every way unique and outstanding and rightly the Celtic fans won the praise of the Spanish Government, the Seville Authorities, The airlines, the travel industry, the press, UEFA, FIFA, Celtic Football Club and perhaps most importantly Porto Football Club and their fans.

No doubt the locals had their own view of their city being taken over by this mad laughing bunch of football fans. Hopefully they will have enjoyed our exuberance and good natured attitude – although occasionally they may have been disturbed by our… well…apparent attempts at bodily self destruction.

One such group of gentle Seville folk will no doubt recall the Celtic fans with what might be accurately described as "mixed feelings" as their dining experience was interrupted by a Celtic fan who found himself in dire need.

The story is taken up by one of the unfortunate fan's closest friends:

"Winchburgh – Edinburgh – London – Gibraltar - Seville. That was our route to get there, by a literal combination of planes, trains and automobiles. Along the way we met an unsuspecting Paraguayan couple (the last of whom we saw were walking around Kings Cross wearing sombreros and Celtic scarves) - Hazel Irvine - who was a great sport - and Baby Spice, whose management had inadvertently booked her on the same flight as countless Celtic fans. Hearing the passengers sing in unison "the front o' the plane she cannae sing, she cannae sing fir peanuts" became a "dae ye remember when...?" moment when our Seville memories were revisited.

However that wasn't our only "dae ye remember when...?" moment. There was one mishap that became THE moment associated with our trip. It all started two days previous...

The eight of us left our room - all eight of us sharing one room with a just a double bed, a bath and no air conditioning - and set off for the party in the park. As we entered the park, having downed our alcoholic beverages at the gates, we spotted the alluring fountain and pond. An opportunity to cool down and splash about was too tempting and we bailed in, making sure our mobile phones, wallets and other precious items were being held by the trusted folks not wanting to get their feet wet.

Dave climbed atop the small fountain and waved a Celtic flag, waving it like he was at the opening ceremony of the Olympics; I splashed around, as did Barrie. Mooney, being an ex-swimmer at school level was doing laps of the pond with the same technique as he would use in a well chlorinated swimming pool: head under water, coming up for breath every two strokes. Mooney was swimming around like a wound-up toy shark in a bath.

Perhaps if we hadn't have downed our drinks pre-entry to the park, or if we hadn't baked in the near 50-degree heat we wouldn't have been so ready to jump into the foostie pond, but at the time it was a great big dollop of fun.

The party was enjoyed by one and all, the game came and went, and our trip was nearing its end. Our single room was given away and we spent our last night sleeping on the grass outside an Irish pub. The journey home was about to begin. And Mooney was about to obtain legendary status.

All morning on our final day, Mooney had been complaining of a dodgy stomach, unable to eat a thing. He was being derided for having drunk too much, for bring half-ginger and succumbing to the heat and generally for being a lightweight.

We were killing time before our bus out of Seville was due to leave and so went for a stroll to take in a few sights the town had to offer. It was hot, so the t-shirts had been dispensed with and we were all in our shorts. Occasionally, Mooney would stop walking, hands on hips, puffing his cheeks and saying "I'm struggling, boys" or "I swear, there's something no' right". The derision continued.

As the group walked on we heard Mooney, who had lagged behind, shout out "Boys! BOYS!! I think I've just shat myself!" We all spun around and saw a distressed Mooney, bare-chested and wearing short baby blue shorts, both hands clasping his arse cheeks. A few laughed, a few disbelieved, the rest pointed to a cafe we were standing outside and told him to get in and get cleaned up or whatever. He waddled to the cafe and saw the sign for the men's toilet, situated at the back of the small cafe.

Mooney weaved his way towards the toilet as fast as he could and slammed the door behind him. He took off his shorts and pants, naked as the day he was born - save for a pair of Nikes - and stuffed his pants into the small wicker bin beside the sink. He turned and sat on the toilet bowl, head between his knees, in one swift movement and not a moment too soon as the dysentery took full effect as his arse coughed, spluttered and trumpeted to an eventual squeak!

How do I know all this happened?

Well, what Mooney didn't realise was that the door he slammed behind him was a stable door and so was split in two. He had only closed the top half and all of the above happened with the bottom half of the door wide open!

There sat Mooney, head between the legs and oblivious to the fact that he was facing out towards the packed cafe looking back at him in complete and utter horror, and with all of us standing pressed up against the floor-to-ceiling glass-front of the cafe unable to scream any warning in time. Most of us fell to the pavement in laughter as Mooney got himself sorted and, red faced, eventually skulked out of the café, past the horrified locals to his mates who offered zero sympathy but rather a chorus of "wait 'til everyone at home hears about this..."

He hadn't even bought anything!

So now, when re-telling the Seville memories, we talk about the small room with eight people, we talk about how Barrie lost his wallet only for a policeman to pluck it from his car's glove box whilst we were in a completely different part of town (money gone, ticket still there) and we talk about dancing to Enola Gay in an underground car park. But most of all we recall the day when, having drank half a foostie pond two days previous, Mooney turned a quaint cafe full of cultured Sevillians sipping espresso into a crime scene.

The Seville experience was incredible and memorable. It remains our number one "dae ye remember when...?" moment, along with 30 residents of Seville no doubt."

After a few days in the Algarve, I returned home and went back to work and told story after story of my trip to Seville and all my travel experiences—as did over 80,000 others!

My client who had bought the hospital site was very keen to compensate me for missing part of my holiday and without me saying a word paid me double the agreed fees.

I thanked the Rangers supporting solicitor who had helped me get to Seville and offered to repay her in any way she could think possible:

"Eh can you get your hands on any signed Rangers strips?"

A couple of weeks later I delivered strips signed by Alex McLeish and Chris Burke as she had requested.

I had been, and always was, suspicious about the stories I was fed about why and how the Pearl Holdings money had gone missing—I thought the whole thing was extremely fishy. Three years later Luqman's business had folded and he and his brother were convicted of various acts of dishonesty and other criminal charges. He spent time in jail on two separate occasions when they could not account for supposed assets of his former company and even when he was released he was forced to wear an electronic tag. In June 2013, the Guardian reported that despite both Luqman brothers being forced to surrender their passports—both had fled the country to Pakistan where they started some other kind of business.

However, he did wish me and Celtic well in Seville!

Seville is where the Celtic support rediscovered itself and what it can do and achieve when that support moves as one body and with one spirit. The football authorities and the travel industry stood in awe of Celtic and its support and for a period of time after 2003 there was great anticipation when Celtic came to town.

I was in Barcelona when we defeated the Catalan giants in the same tournament the following year (and yes I did stay for the second half and was confident that we would go through) and the spirit of Seville was still evident among both the Celtic fans and the Spanish.

However when I think of Seville I think back to Luis in Ericeira and his reaction to Lisbon all those years before and I hope that the people of Spain – and elsewhere—will always remember those wonderful Celtic fans and the party spirit they brought with them.

Over Christmas I heard a story, which although about Lisbon, perfectly captures what I think was achieved in May 2003.

Apparently there is a little old man who looks after the station, which serves the Estadio Nacional. It is not unknown for groups and even solitary football fans to make the pilgrimage to the now disused stadium where we became kings of Europe on the field of play.

However, evidence as to how Celtic Football Club and its fans are perceived away from the field of play is to be found with the little man at the train station. Visitors to the disused stadium sometimes wear football strips, but as often as not they wear nothing that would suggest that they have an allegiance to the football team from the east end of Glasgow.

Irrespective of what they wear, the little man greets everyone with the same toast and using his one word of English.

"CELTIC"!

It is a toast that raises a smile in Seville............ and elsewhere!

Written by Jim McGinley, known to the online Scottish football community as Brogan, Rogan Trevino and Hogan. He is currently editor of CQN Magazine.

CHAPTER 15

THE SEVILLE PROJECT

Douglas, Gould, Hedman, Marshall. Valgaeren, Balde, Laursen, Sylla, Mjallby, McNamara, Crainey, Kennedy. Lambert, Lennon, Petrov, Guppy, Thompson, Fernandez, Petta, Agathe, Healy, Maloney, Miller, Lynch, Smith. Larsson, Sutton and Hartson.

These are the names of the players who played a part in helping Celtic reach the UEFA Cup Final in 2003. This is a moment in the history of Celtic that will stick with the fans for the rest of their lives. Whether they look back on it with envy, or look back on it as a truly wonderful Cup run is up to the individual. I'm not going to look at anything negative from the run to Seville, I'm going to look purely at what an outstanding campaign it was.

Celtic v Suduva (10-1 aggregate)

After being knocked out of the Champions League at the hands of Basel, Celtic looked to their first round tie in the UEFA Cup against Suduva. The first leg came at Celtic Park, with Celtic destroying their opponents 8-1. Henrik Larsson scored a hat-trick and became the joint top scorer for a Scottish side in European competition. The Larsson hat-trick and goals from Petrov and Sutton gave Celtic a 5-0 lead at half time. Lambert, Hartson and Valgaeren added the second half goals to make it 8-0 before Suduva got a consolation goal.

Going into the away game, Celtic fielded a second string side, and they booked their place in the second round with ease, winning the game 2-0. Goals from David Fernandez (remember him?) and Alan Thompson had Celtic cruising 2-0 at half time. John Hartson also missed a penalty just before half time. Alan Thompson and Stephen Crainey both hit the bar from free-kicks in the second half, but the score finished 2-0. Celtic went through 10-1 on aggregate. Attendance: Home 36,824. Away 1,200.

Here's the thoughts of **Noel Kiely**, who was at the away leg:

"Me and my grandfather Noel Kiely Senior went on the official travel for Celtic. There were about 130 Celtic fans and another 50 independent travellers. We landed in Kanuas and it was bitterly cold. The airport was so small and only had one runway. When we got out of the airport the place was like something out an old movie; trams, old cars on the road and nobody spoke English expect a few people at our hotel.

The locals didn't even know why we where there. They considered us with a strange look on their faces because we all had Celtic strips and scarves. It was as if they thought we were like aliens. On the day of the match we got a taxi up to the stadium. It was very run down and we had as many fans as the home team. After being knocked out of the Champions League at the hands of Basel, I wasn't expecting very much success in the UEFA Cup, trouncing Suduva 10-1 on aggregate eased the pain a little though."

Celtic v Blackburn (3-0 aggregate)

Celtic then came up against Blackburn in the second round and again were at home in the first leg. It turned out to be a very nervous game for a Celtic side very much on the back foot for the majority of the match. 0-0 it was at half time, and the game was looking to finish goal-less with neither side looking capable of breaking the deadlock.

Then six minutes from full-time Henrik Larsson scored the all important goal for Celtic. The full time whistle went, to a huge sigh of relief from the home fans, and Celtic had a 1-0 lead to take down the M74 and M6 for the second leg at Blackburn. Going into the second leg, Blackburn were very confident that they would conquer Celtic – Men Against Bhoys headlines were everywhere - but this wasn't to be the case as Celtic silenced both their opponents and the critics with a comfortable and hugely enjoyable 2-0 win.

Henrik Larsson again opening the scoring after 15 minutes, and then ex-Blackburn player Chris Sutton killed off their comeback hopes making it 2-0 for Celtic. So deservedly Celtic went through to the next round 3-0 on aggregate. Attendance: Home 59,553. Away 29,698.

Here's **Bud Adam's** story, from the Blackburn second leg tie:

"We set off early doors and joined the Celtic convoy down on the motorway heading to the so called Battle of Britain, all of us confident that we'd put one over on Blackburn manager Graeme Souness.

The beer was flowing and the tunes blaring as we arrived, Celtic fans had taken over the town, the bars were bouncing and we were all in good spirits. As the day progressed some trouble kicked off when some Blackburn fans tried to take some liberties but it quickly died down.

As word of fake tickets started circulating, we set off to the ground early to avoid the rush only to be met with thousands of fans with the same idea. Police and stewards tried to set up a cordon but too many fans were trying to squeeze through a small gate to enter the turnstiles. A mass crush ensued, panic set in with the travelling hordes and at times I struggled to get my breath as we were packed in like sardines. Tempers flared as people realised they might not get into the game, I was on my own as I lost my friends but my only concern at the time was getting inside.

I eventually (think I may have been one of the last before they shut the turnstiles) got into the Darwin end in time for the huddle and the delayed kick off. Inside the stadium was intense and tensions were running high as everyone tried to find their mates, but after Larsson's opening goal everyone settled down and enjoyed the night. Sporadic fights broke out in the home end as Celtic fans celebrated the opening goal and by the time Sutton added a second the game was already over for the travelling fans-Celtic had won!

This turned out to be the first Battle of Britain on the road to Seville and I was extremely happy at how comfortable the victory was in the end for Celtic.

Celtic v Celta Vigo (2-2 aggregate, Celtic through on away goal rule)

Celtic were then drawn against Celta Vigo, surely their toughest test yet. Again the first leg was played at Celtic Park, with Celtic seeing out another nervous 1-0 win. Martin O'Neill sent out the same team that saw off Blackburn but It took Celtic a while to settle into the game. But it was that man Larsson again who scored after 52 minutes to give Celtic the lead.

The referee had a shocker in this game, refusing to give some decisions to Celtic. Full time saw Celtic secure a 1-0 win to take to sunny Spain for the second leg. We thought it was nervous in the earlier rounds but this was worse. Celta Vigo took the lead through Jesuli before John Hartson got the crucial away goal making it 1-1 at half time. Benni McCarthy then scored to make it 2-1 to Celta Vigo, and it was now a matter of holding on for Celtic.

Didier Agathe played outstandingly in this game. Celtic held on and went through to the next round on the away goal rule, 2-2 the aggregate score. It is the first time that Celtic have survived beyond Christmas in a European competition for 23 years. Attendance: Home 53,726. Away 14,300.

Here's **Toddy McCormack's** story. Toddy was in Spain for the away leg:

"Sitting on the tarmac at Glasgow airport for 2 hours with engine problems, we didn't care as we looked forward to the match against a top La Liga side. Finally were off. Myself, the McGrath brothers Joe and Gerry, big Drewby and Joe "the boss" Cosgrove finally arrive in Vigo, bags thrown into the room, let's go! We headed down into the city and met up with a few Bhoys from back home, for the usual; beer, singing and plenty of great banter. The stadium was more or less situated in the city, which was very handy and as per usual after a few beers we all lost each other!

I met my older brother (Joe) going into the ground, covered in blood with no idea what happened to himself or whose leather jacket he was wearing (after the game he met two Irish fellas who asked how he was as it was them that put him into an ambulance).

After the match we were all in high spirits and eventually found each other in a bar close to the hotel. Dear knows what time we packed in drinking but we were a sorry sight the next morning! Then it was off to the airport for the return flight unaware of the drama that lay ahead. On boarding the plane we were almost immediately taken off.

More engine trouble! After another 2 hours delay we finally get airborne. The flight attendants were mainly fine except for one stroppy woman. A guy was caught smoking in the toilets, and was spoken to by the stewardess. Then we heard an announcement saying that we would all be held back at Glasgow Airport until the culprit was identified by the other Celtic fans. This didn't go down to well, which led to a few questions being asked (not in a threatening manner though) and the stroppy stewardess ran to the pilot and suddenly we were on route to Cardiff! On arrival at Cardiff, we were met by a massive police presence.

They eventually boarded the plane and came face to face with 180 subdued fans, not rioters as was reported. One of the coppers later said that a Celtic fan had told him, there are hundreds of us but we are really nice, just like the Waltons! The police could not have been any nicer and were totally confused as to why a mayday had been alerted due to rioting fans as we didn't look fit for anything never mind a riot. Anyway they gave us something to eat and eventually boarded us on to coaches for a long drive through the night back to Glasgow.

Sky News had covered the event, which was handy in a way, because my 7 months pregnant wife watched me being escorted down the stairs of the plane by a copper so at least she knew where I was!

Looking back on the trip and the whole flight saga and asking myself would I do it all again? I wouldn't change it for the world.

R.I.P. Joe "the boss" Cosgrove."

The first thought I had when we were drawn against Celta Vigo was that we'd go out. It was the most nervous tie we had faced yet, edge of the seat stuff when we were hanging on in Spain with the away goal rule.

Celtic v Stuttgart (6-3 aggregate)

Up next for Celtic was Stuttgart, again with the first leg in Glasgow. The game got underway and there was a big turning point in the 17th minute when Stuttgart had a man sent off. Ten minutes after the sending off though, it was Stuttgart who took the lead through Kevin Kuranyi. If anything the goal only spurred Celtic on more and 9 minutes later Celtic equalised with a goal from Paul Lambert.

Just before half time Shaun Maloney put Celtic 2-1 up. Into the second half and Celtic scored their third through Stiliyan Petrov, and that was to be the final score. The second leg was thoroughly entertaining to say the least. Celtic got off to a flier in Germany, scoring 2 goals within 3 minutes and effectively killing off any hopes of Stuttgart going through. Stuttgart pulled one back before half time to make it 2-1.

In the 75th minute, Stuttgart scored again, and then scored another in the 87th minute, but it was too little too late. A very good Stuttgart side had managed to turn around a 2-0 deficit on the night but they were knocked out by Celtic 5-4 on aggregate. Celtic's fairytale was gathering momentum with notable scalps being taken from England, Spain and now Germany. Attendance: Home 60,832. Away 50,348.

Kieran Daly was in Germany for the away leg. Here are Kieran's thoughts on the trip:

"Stuttgart for me was a wonderful occasion. It began when we arrived in the city and were greeted by a load of German supporters inviting us into the bars around the city. The beer was flowing and the Celtic songs were being sung.

The occasion was special during and after the match especially as we won the tie, I believe that what made this occasion to me was the laughs that we had and building a special bond with the German people in that city."

Fans were starting to get excited at the recent success in this Cup run, and it didn't stop at Stuttgart either. In what turned out to be one of the more comfortable ties, it certainly didn't seem like it in Germany when Stuttgart came back from 2-0 to win the leg 3-2. The 3-1 score line at Celtic Park had effectively killed the tie though.

Celtic v Liverpool (3-1 aggregate)

Another Battle of Britain saw Celtic paired with Liverpool with the first leg again at Celtic Park. There was a now certain expectancy among the Celtic supporters to get through. Celtic started perfectly and found themselves 1-0 up after only 2 minutes thanks to Henrik Larsson.

Liverpool replied though to make it 1-1 just 15 minutes later. This was to be the full time result, but the game was marred by a disgusting act of indecency from El Hadji Diouf when he spat on a Celtic fan. Going into the second leg, it was all in Liverpool's favour and on paper it was Celtic's toughest test. That wasn't to be the case though as Celtic achieved a very comfortable 2-0 at Anfield. Both goals were superb to top a fantastic victory. A low free kick from Alan Thompson and a wonderful strike from John Hartson were the difference in this game. Celtic went through to the semi-final 3-1 on aggregate. Attendance: Home 59,759. Away 44,238.

Here's the story of **Colin Jordan**, who travelled down to the game in Liverpool.

"This Journey to Liverpool started a few weeks prior in Germany. Myself and a few of my friends were sitting in a small Turkish bar after the Stuttgart game talking about the match and who we fancied in the next round. To a man we all said Liverpool. We really fancied our chances especially if we could get Henrik fit.

We got Liverpool and Henrik was fit for the first leg scoring after 2 minutes. The experience of the 2nd leg was phenomenal; we travelled early morning on the day of the game arriving in Liverpool around about 12pm. It was full of Celtic fans singing songs and mixing with Liverpool fans in pubs, all getting on really well.

We went to a Liverpool social club, which was full of Liverpool fans. It was great, the Liverpool fans were very welcoming, telling us how we were going to get beaten easily by the mighty Liverpool. But we remained confident. We got a taxi about 40 minutes before kick off and asked the driver to put some Celtic tunes on so that we were set for the game. We went back to the same social club after the game but it wasn't as busy, I don't know why!

The fans we met after the game were either jubilant Celtic fans who decided they were just going to stay a night in Liverpool to go out and celebrate ie no hotel, hardly any money, just determined to enjoy themselves, or Liverpool fans who couldn't believe the mighty Liverpool had lost at the famous Anfield. To their credit they did congratulate us and wished us well in the semi-finals."

Up against one of Europe's most successful clubs, this proved a stroll in the park in the end. An away goal however for Liverpool had us thinking the worst. At Anfield, Liverpool were clear favourites, but they fell short of expectations when Celtic eased to a 2-0 victory. Watching the game it was just brilliant to see those wonderful goals for Celtic. Big Bad John scored his best ever goal for Celtic that night. Celtic were through to the semi-final, who'd have thought it?

Celtic v Boavista (2-1 aggregate)

Boavista from Portugal came next for Celtic. This was an extremely nervous semi final for both teams as the prize of a place in the UEFA Cup Final awaited the winner. The first leg was again to be played at Celtic Park. The first half was very tense and it finished goalless. At the start of the second half Joos Valgaeren was unfortunate enough to score an own goal in the 48th minute. Celtic fans were thinking the worst. Celtic went into this match as clear favourites with the bookies and it only took a minute for the panic to ease when Henrik Larsson made it 1-1. This was the story up until the 75th minute when Celtic were awarded a penalty.

Larsson stepped up to take it and MISSED! It was a superb save by Boavista's goalkeeper Ricardo to keep the score 1-1. John Hartson had a chance late on but the game finished 1-1. Would Celtic rue that penalty miss? Would Henrik make up for it in the second leg?

With so much at stake this was was another incredibly tense game. Nil-nil would suit the Portuguese side as they had an away goal. Celtic needed to score. Neither side able to break the other down in the first half and it was more of the same in the second half. As the clocked ticked on the closer Boavista were coming to reaching the final through the away goal rule. Then on 80 minutes – at last - a goal from who else but Henrik Larsson! Celtic had the lead and Henrik had scored the goal. Celtic held on to win 1-0 and went through to the UEFA Cup Final winning 2-1 on aggregate. Incredibly Celtic were in the UEFA Cup Final! Attendance: Home - 60,000. Away - 11,000.

Celtic fan **Tony Kelly** made the trip over to Portugal for the Boavista match. Here's his story:

""Claire, where is my passport?" I was frantic now as I pleaded with my wife. She must know I thought. Claire, my wife of twelve years, suffers my trips away to support Celtic without a single moan. Not this time though as Claire would not give me her blessing to go on this trip telling me that our bakery was now at critical point, busy and with too many European away days this year they had taken their toll.

She was adamant she was not helping. I was panicking. Then, I found it. In the very first place I looked an hour ago. Now back to work on Claire, surely she would give me permission to go. Not that a man needs permission but in the home, every man knows it's best to let your wife be boss sometimes. "Claire, c'mon honey." She replied, "No Tony you have been to every game home and away".

It's 8am. I am booked on the official flight to leave at 10:30am. Decisions, decisions. I ask so many times I am beginning to annoy her. I need to change tactics.

"Claire, we will go away somewhere nice when I get back". Claire replies firmly "no Tony." I call Therese Cassidy, through whom just four weeks previously I had booked 16 seats on the one day trip and one on the official trip to Porto. Celtic were playing their biggest game in my lifetime. The Semi Final of the UEFA Cup!

My bakery in Rutherglen was like a supporters club. Every day visitors talk all things Celtic. We had all our staff going to game, even the engineers who fixed fridges. The day before @jamiekerr67 had picked up tickets for travelling. Nicky Fisher our fridge engineer was excited, Brian Hay brother of Celtic great Davie Hay was waiting patiently for his travel details. My brother Paul and nephews and nieces, all soaring in anticipation for their travel details. In comes Jamie, passes out all the tickets and comes to Nicky the fridge engineer.

Now Nicky Fischer has no sense of humour and when Jamie tells him his ticket is wrong and that he needs to go quickly to amend details we all stop laughing, more tension. Then Jamie tells Nicky his name is wrong on the ticket. We ask what's wrong Jamie? Jamie says that his name has been printed on ticket as "Fishy Nicker" - the place erupts!

Today, all jokes were on me. I wasn't going. Claire was adamant. She said you can go on one of the places for one day and back that night. It was her only compromise. I called Therese, told her I would not be on the official flight. She called me a name, told me I was a pest and said she would see me at Boavista. I put down the phone, and sat in my living room watching TV. The build up was amazing. Lead story on Sky Sports News. Headlines in every newspaper. I was thinking I need to go, TODAY. I go back to Claire and ask again, still no. Then I put my foot down. She is livid. I tell her we will deal with it when I get home!

In the car I call Therese who is at the airport; she tells me if I am not at the plane door before Martin O'Neill, I will not be going. She also has someone to meet me at airport. I am racing along the M8 towards Glasgow Airport. I call Claire; she is still angry and puts the phone down. I call again, this time no answer. I get to airport and rush to the plane. I am there just as Martin and John Robertson come behind me. Therese gives me a scud across the head as I get on. The guys I have told I am not going tell me they knew I would be there. How could they? We take off. I have left the match tickets in the car. Aaaaaagggggghhhhhhh.

Jamie was the first person I called from Portugal. "Can you go to my house and get my spare keys straight away. I have left our tickets in car". He replies, "I am not going near your house. Your Claire is raging". Claire had been on the phone ranting and raving to Jamie's wife Dawn. When I informed him his ticket was in the car he duly obliged and got a sore ear into the bargain from Claire!

The game was brilliant; the best sight ever was when the official Celtic party arrived at the airport in Portugal at the same time as the one day flight to return home. The sight of Bobo Balde running into fans and jumping on Jamie's dad whom he knew from his time at the park every day getting strips signed for charity events etc, will live with me forever. Coming home on the flight we didn't need a pilot because we were so high from the victory. I arrived home the day after the game to find my wife standing at the door with the biggest cuddle and the million dollar question. Have we got tickets for the final because we are not missing it for the world? I replied, "Of course darling!""

Talk about nerves. This was painful to watch. Boavista getting the away goal just like Liverpool did, and when Henrik Larsson missed the penalty, would we live to regret it? The game was getting closer and closer to 90 minutes at Boavista's small stadium and they were in the driving seat, as Celtic needed to score. Into the last 10 minutes and Celtic fans go ballistic; Henrik Larsson had just scored the most crucial goal of his Celtic career. We had done it; Celtic had reached the UEFA Cup Final. I never thought I'd see this day.

UEFA Cup Final - Celtic v Porto (2-3 A.E.T.)

Porto. It was one of the teams that the fans wanted to avoid coming up against in any round. They were playing extremely good football throughout the tournament, and they had a fantastic team of players. Going into the game, the bookies had Porto as favourites. Celtic fans travelled in numbers to Seville, estimates of 80,000 to over 100,000 making the trip.

The game kicked off and it was pretty much end to end, but neither side made the breakthrough. It was Porto who did so, the goal coming through Derlei. The second half got underway and Henrik Larsson immediately scored to make it 1-1 with an absolutely wonderful header. Just 7 minutes later though Porto again went ahead, this time through Dmitri Alenitchev.

Only two minutes later and Larsson equalises again for Celtic! Another headed goal puts the fans into delirium. The full time whistle went and the Final was going into extra time. Celtic went down to 10 men after Bobo Balde was sent off, and 10 minutes later Porto had scored again, going 3-2 up with another goal from Derlei. Porto then went down to 10 men in the dying seconds when Nuno Valente was sent off.

Celtic were doing everything they could to get the equaliser, but it was too little too late. Porto had shattered Celtic's dream at the last. Attendance: 52,972.

The last thing to mention about the journey to Seville is that Henrik Larsson scored 11 goals in 887 minutes, while Derlei scored 12 goals in 1,159 minutes.

Here are the thoughts of the one and only Paul Larkin, who managed to make the trip to Seville.

"When I think of Seville, three things come to mind. Heat, cheats and defeat. I don't think I have ever experienced heat like I did that day and was me sitting in the shade and only moving my hand up to my mouth a lot. God knows what it must have been like for the players to play in. Especially for the peely wally ones like Neil Lennon.

Then there was the cheating. Porto were a fantastic side who had a great manager and they were on the up. So, you have to ask, why resort to the diving, the rolling about and the general bitching towards the referee every five seconds. Some of their players were world class and would go on to prove this for many years to come but in my mind they will always conjure up that nasty side of the game that no one wants to see. Most of the Celtic players played like gentlemen that night. Until some woke up...

Ultimately though, in Seville, there was defeat. The fans provided a spectacle that will be remembered by those there, just like the Sermon on the Mount was by those in attendance. The colour, the excitement, the passion, I can still feel it when I close my eyes but not for too long because I will always remember the fact that we got beat and at Celtic, we don't celebrate defeats."

There is a postscript though.

Henrik!

There I was getting home and ready for the Final. The biggest game for Celtic in many years. Could we do it? Would we be able to see off Porto?

I was one of the unlucky ones sat in front of a TV screen in my living room. I was only young at the time so who could blame me for not being in Seville?

It seemed whatever Porto could do, Larsson could do better. I've never been so upset in my life to date. To lose the game in the way we did still hurts to this day. It still remains a very touchy subject for Celtic fans, but I prefer to look at it the positive way, that we actually managed to go on an amazing Cup run. In the end we fell just short, but the Bhoys did us all proud. I will cherish the memory of 21st May 2003 for the rest of my life, Celtic in Seville will never be forgotten.

WHAT THE TWO MANAGERS SAID...

Martin O'Neill said after the game: "I will probably get into trouble for this, but it was poor sportsmanship. The rolling over, the time wasting. But they have beaten us, well done to them and it's up to us to learn from this. It is a steep learning curve, but this was a wonderful, wonderful experience.

The players put everything into it and the fans have been fantastic. We came roaring back every time they scored a goal and, if when we had 11 against 11 in extra time, I think we were the more mentally strong. But it was not to be with Bobo getting sent off. It was a massive blow."

Jose Mourinho had this to say: "I'd prefer to ask whether the behaviour of the Celtic players was normal in your country. What Balde did to Deco in front of me could have ended his career.

The referee didn't affect the result, in that there were no doubtful decisions, but I think Balde could have had a direct red for his foul and Thompson could also have seen a second yellow card on two occasions. The referee wanted to end the game with 11 against 11 and I think maybe he was a bit afraid to send anyone off. There was a lot of commitment in Celtic's game, commitment, toughness and aggression. I'm tempted to use another word - but I won't. We have given a great example to the world and those who love football and we have also made history by taking the UEFA Cup to Portugal for the first time ever."

Later Mourinho could reflect on Celtic in Seville and had this to say in June 2003:

"I fell a bit in love with Celtic, because the atmosphere was amazing and the crowd was magnificent, the way they behaved with the Porto fans."

Then in May 2008 he once again talked about Celtic in Seville:

"When I was at Porto my team also played in the UEFA Cup final against a Scottish side - but it was Celtic. I've never seen such emotional people. It was unbelievable!"

That it was Jose.

Written by Joe Ruddy, a contributor to CQN Magazine, with thanks to BBC Sport.

CHAPTER 16

SEVILLE ON THE BBC

The BBC audience for the 2003 UEFA Cup Final peaked at just over 10 Million viewers in the UK for the live broadcast from Seville. BBC's Head of Football, Niall Sloane said:

"We're delighted that so many people tuned in to follow a British team's progress in the final. We're only sorry that Celtic didn't win."

BBC Scotland's UEFA Cup Final programme was presented by Rob McLean and the main pundit was Sandy Clark, a curious choice given the fact that he had no association with Celtic whatsoever! BBC Scotland had Chick Young trackside in Seville to provide regular updates. It is not known if he had his St Mirren scarf with him in Seville – although it is doubtful!

Meanwhile the BBC provided a comprehensive match report from Seville on their website. Here is what was reported:

SEVILLE REPORT FROM BBC SPORT:

PORTO END CELTIC'S UEFA DREAM

Porto shattered Celtic's hopes of winning their first European trophy for 36 years with a dramatic UEFA Cup final victory in Seville.

Martin O'Neill's side twice fought back from behind against the Portuguese champions on a night of searing temperatures and fluctuating fortunes.

But Porto snatched a late extra-time winner, with Celtic reduced to ten men after defender Bobo Balde was shown the red card.

Derlei and Dmitri Alenitchev twice gave Porto the lead - only for the magic of Henrik Larsson to put Celtic level on each occasion, rekindling hopes of adding to their 1967 European Cup win in Lisbon.

But when Derlei restored Porto's lead with only five minutes of extra-time left, Celtic could not mount another recovery, and O'Neill's gallant side were left disconsolate.

Celtic were backed by a wall of noise from the massed ranks of their fans - and spirits were lifted when Porto suffered an early injury setback.

Influential midfielder Francisco Costinha collapsed making a pass and was stretchered off with a thigh injury.

Porto had the first half's most influential performer in striker Deco, who was a constant threat to the Celtic defence.

He forced Joos Valgaeren into a tackle which earned the defender a booking, then forced a fine diving save from Rab Douglas four minutes before the interval.

Celtic's response was muted, with Larsson's long-range free-kick the only serious threat to Vitor Baia.

Porto deservedly took the lead in first-half injury time - and predictably Deco was the orchestrator.

Deco's cross found Alenitchev unmarked, and even though Douglas saved his volley, the rebound fell invitingly for Derlei to score.

Celtic needed an instant response after the break, and the talismanic Larsson provided it within two minutes of the restart.

He rose brilliantly to meet Didier Agathe's cross to head beyond Baia to score his 200th goal for the club.

Celtic were only on terms for seven minutes before another piece of magic by Deco ended with a pass that opened up the Celtic rearguard for Alenitchev to steer a cool finish past Douglas.

But this topsy-turvy final had burst into life, and Larsson restored equality for Celtic after 56 minutes.

Alan Thompson's corner found the Swede unmarked and he flashed another powerful header past Baia.

Aleitchev had a glorious opportunity win the game for Porto in the dying seconds of normal time when he was gifted the ball by substitute Jackie McNamara, but he blazed wildly over the top from 18 yards.

Celtic were reduced to 10 men four minutes into extra-time when giant defender Balde was sent off for his second bookable offence following a wild challenge on Derlei.

The first period of extra-time - with the so-called "silver goal" decider - passed without serious opportunities for either side.

But Porto were back in front with five minutes left when Derlei collected a loose ball to fire past the stranded Douglas.

Porto's Nuno Valente was also sent off for a second bookable offence in the closing seconds, but by then Celtic's challenge had been snuffed out.

Celtic: Douglas, Balde, Mjallby, Valgaeren (Laursen 64), Agathe, Lennon, Lambert (McNamara 76), Petrov (Maloney 104), Thompson, Sutton, Larsson. Subs Not Used: Hedman, Sylla, Fernandez, Smith.

Sent Off: Balde (95).

Booked: Valgaeren, Lennon, Balde, Petrov.

FC Porto: Vitor Baia, Ferreira, Nuno Valente, Jorge Costa (Pedro Emanuel 71), Ricardo Carvalho, Costinha (Ricardo Costa 9), Alenichev, Maniche, Deco, Capucho (Marco Ferreira 98), Derlei. Subs Not Used: Nuno, Cesar Peixoto, Clayton, Tiago.

Sent Off: Nuno Valente (120).

Booked: Nuno Valente, Derlei, Maniche, Marco Ferreira.

Attendance: 52,972

Referee: Lubos Michel (Slovakia).

The BBC's UEFA Cup Final 2003 player ratings

CELTIC

Rab Douglas: The keeper had an excellent game on his return from injury and made several vital stops - but had no chance with any of the three Porto goals. 8/10

Johan Mjallby: Made an uncertain start but returned to the commanding form that won him so many caps for Sweden. 7/10

Bobo Balde: Improved after a nervous start but was sent off in extra time after receiving a second yellow card following a mis-timed tackle. 6/10

Joos Valgaeren: Another who began with some butterflies, Valgaeren was booked after seven minutes, his poor clearance led to Porto's opener and he then went off injured. 5/10

Didier Agathe: Made some penetrating runs down the right and finally found his man with a cross for Larsson's first of the night. 7/10

Paul Lambert: Was the main creative force in the Celtic midfield and fought hard to add a UEFA Cup winner's medal to the Champions League one he gained with Borussia Dortmund. 7/10

Neil Lennon: Combined his normal holding role with a marking job but had his work cut out matching the pace of man-of-the-match Deco. 6/10

Stilian Petrov: Bulgarian midfielder found it difficult to get into the game or make his normal lethal runs into the box. 6/10

Alan Thompson: The midfielder was forced deeper into defence than he would have liked, although he picked out some excellent passes with his trusty left foot. 7/10

Chris Sutton: Won his personal battle in the air with Jorge Costa, with the Englishman's little flick-ons just failing to fall to his team-mates. 8/10

Henrik Larsson: Headed home the first equaliser superbly for his 200th goal for Celtic and followed it up with his second of the night in what was probably his best-ever game for the Scottish champions. 9/10

Substitutes

Ulrik Laursen (replaced Valgaeren): The Danish defender made some vital interceptions. 6/10

Jackie McNamara (replaced Lambert): The Scotland midfielder found it difficult to adjust to the pace of the game after coming on late and almost gifted Porto a last-minute winner in normal time. 6/10

Shaun Maloney (replaced Petrov): The young striker was introduced in extra time and the Scotland Under-21 international twice came close to setting up a winner for Celtic. 7/10

PORTO

Vitor Baia: The experienced international goalkeeper looked nervous on crosses but had little chance with Larsson's two goals. 5/10

Paulo Ferreira: The defender worked hard, but his poor marking was partly at fault for Larsson's second goal. 6/10

Jorge Costa: The tough defender was bullied by Sutton, was lucky not to be booked for an early foul on Larsson and was substituted midway through the second half. 6/10

Ricardo Carvalho: Made some vital challenges and looked cool and calm at the heart of the Porto defence. 8/10

Nuno Valente: The full-back produced some excellent runs down the left but was sent off in extra-time for a second yellow card. 5/10

Francisco Costinha: The defender was struck down with a pulled muscle after only six minutes. 2/10

Maniche: The quiet man in the Porto midfield peppered the Celtic goal with some accurate and powerful drives every time he was in range. 7/10

Dmitri Alenichev: The destroyer to Deco's artisan in the Porto midfield made some dangerous runs into the Celtic box and finished with aplomb for his side's second goal. 8/10

Deco: Was man-marked by Lennon, but you would never have guessed as the Brazilian-born maestro's breathtaking skills lit up the first-half like a latter-day Maradona. Set up both Porto goals before tiring. 9/10

Nuno Capucho: Started well, winning headers against the taller Celtic defenders before drifting out of the game. 6/10

Derlei: Sullied his reputation with some blatant play-acting but was always dangerous up front and showed good positional sense to open the scoring then score the winner. 7/10

Substitutes

Ricardo Costa (replaced Costinha): Became the youngest player in the final as an early substitute but failed to get close enough to Larsson at both Celtic goals. 5/10

Pedro Emanuel (replaced Costa): Was quiet and efficient coming on in the second half at the heart of the defence. 7/10

Marco Ferreira (replaced Capucho): Introduced in injury time as Porto attempted to take advantage of their extra man. 5/10

Courtesy of BBC Sport.

CHAPTER 17
SEVILLE ON SOCIAL MEDIA

cat - @1888cat epic heat but very much worthwhile, regardless of outcome

Lisbon Lion - @tirnaog09 Press conference post match at Blackburn. Souness growling as Journo's phone goes off, playing 'Grand Old Team' #Priceless

Ciarán Barbour - @CiaranBarbour Crying for hours, being left behind, as I wasn't allowed to go as I was too young.

Steven Fulton - @StevieBhoy8 an unbelievable journey that put our club and fans back on the map! What a team!

stevie bhoy @Stephen24669 very hot, very emotional, ultimately - very proud.

paul leckie - @paul2011l brilliant outstanding showed the English media. Sunburn, disappointment and now appreciation for the good times!

blackjohn - @Sonnyponny73 the King's two magnificent headers in the final that just failed to get us the cup.

Sean Gartland - @SeanGartland biggest regret of my life not going.

Alex Rosenberg - @alexrosenberg83 it's more than a game it really is a family!! :o)

THEChucklesLeVert - @ChucklesLeVert Amazing coming together of the Celtic family. Fantastic host city and a real football occasion. So proud to be a Celt.

Chris :) - @chris_derry Lucky to be at a European Final with the best fans in the world, like my Uncle and his mates in '67. Hail! Hail!

James A-Rab Campbell - @underagemaddog 'The best and worst time to be a Celtic fan' (from my dad)

Johnny_Scotland - @Johnny_Scotland The biggest ever travelling army in football turned Seville into a sea of green and white, but alas it wasn't to be our night.

blackjohn - @Sonnyponny73 sadly we couldn't defeat Porto but we most definitely conquered Seville, our team lost but the fans did not, and they never will.

SEVILLE - CELTIC SUPPORT WINS AWARDS

Approximately 80,000 Celtic supporters, the largest travelling support in history at that time, made the journey to Seville for this game. The exemplary conduct of the Celtic supporters received widespread praise from the people of Seville (there were no arrests) and the fans were awarded prestigious Fair Play Awards from both FIFA and UEFA "for their extraordinarily loyal and sporting behaviour". FIFA president Sepp Blatter also stated that he believed Celtic fans were the greatest fans in the world when he presented the FIFA Fair Play award at Celtic Park.

Sevilla fans travelling to the 2007 UEFA Cup in Glasgow noted that the visiting Celtic fans left them with a "great impression" of Glasgow.

Can we do it again?

It is hard to say really whether Celtic could reach the final again in the future. Of course the competition has changed to the Europa Cup now, but it is still the same calibre of teams. I don't think we can completely rule out the possibility of appearing in a major European final again. It might not happen anytime soon but sometime down the line I'd like to think we could get there again. Maybe even go that extra mile and win the Cup. Henrik Larsson was our hero in this outstanding run and we'd probably need to look at finding another Henrik to get us there again! Remember that Celtic recently finished ahead of Benfica in Champions League Group stages and they dropped into the Europa Cup, reached the final and were very unlucky not to win it. Maybe the trick for Celtic is an elusive third place finish in a Champions League Group and if that happens who knows?

In conclusion, I look to Seville as a truly memorable campaign. It'll always be hard to look back on because of the way in which we lost the Final, but the fact we got to the Final was a fantastic achievement. I just try not to think too much about that game, and think about the occasion in Seville and all the games that led up to Seville. Some of the teams we put out were great sides. Although too young at the time and didn't manage to make the trip to Seville, I will always remember it as a wonderful European adventure.

Written by Joe Ruddy.

CHAPTER 18

SEVILLE – THE PROFESSOR'S VIEW

Professor Richard Giulianotti, then of Aberdeen University, travelled on an academic field trip to Seville and subsequently published his paper titled 2003 UEFA CUP FINAL IN SEVILLE which was published by Scottish Affairs, no.48, summer 2004. We asked Professor Giulianotti for permission to quote from his work and with his approval we have selected the following passages, which are particularly relevant to Seville – The Celtic Movement. In 2011 Professor Giulianotti was elected an academician of the Academy of Social Sciences and moved to the School of Sport at Loughborough University.

SEVILLE – THE WELCOMING CITY

"Seville's suitability in welcoming Celtic fans carried other historical, social and cultural factors. The autonomous community of Andalucia ('state' flag: green and white) has, as its most popular team, Real Betis, founded in 1909, and who owe their own green-and-white kit to a local man who returned to Seville with Celtic strips that he had found attractive during a Scottish sojourn. In symmetry with the fervour of Celtic's supporters and the traditional enthusiasm of their players, Seville possesses a popular culture that is appreciative of those who personify the key folkloric term of duende, that was originally associated with flamenco, and which refers more broadly to the spirit and passion of dancers and other artists who express themselves beyond technical routines. More specifically, Seville's public geography ably staged the transformation of the UEFA Cup final into an elaborated social event for Celtic supporters. The highly intimate, baroque Barrio de Santa Cruz, and its surrounding districts, is filled with tapas bars, hotels and pensions that accommodated some of the supporters. The themed Irish pub, Flaherty's, did a huge trade among the hundreds of Celtic fans that were massed outside, selling a reputed two months' worth of beer in five days."

Professor Richard Giulianotti

WORSHIP

The collective consciousness of the supporters was strongly promoted through the wearing of identifying attire. On match day, an overwhelming majority wore the sacred 'hoops' shirt, forging a heightened sense of unity. One fan from north- east Scotland recalled his walk towards the stadium as an entrancing communal experience: 'To look around, and then behind you, and see thousands and thousands in the shirts, the hoops, walking alongside you... . I was living the dream, that's what it was, living the dream.' The songs – especially the constant rendition of 'Hail, Hail, The Celts are Here' – constituted positive rites of self-worship. Other songs, notably about Henrik Larsson, highlighted the totemic qualities of the club's representative players.

Professor Richard Giulianotti

"NOTHING TOOK PLACE"

In Seville, the public authorities had taken the customary precautions for a major European fixture. Police reinforcements had been drafted in from as far away as Valencia, and several mobile units were stationed around the centre. On the Monday outside Flaherty's, police kept an eye on Celtic fans, and in the one incident of any note, a supporter who had climbed a small tree to retrieve a trapped beach ball was beaten down by an officer's truncheon blow to the ribs; a teenage boy caught the assault's aftermath across the eye. While dampening the atmosphere temporarily, the supporters did not allow this incident to define their relations with police over the next few days. Throughout the week, only two fans were detained: one for allegedly wrecking a hotel room, the other for a minor assault on a fellow fan that produced a £92 fine (including compensation) and a reported handshake of reconciliation between the two parties (The Herald, 23 May 2003). Thus, the dominant discourse, that this mass migration produced only exceptional and isolated incidents, was sustained by other parties. In discussing public order on the day of the match one local reporter professed that 'nothing took place' except a solitary incident whereby a Celtic fan attempted to pilfer a match ticket from a Portuguese tout.

Professor Richard Giulianotti

THE MSM IN SEVILLE – "NAEBODY READS IT!"

The Sun and the Daily Record became embroiled in a struggle to produce the defining images of the Seville event, and to project themselves as key facilitators of the supporter communion. The Record, derided by many Celtic fans as the Daily Ranger, started from a particularly weak market position. All football supporters are wary of systematic bias against their specific club within key institutions, such as the football authorities and the national media. All fans practice what the Italians call dietrologia, that is, the science of observing or speculating upon what goes on 'behind the scenes' among powerful groups, and usually to the perceived detriment of the supporters' favoured club. Earlier in the season, the Record ran a front-page lead story that, in the eyes of Celtic fans, seemed to provide irrefutable evidence of its suspected systematic bias against their club. Under the headline 'Thugs and Thieves' that was printed adjacent to the club crest, the main article accused Celtic players of criminal misconduct against the newspaper's photographer at a Christmas party in Newcastle. In response, Celtic fans attacked the newspaper for its premature, unjust judging of their players, and initiated a 'Bhoycott the Record' campaign that reportedly seriously damaged the paper's circulation figures. The police investigation concluded that criminal charges against the players were untenable but the boycott remained in place after the Record editor had been fired.

Both redtops sent open-top double-decker buses to Seville, equipped with the standard publicity 'girls' and blaring public address systems, to track down stories, snap photographs and generally ingratiate themselves within the supporter carnival. The Record bus carried an appropriated image of Henrik Larsson emblazoned across its side, but still met with scepticism from supporters: on one particular occasion, as the bus drove through the centre, a passing fan shouted 'Naebody reads it' several times to the driver.

Professor Richard Giulianotti

SEVILLE – THE AWARDS

Socially, Celtic fans constitute a relatively exogenous community that attracts followers who enjoy the expressive, participatory, non-violent elements of passionate fandom.

The social dynamics involving Celtic supporters were highly positive. Seville enabled the fans to translate their sense of belonging to an imagined community into full celebration within a vast communion, while creating some arresting spectacles that did not fracture public order. In relations with other groups, the support established a good accord with Spanish police, delighted the local mayor who raked in some €17.3 million from hosting the event, and made effective and selective use of Scottish media while there. Three months later, UEFA awarded Celtic fans the 'Fair Play' trophy for 2003, in recognition of their activities in Seville.

Professor Richard Giulianotti

Academic quotes from CELTIC, CULTURAL IDENTITIES AND THE GLOBALIZATION OF FOOTBALL: NOTES FROM THE 2003 UEFA CUP FINAL IN SEVILLE, Scottish Affairs, no.48, summer 2004, by Professor Richard Giulianotti. Thanks to Professor Giulianotti for permission to quote from his work in this book.

CHAPTER 19

DON'T TELL THE BILL HOW WE WATCHED SEVILLE

25th April 2003. ANZAC Day in New Zealand. A public holiday to commemorate the fallen in wars. Dawn Ceremonies are the usual order of the day. However for around 75 Celtic supporters the early start to the day was for another purpose. Celtic were playing Boavista in the second leg of the UEFA Cup semi-final.

Our venue to watch the game was probably appropriate for the day-The Newmarket Returned Services Association clubrooms. Possibly an unusual meeting place for a Celtic Supporters Club with a large portrait of the Queen on the wall. However the management and staff were very supportive and always prepared to open at odd hours to accommodate us.

So, along with my 2 sons Sean and Stephen I made my way there in the early hours of the morning. We sat at a table alongside Bob Cairney and his son James. With 13 minutes of the game remaining Celtic scored. Watching on an internet stream made it seem as if the ball would never cross the line – but it did.

The 5 of us hugged each other in a huddle of joy. Myself and Bob who had seen Celtic in previous European Finals and our boys. Boys who had all been born in New Zealand and had never yet seen Celtic in the flesh. The remaining minutes lasted hours but at last the final whistle blew and the whole room erupted in one huge huddle.

However celebrations were relatively low key. The RSA would soon be busy with people arriving from Dawn ceremonies. We had agreed to tidy the rooms up and have it ready immediately the game finished. Also the NZ Celtic Supporters Club football team had an important game later in the day. A first round tie in the Chatham Cup - the NZ equivalent of the Scottish Cup.

A few hours later many of the guys who had watched the Boavista game were getting ready for their own Cup Tie. Coach Ian Donnachie had a job getting the players focussed. All the talk in the dressing room was about getting to Seville. Eventually Ian managed to get the players to concentrate on the game in hand. He need not have worried. The opposition was only another non- league team but we would have beaten anyone that day such was the high the guys were on. A 12-2 win rounded off a great day.

Now everyone's attention turned to Seville. Many of us made calls to the other side of the world but it soon became clear that getting tickets would be almost impossible. A long and expensive trip with no guarantee of seeing the game. We then found out that copyright concerns meant that there would be no internet coverage.

Phone calls to New Zealand TV Channels were frustrating. No one was interested in screening a game involving Scottish or Portuguese teams. The game was going to be shown live in Australia and thoughts turned to flying over the Tasman to watch the game. Several NZ fans had done this before when live Scottish Football first screened there. The Club's resident Travel Agent – Gavin Findlay - looked at the costs of chartering our own plane. It seemed the only option but it was frustrating to think that the rest of the world would be able to watch in their own countries.

Then Kevin Everett stepped in. As well as being the NZCSC secretary Kevin was the IT expert and, importantly, the eternal optimist. A few years previously we had been able to watch live games by travelling up the small

196

Northland township of Monganui. There a local resident- an eccentric American- had set up a large satellite dish and broadcast pictures from TV stations around the Pacific. The local Hotel was part of the network and we had on several occasions seen live games there in the early hours. That "facility" had closed down but Kevin had heard a rumour that a motel in West Auckland now had a similar set up.

The rest of us were sceptical. We had heard these stories before. Mostly from soccer –starved ex pats who were desperate to see their teams play. It was always a case though of somebody telling you that they "knew someone who knew someone who had heard of…" We were not confident that Kevin's search for this latest mythical motelier would bear fruit.

Then one evening he phoned me to say that he had that afternoon found the very motel and had seen for himself the Australian TV channels it was capable of showing. "Brilliant" I thought. However there was a problem (well of course there would be!) The motel was small and all the rooms were taken for the day of the Final.

There was only a tiny reception area and even if a TV was installed there it would not be capable of holding more than a dozen people. So near and yet so far. Not for Kevin though. He had explained to the owner how desperate we were to see the game and there was a way he reckoned how it could be done.

I asked Kevin for the details on how it could work. The first thing that would be needed would be a venue that was within sight of the 2 TV masts that were near the top of Lincoln Road in West Auckland. The second thing that would be needed would be cash.

Quite a bit of cash! No cheques. Not exactly a request for used notes only but close to it I thought. Kevin then started to tell me what the motelier would need to do to get the pictures. However I thought it better if I did not know too much and suggested that we keep the knowledge of how we were going to get the pictures to as few people as possible.

The venue sprang to mind right away- the clubrooms of Oratia Utd FC at Parrs Park. We had played there before and knew some of the committee.

A quick phone call and we had a booking organised. There would be one slight problem. With such a short time to the game there would be no chance of getting a special licence for the bar to open early in the morning. It would be a tea and toast occasion!

Now to spread the word. It had to be done with some caution as we could not exactly let people know how we were getting the pictures. Phone calls, emails and word of mouth got the message out. We had to be careful when answering calls from people asking if it was true we were showing the game and how we were able to do so. I received a call from a Portuguese guy asking if he could come along with some friends. I assured him they would be most welcome.

A few days before the game I got a call from Angus Gillies a reporter with the TV 3 network. Angus's dad Iain had actually been on Celtic's books for a brief spell in the 1950's before emigrating to New Zealand. Angus was certainly a Celtic sympathiser and had played for the NZCSC football team for a few seasons. He had heard we were showing the game and wanted to do an item for the News programme that day. I told him that I was reluctant to agree in view of the manner in which we would be getting the pictures.

He accepted my decision then but I would discover later he would be more persistent!

The enquiries we were getting indicated that it would not only be Auckland based fans that would be coming. Even the South Island would be represented. The night before the game I made the trip to the Oratia Utd clubrooms to meet the mysterious motelier who would be responsible for the transmission.

On the way I stopped off at a couple of ATM's to withdraw the necessary cash. Kevin had continued to be busy and when I walked into the club the first thing I saw was the huge screen he had hired. He had also arranged for large speakers to pick up the sounds.

His wife, Karen, had been busy too. She had discovered a fabric shop in Auckland that also sold fancy dress and novelty items- including sombreros! An astonished shop owner was incredulous as she bought all his stock. Some were used for decoration while others were bought by members to add to their attire for the occasion.

At last I met our technical assistant. I gave him the envelopes with the money. He did not bother to count it! Now we would see the technical wizardry that would bring us the pictures. He produced a plastic bag out of which he pulled a small length of cable, a small square of light metal- technically known as a "receiver unit" and some sellotape. Unbeknown to me at the time was that there had been some concern over the receiver unit. It did not seem to be working when tried a day earlier and getting it repaired could be difficult.

Kevin's ingenuity sparked off again. He knew vaguely an Irishman who worked on the TV3 Soccer show. Surely a Celtic sympathiser? And he was. Thanks to him the unit was sorted but there would be a price to pay as I found out later, Kevin had not wanted the rest of us to worry or indeed to know too much about the technicalities of how we were getting the pictures so had not told anyone. So when I arrived I was blissfully unaware of how close to disaster we might have been.

We went up to the mezzanine floor with our technician and he attempted to stick the piece of metal to one of the large windows. It did not hold. "Have you got a cardboard box" he enquired. I went and got one from the boot of my car. It occurred to me that we were now supplying some of the "technical" gear! This must be the most expensive bit of sellotape and bit of metal in world history. However a few moments later I was thinking what a bargain! He stuck the metal to the box near the window, fiddled about with the cable and there on the big screen were pictures from the Australian TV station that would be screening the big game in a few hours.

Just as he had finished the set up there was a flash of lightning and a roll of thunder. At first my only thought was there might be some wet weather on the way. Then it was pointed out that an electrical storm might interfere with our broadcasting ability! Something else to worry about!

To help with security a couple of lads stayed on the premises overnight. I headed home via the supermarket to pick up some groceries. Just as

I was heading for the check out my phone rang. It was Kevin. I knew what he was going to ask. "Get some champagne" was the request. I had thought of that myself earlier but put the idea out of my head. It was bad luck to tempt fate like that. Kevin's optimism was unwavering though. He assured me that as Martin O'Neill and the players would not know that the NZCSC was buying champagne there would be no bad luck. I was not sure that fate worked like that but agreed to his wishes.

A short time later I was in bed and trying to get a good night's sleep. I then realised that we had all been so busy worrying about getting the game on that I had hardly even thought about the actual match itself. What would the line-up be? How would we cope with the heat? Eventually I nodded off.

At 6am the alarm went off and I was up immediately. So too were Stephen and Sean. On a normal school morning it would be another hour or so before they would reluctantly get out of bed. Not today. 10 minutes later we were in the car and on our way across the city to Oratia. I reminded the boys that as soon as the final whistle blew we would head straight to the car and make our way as quickly as possible to their school at the edge of the city centre. With decent traffic we should get there just after 9am – not too late for their classes. Both had their school uniforms on with Celtic tops over their shirts and Sean sporting a large sombrero on his head.

It was a dark May morning but soon we were in the lights of the Clubrooms. At the door Gavin Findlay and Scott Morland, resplendent in green wigs were taking the $25 admission. They told me that a couple of people had actually complained at the charge but in fairness they could not have known how much it had cost us to put it on and we could not exactly announce the details of our expenses. Inside the first person I met was Angus Gillies with his TV crew. The price for the assistance with the receiver unit was him being able to do a news item on the occasion. He had also offered his outside broadcast unit as a back-up should we have technical problems.

A few guys were not so happy to see the cameras. Not everyone had arranged time off work legitimately!

Around 180 were in the hall including about half a dozen Portuguese fans. The atmosphere was a mixture of tension, apprehension and yet happiness that we were part of the worldwide Celtic family. I said a few words of welcome using my rusty Spanish in recognition of the Final venue and then made my way to a good vantage point. The bulk of the crowd, including Stephen, were in the main hall but along with a few others Sean and I made our way up to the mezzanine floor. A few moments later all eyes were on the big screen and as the teams come out we roared in unison with thousands of other Celtic fans around the world.

Once the game was underway all the previous weeks concerns were forgotten and I could concentrate on the game like everyone else. At half time I reflected with Scott Young who had driven the 130 kilometres up from Hamilton that morning. The journey was for a large part through the fog alongside the Waikato River but he was determined not to miss this game. Like a few others he was born in New Zealand but had Scottish parents and his grandfather, a miner, had known Jock Stein. He was as steeped in Celtic as someone from the Gorbals.

Not long into the second half of course Celtic scored, Henrik Larsson's header equalising Porto's first half counter. The hall erupted. I watched Sean dance animatedly with sheer delight on his face. At that moment any regrets I still had about not actually getting to Seville vanished. I would not have wanted to have missed the chance to celebrate with my own, as well as, the Celtic family. Emotions were high as the game went into extra time. Stephen and Sean also had the concern that we might have to leave after 90 minutes to get to school. But there was no way that was going to happen that day. Of course it did end in disappointment.

Bobo Balde's sending off seemed to subdue the crowd and it was just not to be. As the final whistle sounded there was a short burst of applause at what had been achieved but also a feeling of being so close.

The crowd started to drift away. As the Oratia Club could not get a license the Newmarket RSA had agreed to open as soon as the game finished. Most fans began to head there. Others still had work commitments. Stevie Deacon and David Hepburn had been up since 4am to drive down from Whangarei with a couple of other Northland based fans.

For them it was straight back up the road for an afternoon shift. I at last got the 2 boys to school. It was so late now that there was no chance that a "the bus was late, Sir" excuse was going to work. I took a piece of paper and wrote on it "Please excuse Stephen and Sean's late arrival due to family commitments" It was the most appropriate thing I could think of!

After that I headed home for a quick, much needed shower and a post –match fry up! Soon I was on the bus heading to the RSA. On the way I felt a curious mixture of sadness and happiness. Sad that we had lost a European Final and would likely end the season with no trophies at all.

Yet happiness at what the NZCSC had achieved and seeing so many Celtic fans in New Zealand having the chance to enjoy watching their team in such a big occasion.

Any remaining sadness vanished as I walked in the door of the RSA Club. It was more like Gallowgate, Glasgow than Newmarket, Auckland. The place was full of fans bedecked in green and white. The background music was that mixture of football songs and Irish ballads that have featured on Celtic buses and in Celtic pubs for decades. Someone had draped, in a not too irreverent manner, a large tricolour around the portrait of the Queen!

It was great to spend an afternoon in that atmosphere. I bumped into 2 of the NZCSC's founder members, Des King and Ants McVey. Des had been born in Scotland but had come to New Zealand at a young age. Ants was a kiwi by birth and had never even been to Scotland but like the whole McVey family had inherited a passion for all things Celtic from his Scottish father and Irish mother.

I was a bit surprised to see Adrian Moran was still there as he had earlier told me he would be going straight to work. However he decided an afternoon with the Bhoys was needed and had phoned in "sick". He had not long returned after a bad leg break while playing for the NZCSC football team so had advised his boss that the injury was playing up and he could hardly walk never mind drive to work.

The craic and the beer flowed. The RSA sold more Guinness that day than they usually did in a month! Just after 6pm we turned on the TV News. Normally Scottish Football attracted no interest in the New Zealand media but things were different for this short period. Celtic's defeat of Liverpool got good coverage and for the last few days local TV was covering the arrival of so many fans into Seville.

The room went silent for a short while as Angus Gillies' item was screened. As promised Angus did not reveal how we got the pictures although his statement "we cannot tell you how they got the pictures" ended up causing more curiosity than if he had shown them. (Kevin later informed me that for some time after the game he was having to diplomatically field questions on where the pictures came from) Angus's item mostly concentrated on the NZ fans and their passion and desire to see their team. There were a few cheers from guys who saw themselves on the screen.

Unfortunately one who featured on the item was Adrian Moran who was seen leaping and dancing with delight at Celtic's second goal. Sadly for Adrian he would later discover that his boss was watching the news that night and a week after Seville Adrian would be looking for a new job!

Around 7pm I took advantage of an offer of a lift home with a few of the lads. In the car Sean Hird reminded for about the 6th time that day that it was his birthday. Jon McGrinder opined that these early kick offs were great as you could spend the day in the pub and still get home in time for dinner and a good sleep before work the next day!

I was soon sitting down to a dinner (and a few more beers) with my family. My wife Christine was NZ born and not particularly a football fan but we had lived together in Glasgow for 6 years so she knew the passion that Celtic fans had. If the boys ever mocked her about her lack of football knowledge she would retort with "well I was at the 4-2 game". That would usually quieten them.

Nevertheless I was not sure she would have been happy to know that the boys were over 2 hours late in getting to school so I waited until she was out of the room before I asked them what the teacher had said when they handed over the note I had written. They told me he had just asked them what the final score had been! I was right after all - Seville was indeed a family commitment.

PS – some months later I was reading a book while the TV was on the background. The programme was covering local TV awards, not something I would normally be interested in. However my ears picked up when I heard cheering Scottish voices. I looked up and saw a brief clip from the item Angus Gillies had done on the UEFA Final. He was receiving an award for his work. So I suppose Celtic did have one winner from Seville!

Written by Mike Maher, a New Zealand based Celtic supporter and contributor to CQN Magazine.

CHAPTER 20

THE SEVILLE TICKETS

Where to begin? I always said I'd keep this story to the select few who knew the details, however with the passing of ten years (so hard to believe), I guess I can finally put the facts as I remember them down on paper (virtual, that is).

Following our magnificent win over Liverpool, three of us ardent supporters were of the unshakable belief that we were going all the way this time. So confident, in fact, that we booked a week's package holiday on the Portuguese Algarve to coincide with the UEFA Final in Seville. We figured, sure if the worst comes to the worst, at least we'll have a "lads" holiday in the sun. So, after the plan was hatched and a gallon of porter drank, we informed our respective wives/partners of our plan. Glad to say that the news was favourably received, although a large amount of Brownie points were used up. Consequently, we watched the first leg of the Semi-Final in complete confidence, in the certain knowledge that Celtic would be once again in a European final.

Sadly, in between the games our greatest supporter, Charlie Murray, passed away. Only those who knew Charlie, a beautiful wee Belfast man, can understand the grief this caused. He was the originator of the idea of a Celtic Supporters Club in the Irish Mid-West. His club, The Charlie Tully CSC drew members from Clare, Limerick, North Tipp and North Kerry. These eventually formed their own clubs, but back then, Charlie was the heart and soul of Celtic. I am delighted to report there is now a CSC named after this humble man. After his funeral we watched the second leg against Boavista, but I have to say, we barely registered the result. Within a few days, however, we were back on track; we now owed it to Charlie to represent him at the game.

It was then the hunt began. We knew that every Celtic fan and their cousins would be scouring the world for the precious tickets. Our own supporters club had 16 season tickets and could therefore hope to get a small amount from Celtic FC, these would have to be raffled amongst the season ticket holders, of which I was one. Our band of three decided to write, phone, email everybody that had the remotest of chances getting tickets. I unashamedly used my father's connections to the GAA to obtain a promise of All Ireland hurling or football tickets for whoever came through for us. I got in touch with several well-known international politicians whom I persuaded owed me big time. The word was out.

I had a friend who was fairly well got in the Vatican and so I had him contact all the bishops and priests he could, both in Rome and on the missions (he was really well got). In fairness and despite him knowing my religious beliefs had long gone from the Catholic faith, he did what he could. In the meantime, May was drawing ever closer. My comrades were having no luck either and it seemed like the club draw would be our only chance. It was then I had divine inspiration!

I had heard that our largest shareholder, at a personal level, was a sound guy, not remotely like the media image that had been built around him. But how to approach him? Well, first I obtained his home address through a very old story in a national newspaper. That done I now had to compose the correct type of letter. Begging? No way, demeaning to both him and I. Boisterous? nah, to crass. Humble? Mightn't get the correct result. I know, sez I, humour mixed with business. And so it was that I composed the following .

A Chara,

As a fellow Shareholder and indeed, supporter, I wish to address you with regards to our upcoming UEFA cup final. I could write for hours on how much

Celtic means to me and tell you hair raising stories of our numerous trips to Glasgow over the years but that would only be taking up your valuable time, so I will cut to the chase. Having booked a package holiday on the strength of our win over Liverpool, myself and my friend find ourselves in Praia da Rocha, with a night booked in the San Pablo hotel, but with no feckin match ticket. I have called in favours from mates going back over the years, but all to no avail and since it appears that selling ones wife and children into slavery is now illegal, we are up the Swanee. After some soul searching and meditation I decided on offering you a deal. Having read various articles about you over the years (although I take newspapers with a large dollop of salt) I came to the conclusion that offering money would not get me the two desired tickets. So here is the deal. I have two possessions that may be of interest to you. I must admit I do not know the monetary value of either, but I do know the value to myself and my friend of attending this upcoming magnificent occasion in Seville.

The first item is a pristine condition programme from the Ireland v England rugby international in Lansdowne road in Feb 8th 1947. The second item is of huge sentimental value to me and indeed should show just how important this occasion means to fans like me. It is a postcard sized photograph of the Celtic team that won the double in 1954. What makes this photo invaluable is the fact that all the players autographed the back of it! Including Bobby Evans, Sean Fallon and Charlie Tully. It breaks my heart to offer this photo, but to see Celtic run out on the pitch in a European cup final would be amazing. If you are interested perhaps you could contact me at the above address or even phone or Email me. If not, so be it. I genuinely hope you have as much craic in Seville as we intend having, win, lose or draw. Hail Hail.

Well, letter sent, calls made to the Vatican and GAA carrot dangling, there was nothing else to do but wait. Two days before our flight, my boss tells me there was a guy looking for me on the phone during my lunch break. Fifteen minutes later they called back.

"Is this Blaise Phelan." Says this strong voice, (indistinguishable accent).

"Tis" said I. "Who am I talking to "

"This Dermot Desmond, I received a letter from you a couple of weeks ago. Sorry about the delay in getting back to you."

"Tom, is that you. This isn't f*&king funny, I have work to do".

Laughter. "No it's Dermot Desmond, honestly".

"Billy, you bo**%x, don't joke about this".

More laughter. "Seriously, it's Dermot Desmond".

The penny began to drop, jayzus, this might be genuine! And so it was. I sat at my desk and had a conversation about team tactics, Martin O'Neill and Celtics future with my new friend, Dermot Desmond. After a bit, he excused himself, he had a meeting to go to and then informed me that indeed he did have two tickets for myself and my buddy, Tom. I asked to what address would I send my offerings, but was told that this was not necessary, the tickets were a gift. He offered to have them mailed that day, but with two days to the flight, I told him I would be in Dublin before close of business. And so it was that Tom and I drove the straight to Dublin, hitting the road in the odd spot, we arrived in time to receive our precious tickets in the plushest office of the Irish Financial Centre.

Ironically, I won a ticket in the Club draw, but was able to have it re-raffled so another member could benefit. There is more to the story, about the offers I received for the ticket, offers I had from two Scottish newspapers for the story with a copy of the letter. Then there were the adventures in Seville and the Algarve, but they are for another time. On a very sad note my great comrade, Tom, passed away last year leaving a void that has yet to be filled. But I do have the great memories of him. The one thing I'll say is that on entering the stadium, I took out a photo of the late Charlie Murray and let him look around at the awe inspiring green and white, knowing that his spirit was somewhere with us.

A strange thing happened to the 1954 photograph. I donated it to the original Kano fund, to be raffled. However, it never reached the organizers. On contacting the Post Office I discovered there was an industrial action taking place and mail could be delayed up to several months. There has been no word since.

There are various views on Dermot Desmond's stewardship of our club. I for one am extremely happy that he didn't allow us to take the route of others and leave our club in dire financial straits. On a personal note, I have always thought that his gesture, not so much giving me the tickets, but to take time out and phone for a chat, shows him to be a man of character and decency. The kind of person I would wish to be in charge of our beloved Celtic.

Written by Blaise Plelan for CQN Magazine.

CHAPTER 21
MY SEVILLE STORY

Fans of The Beatles may remember when their 'Anthology' was shown on TV in the mid 90s. One instalment dealt with the legendary Shea Stadium gig. I recall being quite impressed with the editing of one trailer, in which all surviving members of the group name checked the venue in quick succession with faces still betraying a sense of awe at the gravity of an event held thirty or so years prior.

I think that's the way it's going to be with Seville.

My Seville story really started while I watched the Boavista away leg with my wife at home. This had become a superstitious arrangement through progressive away ties in the competition. I'd come to feel that we wouldn't win if the dynamic consisted of anything more than her and I. Irrational yes, but hardly unusual for someone who dribbles a mini football around the house during live radio commentaries somehow believing that I'm contributing to the match in progess.

Of course we'd loved Blackburn, Stuttgart, Liverpool etc, but with twenty minutes to go in Oporto, I sat with my stomach recreating a range of football related sinking feelings from the past. You know, being told I was 'rubbish' by the high school team prima donna as another of his cannonball passes rocketed out for a shy under my foot, or the time I ran home from primary school to watch Celtic lose to…. someone…on a black and white television during the seventies. I've never wanted to find out who we lost to or what year it was. The memory is more intriguing left blurry like footage of the moon landings.

Back in 2003, I'm out of the seat, whole body wound in tension. I've only breathed in. I'm gonna have to breathe out eventually. The ball, the ball… it's hit off Hartson, no he passed it…wha'?.... HENRIK, PLEASE, PLEASE!

I never stopped to think about dad's instructions. Toughen up? Stop greetin'? When you love Celtic you've got no chance. BANG, my head went off like a beetroot grenade. I got those wee stars and psychedelic patterns in my eyes as I let out a throaty skrike again and again. Still, hold it, calm it, easy baw etc. We're no' out the woods yet. The spell at the end was sheer hell. I celebrated Bobo's clearances louder than I do goals at most SPL home games.

The final whistle blew. I'd look at a tape of events later I thought. I always love scrutinising the scenes and interviews at the end of Cup Finals but now is just for us to enjoy I kept repeating to a still seated other half 'We've done it, We've done it'. Now, most of the time I speak (a lot) without thinking about it but I really felt the 'we'. Not just in our living room but in Oporto, crofts on Barra, downtown Boston and all the Celtic bars I'd ever drank in.

I threatened the mood a wee bit by getting herself in an affectionate headlock. Obviously, a gallon of adrenaline wasn't jetting through her system as a stupid, tearful ape flew at her from the other side of the room. She forgave me though after much apologising. I mean, I had to keep on her good side – Seville wasn't going to come cheap.

As I lay horizontal on the living room floor, necking the last can of celebration Stella from the fridge, I beamed as yet another bevvied 'tic fan challenged the panel to deny we were brilliant on the post-match phone ins.

Two hours after the final whistle and I was still clenching my fist and spitting 'Yessss' every now and then like it was a twitch. How was I going to get there and how might I get a ticket? People all over the world were thinking the same thing. It was to be a big exciting, nervy, and periodically depressing game of musical tickets (and flights). During my quest to reach Seville I would see the best and worst of human traits (in context you understand) and also rediscover what I already knew – Celtic is not just a football club but an ideal concerned with fair play for everyone.

Flights were fairly easy. I queued outside a travel agent on Cathcart Road in Glasgow on a drizzly Monday morning before work along with a dozen or so other hyper hoopites. I was to end up on a French jumbo more used to taking Serge and Monique long haul trips to Tahiti than carting 500+ Celtic fans to Andalusia. It's quite a sight to see that many people on a plane wearing the same top. Still, I don't imagine anyone thought 'damn, I must change'.

So far so good. I'd resigned myself to simply making a pilgrimage to Seville, ticket or no ticket. Over the next few weeks at work I tried to make connections via email to every long shot I could think of. Two lines of enquiry remain with me for different reasons.

Cesar is a Basque doctor who lodges with a mate of mine in Edinburgh. When I explained my dire need he asked his father to suss out the ticket scene across there. The old boy called his business contacts in Seville only to draw a blank. Even though he looks like an able Bilboa centre back, Cesar's not really a football fan. The fact that he tried to help was much appreciated though.

Maybe I should have known better but keeping tabs on the various CFC message boards really brought me down. I realise there would be a proportion of wind up merchants and full time touts on the sites but I also caught a whiff of some selfish, profiteering fans. The popular line of argument seemed to be 'what would you do in my place'? That's easy – sell at face value.

The weeks drifted past and all my options dissolved one by one. It would be the big screens for me. In the days leading up to the final, TV reports were coming live from Seville. I was just desperate to get out there. Everyone in the office was talking about it all the time. I got the impression that fans of all other teams (except the obvious) and none were as excited as us, and that the whole event had become one for Scotland. I think it's worth remembering that we don't, and have never felt the need to sing 'no-one likes us we don't care'. Many do like us and we do care.

Monday 19th May 2003 was like any other day at work except I was chain guzzling coffee and pacing the floor like an expectant father. The phone went. Call from a colleague:

Caller - 'What are you doing on Wednesday?' (Yeah, nice one smart arse)

Me – 'Erm, I'm on annual leave'

Caller – 'I'm your fairy godmother' (Whit?)

Me- 'Sorry, in what way?'

Caller – 'Och, I'm kiddin' you on – just phone Tommy on his mobile'

Tommy's speaking to me from Spain when he answers. After denying all knowledge of me for a minute he casually tells me I've got a ticket - from Jesus.

ALLLLLLLLLLLLLLLLLLLEEEEEEEEEELLLLLLLLLUUIIIAAA, ALLLELLLUUUIIIAAA

Now that might sound cornier than a cornfield in Cornwall but it's literally true. Tommy's brother works for a multi-national company. He had asked his Spanish colleague Jesus to secure some extra briefs if possible. After copious thanks, I retired to the male lavvie to punch the air in delight many, many times and croak out 'yes, ya beauty' over and over.

So this was it. I was going to be there. After a trip to the Celtic shop to get freshly togged out the next day, it was just a matter of counting down the hours.

Eldorado. Yes, I know it was the city of gold but we all hoped Seville was going to be the city of silver for Celtic. I'd ordered a 5 a.m. taxi to Glasgow Airport. Naturally, my cabbie was a kind of tattooed, bluenose caricature who wouldn't talk to me all the way there. I was desperate for some banter. Imagine if I'd puked in the cab with excitement. Tempting.

I soon met up with my mates and we got the breakfast pints in. There was a brilliant match atmosphere in the airport. The teeming departure lounge was chaos with ad hoc green hair-dos being administered to half cut punters and fans of all ages chatting nervously and laughing at any patter at all.

The journey on the plane was just something to get through. I'm not a great flyer. I do remember using the toilet about 23,000 times and discussing the merits or otherwise of violent horror films with a mates' 11 year old son.

As the aircraft door swung open it felt like standing in front of a hairdryer firing squad set to hot. We were escorted to our buses and conveyed through the scorched outskirts of Seville. The stadium looked small and compact to me as we were dropped off. Little did I know that I would later walk into the coliseum scene from Gladiator, complete with CGI-like animated hordes of Celtic fans.

A group of us walked up to the centre of town through the EXPO site complete with Arianne rocket. For some reason the whole area seemed like a ridiculous theme park from an episode of the Simpson's. What do I know? – it's better than the shows across from the Victoria Infirmary in Glasgow.

I took my first picture on the bridge over the river. We'd heard that a Porto fan had died after falling from this bridge. It's too easy to dismiss these things in among mass human traffic but I remember feeling (not for the first time) how profoundly sad it would be to leave home for a football match and never come back.

We found a neighbourhood bar and settled down for a while. I still had to meet the Bhoys with my ticket, so made a series of shouty mobile calls as the mobile reception was so poor. The plan was set. Cathedral at three.

After a couple more Cervezas we began to wind our way through the narrow streets. I was lagging behind the others and I took my favourite picture of the trip. It shows many of my friends filling a sunny street lined by distressed orange trees. Everyone is walking tall in the hoops. All my people right here right now. D'ye know what I mean?

The night before I'd made myself a t-shirt tribute to my Grandfather. He died in 1990 but I wanted him with me today. Younger fans feed off stories from the past and I love that he lost his false teeth in 1957 and had to be brought home pallbearer style by three or four neighbours. I also remember when he was older and much frailer after a couple of strokes that the old fire was still there as Charlie scored his second penalty at Ibrox in that 4-2 game from the early eighties.

In any case, as we moved through the town and the crowds got bigger, I felt great in my home-made t-shirt with hoops tied round my waist.

I met Tommy and the Bhoys who had just hoovered up armloads of left wing freebies at the local offices of the Spanish Socialist Party. After being offered a fraternal fan to cool myself down, I received my ticket in the entrance of a pub that Billy Connelly had apparently cleared for a private party. The owner shooed us out of the place but I didn't care, I was Charlie Bucket with a golden ticket. Recently someone gave me a framed photo of a celebratory me after being passed the brief. The face is in its thirties but the body language is in its early teens.

After more beer in a bustling wee bar, we began the walk back to the stadium. The nerves started then. I hadn't thought about the football much all day. Now the cold fingers of fear and doubt gripped my guts. The jokes were getting less frequent and the smiles nearer grimaces. Some of our party were suffering from kilt rash and walking decidedly bow legged. I spotted Jim McInally and his kids all decked out in the hoops as we neared the stadium.

With time on our hands we stopped by a fence and quaffed a few beers bought from a vendor with a bin full of bottles. The crowds were massive by this time. We had to move on. I remember thinking the security seemed fairly lax until I realised that the bar code on the ticket really did have a use.

Then I was in.

I had a great seat between the main stand and the Celtic end. Next to me were three empty seats that stayed that way all night. Unbelievable. The hour before kick off went past like a three minute pop song. I just couldn't get my head around the sheer mass of Celtic fans. This was where it was at in world sport that night.

We all know what happened on the field.

At both goals I was showered by crash test dummy Celts firing all over the seats as if out of cannons. If I'm being honest, once Bobo went, I was just waiting for them to score. We came close but I think we just came up short on the night. That allied to a weak referee meant we didn't win the UEFA Cup. The cup though is all we never won. We gained new respect for our team, club and ourselves. We proved we are big time. On the way out I was sad but proud. A teenager walked past me crying and unconsciously I clapped the back of his head and said 'never mind son – we done well'. I never told him to toughen up and stop greetin'.

With wet eyes, I would have had no credibility.

Written by L Monaghan for CQN Magazine.

CHAPTER 22

TEN YEARS ON FROM SEVILLE

Setting the scene.

BROGAN ROGAN TREVINO AND HOGAN - SEVILLE

Seville: a town with all its history, all its culture, all its tales to tell and all those influences but where just one word is guaranteed to bring a smile to the face of any local:

CELTIC!

Any discussion about modern European Football and cup competition will eventually throw up the link between the Andalusian capital and the team founded by a Marist brother from the east end of Glasgow.

What makes the link between the two all the more remarkable is that the connection was made over only a few days in May 2003 which culminated in the Glasgow club coming to Spain and losing a football match. The Victors on the day were F.C. Porto who, under the guidance of an audacious young manager called Jose Mourinho, would go on to lift the big Prize of the Champions League Cup the following year.

It was a Golden period for Porto, yet it was the losing side who would stamp their name, if not in the history books, then in the annals of endless folklore, because in truth there was no real story in Seville were it not for the Glaswegians.

As a result of those few days in Spain, the major players in the sport, the European and World bodies who govern the game, would depart from all previous convention and practice by honouring, commending and, to be frank, standing in awe of the football fan—or to be more precise—The Celtic Fan!

They say there were 80,000 there.

They say it is or was the biggest travelling support in the history of Sport.

It remains the biggest travelling support to trek across Europe to support a football team.

As mentioned earlier, CNN reported that on the day before the game 3% of the earth's flying population were all headed for Seville and were sporting a Celtic scarf.

They say that the Celtic support was worth 600 Million Euros to the Spanish economy—they didn't count the money spent by the thousands of us who crossed the border from Portugal to support the hoops—the Portuguese just got a wee spin off.

There are literally thousands of stories surrounding the trips to and from the Spanish City.

Long lost friends who somehow bumped into one another after years apart: People who turned up on the spur of the moment yet who managed to find friends and family among the mayhem—like homing pigeons who somehow mysteriously know their way home.

People who missed flights, arrived by car, left their desks at the last moment, lied to their bosses about where they were going, met a girlfriend or boyfriend to be at the airport, had a ticket, didn't have a ticket and couldn't care less!

Seville was a town where football came to learn the value of "The Green Pound" and as a result many a civic authority would take an interest in an approaching UEFA draw in the hope that the word "Celtic" would be matched with their local heroes.

However, the most important thing about Seville in my eyes is that Seville is the town where Glasgow Celtic Football Club rediscovered itself, its value and its wonder.

Blessed with a team that could hold its own in any competition, Celtic would come to the heat of Seville and face a team that were to be the Kings of Europe within the twelve month.

Twice they would fall behind, and twice they would fight back through the talismanic head of the King of Kings, The sporting hero of Sweden, the once dreadlocked and now balding Rastafarian Larsson.

Whilst Deco and Derlei of Porto would rightly be praised for lovely football in the course of the final- though their memory may be tarnished by play acting and gamesmanship- any examination of the 2003 UEFA cup final shows that the Swedish born son of a Cape Verde Father was in a class of his own in his chosen position.

Over and above showing a determination to play and win which was draining just to watch, Larsson would score a goal which should be the object of study by anyone with serious ambitions to play professional football in the striker position.

As Didier Agathe crossed a high loping ball towards the Porto back post, a study of Larsson's movement and guile shows the perfect striker's motion and execution of a football move.

The manipulation and manoeuvering of the defender, the seemingly impossible leap and never ending hang in the air, is only bettered by the vision and ability which enabled him to head the ball back across the goal and into the net via the inside of the far post.

In essence, Larsson defeated two central defenders, a fullback and a goalkeeper by using one elongated twisting leaping motion which culminated in his placing the ball into the one exact spot where it could not be saved.

In sheer striking terms it was perfect—with no one in the world being able to say that they would have executed that piece of football any better. This was the King of Kings scoring the goal of goals.

However, despite Larsson's heroics, the team from Glasgow would lose the match.

Yet, the club from Glasgow would win everything – everything from respect, to admiration, to awe and wonder—from the city, UEFA, FIFA, Governments, Porto, broadcasters, airlines and anyone else.

If Football and Europe had needed reminding just what Celtic Football Club bring to any major event then Seville was it. Equally, for different generations of Celtic fan, Seville afforded them the opportunity to see, be part of, and feel the experience of the Celtic support acting on instinct, en masse and with one purpose—to support—with a smile and a song.

Recently, after the defeat of Barcelona at Celtic park, one Spanish magazine described what they saw as " The Greatest Home advantage" in European Football— in an attempt to describe the atmosphere at Celtic Park.

Those few days in Seville saw the Celtic support conquer a European city whilst at all times remaining guests, visitors, customers, partygoers and most of all Celtic fans. They brought that atmosphere and spirit from Kerrydale Street and unleashed it on the unsuspecting and bemused Andalusians. They came, they saw, they sang, they drank, they spent, they laughed and they conquered—with sheer weight of numbers, spirit and the Celtic personality.

This was a festival, a carnival, a party, an audience, a crowd, a family and a club all rolled into one.

There were no strangers, just members of a family that you had not yet met and who were all there with the one purpose, one goal, one intention and one vision—and that was to be part of Celtic Football Club.

Yes, the players took to the field and the management managed from the sidelines, but the spirit of Celtic stood in the stands, the fan zones, the pubs, the parks, the airports, the hotels, the bus stations, train stations, petrol stations—everywhere—but the Police stations.

Celtic—a name that was meant to be all inclusive from the beginning, which said that everyone and anybody was welcome, and which has meant and always will mean that those who follow this club are not and never will consider themselves THE people but A people—a body of support—a brotherhood or family or a club in which we are all members.

As each member of that family rolled into town by whatever means, the cumulative glow and presence increased with powerful effect. If Smiling and singing were a currency then this Green and White brigade were the richest of the rich—so rich that media moguls and TV crews from all over the world could not ignore the remarkable gathering—and all for a football team who had not as yet kicked a football.

I often think of Seville and want to shout:

"See! – See what we can do when we all act together? - as one body, as one support, as one club, as one movement, as one spirit?"

I am not sure that the "Celtic" effect is truly understood or realised by those involved with the "business" of football or even the "Business" of Celtic Football Club or PLC.

There is little that the Celtic support cannot achieve when acting as one. Whether it be raising money for charity, being the twelfth man in a stadium, being an economic force to be reckoned with, or just being the world's biggest infectious party— all of which was shown in Seville.

For me, Seville is not a city or a town—it is a feeling—an emotion—an experience—when I for one felt as if I was a king of kings!

Many will wonder will it ever happen again?

I genuinely don't know.

I only know—that if there is going to be a show—then the Glasgow Celtic will be there!

20 MAY 2013 on the Celtic blog, Celtic Quick News, something remarkable happened. The Celtic support, who had kept their emotions about their experiences in Seville bottled up for more than a decade, decided it was time to talk. The founder of Celtic Quick News, who writes the closing chapter in this book, started things off:

PAUL 67 - 10 years ago today five of us filled a car and drove to Bristol Airport, the nearest available departure point for Scot's leaving for the Spain; more-local airports were booked out within minutes of the event ahead being confirmed. Bristol is a small airport but the place was full of other Celtic fans who had travelled south for the same purpose. Every departure point in the land was filled by green and white. A remarkable exodus was underway, it was a privilege to be part of it.

LIVI BHOY - We flew to Malaga from Manchester two days before the game in Seville. There were only two groups not going to the game on the whole plane. An old Welsh couple who were hitting the bevvy and enjoying the spectacle and a family who looked pretty well off who were enjoying it slightly less. I am sure Charlie and the Bhoys were on our flight. They were certainly in the airport bar.

MORNSY- When Henrik scored, I have never heard such a noise. After the game, we made our way back up to Lisbon and obviously, the Estadio Nacional… loads of supporters just popping in.

Walked up the stairs onto the pitch, worked out where big Tam had been when he hit that shot … just brilliant. Then back on a plane full of green and white to Frankfurt. A few beers with lots of regular travellers in the bar wanting to have a chat – then back to Manchester. All done in just over 48 hours.

Unbelievable experience and if nothing else – at the start of the season, every player should be shown the documentaries and game clips that are out there – just so they know what their responsibilities are and also what they could be part of.

MIDFIELD MAESTRO - 10 years ago today I flew to Seville from Prestwick with my son & daughter, 12 & 11 at the time. Stayed in Hotel Monastario in Puerto de Santa Maria, Cadiz. Spent day by pool. At night I took the kids in a taxi up to the team hotel in Jerez. Sneaked in back door & got to meet all the players & management. Then went to Hotel Trype & met the Lions that were there. Have plenty of great pictures. Back to our hotel & off to bed to dream of what might be the following day.

THE BATTERED BUNNET - Our crew – 6 of us – drove down to Heathrow overnight and got the early flight to Milan. From Milan we flew to Malaga, and drove the few short miles to our billet in Benalmadena where a 7th member of the troop joined up.

Following day we drove up to Seville for the game in a convoy stretching a hundred miles, arriving in the city about midday. The purple blossoms blowing across a forest of green and white remains a vivid picture amongst many. I texted a pal who couldn't make it, as follows:

"Seville bears witness to the re-emergence of the Celtic phenomenon."

Ticketless, I watched the game in a park with 10,000 odd Celtic and Porto fans. It was 42 degrees celcius an hour before kick off. With the giant screen facing the setting sun, we couldn't make out the picture but for a small strip in shadow at the bottom of the screen. As the sun sank ever lower, so the shadow of the city it cast moved inexorably up the screen, such that by the start of the second half the picture was complete.

For that first half, we were reliant on assorted texts and phone calls home.

Wandering around the city in the early hours afterwards was extraordinary, the sun rising to reveal the main railway station looking as though it had been hit by a chemical weapons attack, so many people lying asleep wherever they had dropped.

Back at Malaga airport 2 days later, bumped into a chap who was flying to Prague to catch a connection back to Edinburgh. I reckon he got home before us, but I doubt many took a more out-of-the-way route than he.

Wherever you are Frank, Hail Hail.

Our last leg – the overnight drive back up to Glasgow from Heathrow – was a tough one, combination of beeriness and weariness stalking us all the way.

Would only change one thing about that odyssey though – the result.

CHAVEZ - A couple of months before the Seville final I was out in town with a pal and we got talking to some Spanish people in a bar. Two of them lived in Glasgow, the rest were visiting. Anyway, as the evening wore on they introduced me to their mate Juan, who said in pidgin' English that he really wanted to see Celtic. At that time I had two season books so told him I'd take him on the Sunday. I met up with them all in McChuills. We then went to Bairds, had a quick drink and I headed off to the game with Juan while the others stayed in Bairds. The game was pretty flat but Henrik scored twice and we beat Killie quite comfortably. When we got back to Bairds his pals were all blood-red. They'd been drinking some mental sherry, or it might have been Buckfast. Anyway, we went our separate ways.

I didn't get tickets for Seville until about 10 days before the final. By then all the hotels were full everywhere but we got flights ok. By the next day I thought we'd have to stay miles away in Cordoba or somewhere like that when I thought, why not text wee Juan, see if he knows of anywhere. Straight away he replied that his brother lived in Seville and he'd ask him. The next morning he'd sorted us with a twin room in a wee hotel five minutes walk from the cathedral. Result! Great trip. Great memories.

BLANTYRETIM - Midnight drive from Blantyre to Manchester airport, plane to Madrid the express train to Seville all on day of final, plenty of Celtic fans stuck in Madrid as they hadn't booked seats on the Express. Left luggage. In a wee bar and went to the match. Slept in train station before heading back on express train next afternoon.

Hotel booked in Madrid and had another night out there. Flight back to Manchester then drive back home. Passed a Parks bus on M74, those poor souls had driven all the way back from Seville.

FISHERMHAN - TBB, I was in that park also I can remember someone appeared with a portable tv and a guy grabbing a mic and giving us a running commentary of the game

We flew from Glasgow to Amsterdam then on to Madrid where we got the fast train to Seville – what a journey. Hoops everywhere we went and what a blast that train journey was!

Spent the night sleeping in an oven of a hire car in the train station car park had to get out for a wander around 04:30 and walked into the train station to see a green and white blanket of bodies covering the station concourse.

TOMMYTWISTSTOMMYTURNS - Seville memories: After BBJ did the business at Liverpool, I decided to take a bit of a gamble and booked flights to Malaga for a week with the UEFA Cup final slap bang in the middle. The idea being that if we didn't make the final, then me and the missus would have a week in Andalucia.

I managed to get bookings at two separate Seville hotels (just in case) and I "won" an ebay auction for two Cup Final tickets costing £160 each! We booked hotels for the other days in the beautiful villages of Ronda, Gaucin and Benahavis. After that it was a case of sitting at home waiting on the result of the Semi against Boavista....we went absolutely nuts when Henke scored in Portugal, knowing that we already had all the necessary arrangements in place!

We flew to Malaga the weekend before the final, picked up a hire car and headed off for two cracking nights in Ronda, an amazing place. The day before the game, we drove to Malaga airport and picked up my mate and his wife, who had managed to blag two tickets for the game. I still had the two hotel rooms booked, so we were sorted.

The drive to Seville was just magic, we passed loads of cars with Hoops scarves and tricolours out the windows. After settling into Seville, we joined the many thousands in the park and got quite plastered. The combination of hangover and 42degC/high humidity meant that I only drank water the next day during the build up to the game, even after we met up with more friends who had flown into Seville that morning! We even had to go back to the hotel as the wife ended up with heat exhaustion and she got bundled into a cold shower!

After the Tenko type march out to the stadium, I sank to my knees after entering the stadium. I never ever thought I would get to see Celtic in a European final. It was very emotional, even more so when we found our seats and looked along at the massed ranks of the Hoops support. After the game, we picked up a few cold beers and crashed at our hotel, too worn out for any partying.

The next day we drove back to Malaga airport and dropped off our friends before heading into the hills and the white washed walls of Gaucin. Back into holiday mode, but heads filled with what could have been!

We were really lucky with the gambles we took on tickets/hotels/flights, but it all added up to an incredible week for us and we just felt blessed to be a part of the amazing migration of the Celtic family.

MADRARUA - 6 of us booked a week in the Algarve the day after we beat Liverpool, such was our confidence. What started out as an attempt to see a match became the trip of a lifetime, an adventure that led to friendships and stories that are still repeated when a few of us get together. Not to mention the amazing way I obtained the precious tickets for the final, but that's another story.

TEUCHTER ÅR LÅ - I watched the game on the screen in the big park and was absolutely in awe of the magical, hypnotic effect of marching Celtic supporters, clad in the hoops, walking back to the city centre over the bridge. It gave the illusion that the whole bridge was "alive".

HENRIKS SOMBRERO - Leaving the house at 4 in the morning to get to Glasgow Airport. Departure lounge a sea of Hoops all on the beer. Hotel in Torremolinos. Bus to the game stopped off in the middle of the desert at some wee diner. About 20 buses parked outside it. A sea of Green and White Hoops everywhere. Standing waiting to be served and big guy walks in with Hartson printed on the back of his hooped jersey. Turns out it was Big John's da. Spitting image.

I'll never forget Lenny that day. How that wee ginger hieded Irishman could cover every inch of that park for the entire game is beyond me. He was immense.

GARCIA LORCA - I am just a few miles south of Sevilla today and if only the weather then had been like it is today we may just have won it. Anyway I have lots of fantastic memories of Seville (as I have of Lisbon and, to a much lesser extent, Milan). However, the morning after the game I came downstairs in my hotel and recognised a young man at reception checking out. He had previously worked for me in London. Turned out he had started a new life in Australia and was getting married in 6 weeks time. He flew from Australia to London. Flew to Madrid and took the fast train to Seville. He had no ticket but watched the game in the park. He simply said. "I had to be here." We will have our time again. No fear on that one.

BOBBY MURDOCHS ANKLE - Seville, about 20 of us from the Greenock Celtic were staying in Benalmadena and Torremolinos. My 2 brothers (one had flown in from Canada) and sister had taken my father with us. He had missed Lisbon and Milan as the 6 kids he had came before his beloved Celtic, so he loved it. Day after the final, which we all had tickets for, we're sitting at the pool, he's got this contented look on his face, so I ask, he says, "ma weans have took me to see ma team way the rest o our family, disnae get any better. Lost him 2 years ago next week, but he died a very happy contented mhan.

NORTHBHOY - Ah Bristol, stopping off point to Seville via Malaga…

Great memories Paul, I also got to Seville via Bristol. I travelled by Easyjet to Bristol with only the one ticket from our 3 season tickets and then on to Malaga to join my brother, his wife and godson at a hotel in Benalmadena, which was fully packed with Celtic support, mostly Irish and what an atmosphere, Seville was even better!

On the way back I spent the day in Malaga and the Saturday in Bristol with friends. We had a hillwalk round Bristol pubs before a lovely meal and headed up just in time to catch the Sunday match. My own two bhoys were too young to go!!!! Only one ticket mind - and they have not spoken to me since. Only joking, they text me and send me threatening e-mails.

Can't believe its 10 years - need to go again, might take the bhoys this time!

ESTORILBHOY - Seville, so many great memories.

Met the big tall guy from Still Game (Greg?) at Madrid train station heading towards the game.

Stayed in Occidental hotel in Seville next to main train station. George McCluskey and Patrick Kielty also stayed there - brill atmosphere - can't believe 10 years ago though.

Biding memory was the heat at kick off time, couldn't believe that people could play football in that, sweat was pouring off us just sitting in the stadium.

Also coming back home via Madrid and sitting in plaza major on the evening after the game and little pockets of Celtic fans in all of the open-air restaurants. The violinist playing along with the songs coming from all areas of the square felt like a piece of heaven on earth with all the smiling Tims and locals enjoying the great atmosphere. And that was after we lost!! :))

Can't buy that stuff.

YORKBHOY - Sitting outside a cafe in Seville and we had about 30 verses of the Watching The Bill song then someone comes out with "We'll be eating alfresco …When you're working at Tesco…"

COWIEBHOY - 10 years ago today, and its a wee trip from Islantilla to Seville (58 miles), to find our bearings and parking for 21st. Place already bouncing with Hoops, Welcome party in the park, to see the Big Cup Winner, King Billy "McNeil" followed by Shebeens. On walking into the park, I bump into half of my parish, walk another 50 yards and it's the Cowie rebels, with my brother in law, all the way from Toronto.

Incidentally I have already come across the big kilt wearing red heated Mohican, mentioned earlier, and have seen the huge Grampian Emerald Flying Squad banner, hanging from the top to half way down a hotel.

THERE IS ONLY ONE TEAM IN GLASGOW AKA 67 MOULDY 67 - UEFA Cup Final day before / night before and early morning of…The UEFA Cup Final trip started for me the previous week on the Wednesday 14th when I had to travel down to Cork for my brother In law's wedding which would be on the Saturday.

A large group of my friends were leaving Glasgow on the Monday, as I would only be travelling back in the car from Ireland on the Monday. After negotiating the early return from our trip to Ireland, it was decided that the safest bet would be to book flights for the Tuesday from Glasgow. After dropping the wife off at the in laws in the midlands of Ireland on the way north, headed home on the Monday afternoon, caught ferry, got home late Monday night.

Early start on the Tuesday from Glasgow Airport, normally busy for Euro away trips, but this Tuesday morning was something else. The check-in or pre check-in area was right out in the main car park. Unbelievable! The airport was buzzing with excitement and could be here all day talking about it.

Having been taken to my first games by my dad back in 1980/81 (although he tells me he took me to a match in '75 down at Ayr) it was a great experience to go Seville with my dad, a friend of his and my best man. So the four of us are on the plane, two of us wearing the sombreros as purchased in the Celtic shop, (me and mate) and the other two wearing the really classy Mexican style ones, (that was dad and his mate Peter).

The crew from Transavia (NL) were a lovely friendly bunch (one of the many hundreds of charters, we were with the Hinds group).

After arriving in Seville, we noted that our hotel was a good 20 minutes up the motorway from the city centre, accessible by the hotel shuttle. After quick look around the hotel, we opted for local bar, beautiful day in the sun. Some cold beers.

As afternoon moved on, the older heads stated that they may go for a sleep, and then catch the shuttle bus into town. Memory of the afternoon had to be my father trying to explain to the waiter on how to make his steak well done, hand singles and lighters coming out, "fire, fire" – what a laugh!

The younger two decided to opt for "one for the road " eventually getting back to the hotel, after deciding to set the alarm for about 1800 or 1900 hrs, next thing we know and it is 2300 hrs. Oops!

Quick shower, down to reception and we meet dad and his mate coming back from the town LOL. So we decided to catch the shuttle bus into the city about midnight,

After walking about various bars trying to catch up on everyone else, before we know it is 0400 am and we have sore feet, walking about looking for bars (that were still open) and trying to work out where the bus meeting point was. Amazing banter along the way and just an unbelievable amount of Celtic fans in the city the night before the game. Sensible heads on we go back to base camp.

Day of the day game to follow…

COORSLAD…Went to Albuferia for the week with my wife and son. We were joined by a fine couple we met in a Blackpool hotel the previous year. What a week. The guy arrived at the pool to meet us with a grass skirt on. He then bought a Blue guitar and rocked, rolled and rebelled a small English pub. Went to Seville on the day of the game on a bus from the hotel. Think there were only 5 tickets on the bus, 2 of which were mine and my son's. Anyway my good friend from Blackpool travelled to Seville in his grass skirt, green curly wig and plastic boobs. Even the local police asked for photos of him…some stories from that week. Nearly lost my job - pulled a sickie and was caught…my only regret was I hadn't a ticket for my friend…that wonderful guy is my good friend Vmhan…We had a ball!

POGMATHONYAHUN AKA LAIRD OF THE SMILES - The night before the game we were standing drinking outside a wee pub in a tree lined square, the trees being the ubiquitous orange trees found throughout Seville. Suddenly an orange dropped out of one of the trees and hit a Bhoy who was standing under the tree on the head. This started a spontaneous chant about the falling orange from those of us who witnessed it.

CELTFISH –Was lucky to be in Porto for the Boavista game. A friend had managed through a tenuous link to the Benfica doctor to get tickets for the game. We were situated on a small terraced area to the right of the dug-outs. Never experienced a more tense game, ever, especially the last ten minutes. When the final whistle blew, I saw Big Bobo fall to his knees in front me. That was it, what an unbelievable journey, we had made it to Seville. Now, this is when I made a complete erchie of myself where I still wake in the middle of the night, squirming. A plastic tunnel was pulled out to the edge of the pitch and the players began to run back into the changing rooms. I had climbed up onto the glass partition and saw MON heading to the tunnel and began to call over to him. He dissappeared and then his head popped out and saw me on my own hanging over the glass. He came over and we clasped hands, and he said "thanks for coming." I was stunned and dumbfounded. All I could say in return was "Martin we love you !! " Oh well, what a night, at least I got his name right !.Seville, here we come.

!!BADA BING!! - 10 years ago right now me and the guy I was in Seville with panicked - "taxi take us to Seville big man ". We were in Fuengirola and fellow Tims were saying all buses and trains to Seville were full on the day of the game. We were terrified of being stranded.

ONE MALLOY - Reading the stories of Seville brings back lots of memories. Like others I was too young and couldn't have afforded to go to the two previous finals so Seville was a must go to. A 5 day trip with my oldest daughter - Glasgow to Malaga - then on to base in Benalmadena. On the day of the game the bus from our hotel joined the convoy north. We parked in the bus park at stadium, walked back into the city. It was a sea of green and white, wow, heavenly! Had 2 tickets purchased online from the Liverpool area for £900, face value 15€ each, though later got £200 back. To have been there is the memory of a lifetime.

TALLYBHOY - As it's the tenth anniversary of Seville here is my recollection. When the ref blew his whistle to signal the end of the Boavista game – and we knew we were in the final – about twelve grown men whose ages ranged from mid-30s to late 40s, hugged and kissed each other and started doing the huddle in the middle of the floor in a Troon pub, knocking stools, chairs AND tables flying! At the time the pub was a Tim shop – less so now. BMCUW has been in a couple of times!

We all decided that we would go to Seville, but over the course of the next few days the numbers decreased to three – me and two others. Things like work and family commitments meant that most would stay at home.

My big mate started to make all the arrangements and booked a flight from Glasgow to Alicante, sorted out a hire car there and found a hotel in Seville. We handed over a deposit, and everything – except match tickets – was arranged in a couple of days.

At the time I was running the family business and, unfortunately, for a variety of reasons had to pull out at the last minute my place being taken by another ghuy – never got my deposit back!
I was gutted to put it mildly – but that's life!

The build-up on the day of the match was incredible, and we had made arrangements to watch the game in the same pub which was bedecked in Celtic flags, beach balls and sombreros. The place was heavin'. Not quite the same as being in Seville of course, but better than nothing!

Huge disappointment on the night, but an amazing experience nonetheless.
At the end of the game we all trooped off to another pub in town where a VERY well-known local Tim – who hails from Kilwinning – had hired the premises for the evening from the owner. The 'celebrations' continued into the early morning.

I had about three hours sleep, and at about 0830 went round to the business premises to ensure that everybody had turned up – they had, and I promptly went back home to bed to nurse a raging hangover!

MCGRORY1888 - Went to every away game except the semi against Boavista. Bought tickets on line as soon as they became avail. Flew to London the day before the game, flew from there to Madrid. Sat outside Madrid station waiting for the rest of the clan to gather. Fantastic train journey to Seville (well what I can remember of it anyway). Spent the time in the "refreshment" area singing etc. Taxi from Seville station to our hotel. We stayed in the same hotel as the BBC crew, big Billy, Jim Kerr etc...Fantastic place. Best memory was just outside the stadium where a tout stood with a wad of tickets waving them about when out of nowhere a wee boy ran out of the crowd, grabbed the tickets and melted into the crowd which mysteriously opened up swallowed him amongst howls of laughter. Wonder who he was? Did anybody else see that?

PAUL 67 - In the months afterwards I made a trip to the Celtic Superstore to buy the DVD of the match. I wasn't ready to watch it but needed to have it nonetheless, for when the time came. I've still not opened the box.

I watched the game from high up in the Porto end. The Porto fans were great, allowed us to celebrate with all the enthusiasm you could muster for goals in a European final, then wished us well as we made our way through them and out of the stadium. Had Celtic won while dropping like flies whenever an opponent coughed, it might have been different.

Porto were favourites and would go on to prove how good a team they were by winning the Champions League 12 months later. Their players would demonstrate their prowess across the world for the next decade. They had fabulous talent, so much so, that they should have aspired to better than the gamesmanship used during their run to the UEFA Cup and Champions League wins.

On the field it was a tale of great goals and heroic defeat, off the field, it was one of the most spectacular events in sport.80,000 Celtic fans made the pilgrimage to Seville and treated the world to a carnival. The city became the scene of one of the largest parties the game had ever known. For me the pre-match schedule involved a two hour trip north before a panicked dash across the city collecting match tickets. What a stress!

238

There were 10 in our party and collecting the tickets took priority. Once we had them we could afford time to eat, but what? Several restaurants were sold out but we eventually found a café with frozen chips and a meat-based slab of something or other. No choices. No beer, wine or cola either, it was diluting orange juice or water. An entire city was pretty much emptied of food and drink.

You could forget about motorised transport to get to the game, we had to walk from the city to the stadium on the very outskirts of town. It was hot and dry. An enterprising local was selling a retained stash of cola at the side of the road at a hugely inflated price. No one passed him without buying.

This was a journey to a football game that none of us were familiar with.

The long walk home from the game was memorable for the incredible reaction we got from the locals. They applauded each of us as we walked past their homes in recognition of what took place in their city throughout the day. Things like this don't happen but that day was different. Seville, like Lisbon, will always remember Celtic. FIFA and UEFA made their Fair Play Awards the following year to Celtic fans, a nomination normally reserved for clubs.

I met a German couple in the hotel elevator. "Are you disappointed?" they asked. "No. We were beaten by a good team". I had celebrated two Celtic goals in a European final and watched as we pushed a tremendously talented team to the brink. Disappointment comes a lot worse than this, although time brought regret.

Seville 2003 was not Lisbon 67 but it was a wonderful occasion in our very proud history. Let's do it again.

ART OF WAR - Still got my Seville Survivor t-shirt that someone gave me when I got back – Oh and my sombrero from Torremolinos!

YORKBHOY - I remember sitting in Seville airport for a much delayed flight to Glasgow when King of Kings was being sung. The acoustics of the airport made the song sound like a hymn (I know it is one) than a football song. It was an incredible experience. I must admit I did shed a tear or two…

SOUTH OF TUNIS - Seville? I have never watched the game. I have no desire to watch it. I was never one for overconfidence but that tournament - I had no doubts re Suduva .. .I knew that Blackburn were no big deal.. . I knew we could beat Vigo… I knew we could beat Stuttgart... I knew we could beat Liverpool... I knew we could beat Boavista.

Come the final —I didn't think we could beat Porto – the heat / the class of the Porto players / the belief that the Officials would indulge Porto and the belief that 2 of the Celtic team simply weren't good enough [and yes those 2 players had contributed greatly in getting us to the final].

I took a week to travel from Sicily to Seville. Palermo/ Napoli / Genova / Nizza / Marseille/ Barcelona / Algeciras. Accompanied all the way by the belief that we would lose.

Great trip, great memories, a fabulous life affirming experience but the behavior of the Porto players absolutely sickened me.

BROGAN ROGAN TREVINO AND HOGAN - The old city has been invaded by the Roman, Carthaginians, The Moors and the Arabs— but never have they seen an invasion like this!

SUPERSUTTON - don't have the skills to evoke the memories of Seville in words. I have them in my head and in photos.

However I can recant the tale of how I got a ticket for the final. Two days before the game I got a call from the fine gentleman who sat beside me for years in the North Stand. His son worked / lived in Spain and had bought tickets for their entire family, comprising sons, wives, girlfriends as well as his own wife. The tickets weren't all together but they had them. And he had been effusive in his delight when telling me this at the last home game.

Sadly, while they were in Spain as a pre-final holiday, his wife received news that her mother had died and therefore had to return home.

He called me from Spain and said if I could get transport over there, I could have the ticket.

Whilst money was tight for me at that time, my wife was first to get on the phone and seek out travel. I was again lucky in that the travel company had just put on ANOTHER flight out of Prestwick. I got a seat on that, leaving early in the morning and flying home directly after the game.

I had already given my Celtic top (the yellow one) to a colleague who was going to Seville without a ticket just to savour the occasion.

So a quick scoot over to the Celtic Superstore was required to purchase the Hoops. I have never worn a Celtic top other than when playing 5s. A throwback to being attacked when walking through Bridgeton Cross after an evening game in the 70s.

But there I was before dawn at Prestwick. Celtic top, shorts, socks and trainers. The form I was in at 5s must surely get me a place on the bench I thought.

In Seville I happened upon my work colleague; what are the chances of that. I saw the spectacle of a water fountain adorned by Celtic fans. Remember fondly greeting the guys form Oz with their boxing kangaroo, in Celtic colours of course.

The singing, the heat, the noise, the jubilation, the disappointment, the pride. And then more singing and pride.

Like you Paul, I have never been able to watch the game. Some day I probably will. Might even spot myself in the crowd.

To Alex whose family tragedy became my good fortune, thank you will never be enough.

31003 - If my memory serves me right there were two turnstiles to go through. There were also a helluvalot of forged tickets on the go. These tickets seemed to get you through the first turnstile, but, alas, not the second. Seen many fans, resplendent in replica tops being chased by security through the concourse. Other Celtic fans were side stepping any fugitive Celtic fans then inadvertently bending down to tie shoelaces etc as security tried to get past. Saw a few poor ghuys getting thrown out but at least they were released as soon as they were outside.

I had a seat next to a gangway....just in line with the back post that Henke scored at. A ghuy sitting nervously opposite me stood up about 2 mins before kick off. He turned 360o to take in the full spectacle of Celtic fans taking up most of the stadium. He knelt down on the stairs facing the fans, blessed himself and said a few prayers....then walked out never to be seen again.....nerves must have got the better of him and he couldn't watch the game.

LIVIBHOY - So many memories of Seville. The drive from Benalmadena to Seville will live with me forever. We had managed to get a guy from a boozer in the town to drive us to Seville the night before the game. 4 of us in the van plus the driver. The guy was a Scouser and seemed to be well known to the locals who thought we were mental to agree to go with him.

A great night was had in the 24 hour square with a guy in a kilt and hoops playing Celtic songs on bagpipes and making what must have been a small fortune in the process. Back to the hotel at what time I have no idea. Woke up in a panic. We had slept in.

ARGHHHHHHHHHHHHHHHHHHHH! The biggest game of our lives and we had managed to sleep through the alarm. Checked the phone and the Scouser had been in touch. As good as his word he was outside in the most clapped out van I had ever seen. He had a mattress in the back and I took my seat in the front as group leader and co pilot as none of the other lads had a driving licence.

We had to stop every 20 miles to put water in this thing. Turns out the guy was a handy man and all round decent bloke but did admit to getting involved in things he shouldn't but he appeared to have kids all over the place and wanted to give them what they wanted. Fair play to him. He took us to Seville and will always have a special place in my heart. Every car and bus that passed us had green and white in it. It was like driving along the M8 to a cup final. I have never witnessed anything like it. I had thought that everyone was coming in via Malaga. That road was a scene of green and white and every garage/bar/restaurant was too, on the road to Seville. It was mind blowing. When we reached the city the traffic began grinding to a halt.

It was obvious that the city was gridlocked. The surroundings reminded me of the gas tank in Glasgow. Slightly industrial. We then moved at a snails pace and although we were now buzzing and eager to exit the van, our driver assured us we were still far from the promised land. As we shuffled along a bit we seemed to reach a street full of schools. There were schools along both sides of a dual carriageway and the kids were all out waiting on their buses to take them home. There were hundreds of them. They were all chanting Celtique, Celtique, Celtique.

There were guys exiting their vehicles to give these kids scarves and jerseys and flags. By the time the traffic shuffled along the kids had more Celtic stuff than we did! Something I will always cherish is that memory. We had taken over. The city itself was a mass of green and white. I'm not quite sure what the Porto fans must have thought when they arrived. They must have felt like the away fan at a game in Glasgow. We spent more time looking for mates, acquaintances and work mates than we did enjoying the city to be honest.

We managed to hook up with quite a few old friends and then settled in a nice wee bar near the river. Drank many beers and sang a few songs before making our way on foot to the stadium. Met my old man outside the ground who was in the full Celtic kit. I was just slagging off this guy to my mate saying, "Look at that old bloke there in the full kit. He looks like a Subutteo man". Turned out it was my dad and we hugged and shed a tear. We were altogether as most of the guys from our CSC had met him and heading to a European final. Our CSC was 5 years old. We had our flag and we were ready to watch our team lift the cup.

Negotiated the security checks and got into the stadium perimeter. They had a Soccer AM type put the ball through a hole or hit a target. Everyone had a go and we all did it and won some throw away radio that most of us probably lost before we made it home.

Through the turnstile and up the mountain of stairs en route to our seats that were in the very back row of the upper tier. I will never forget walking up the stairs to of the wee tunnel to enter the arena for the first time. I was met with a sea of green and white that covered two thirds of the ground and there was a small pocket of blue and white at the right of me. I am not ashamed to say I wept and had to be helped to my seat. That is my proudest moment as a Celtic supporter. It was the most amazing sight I have ever seen in football. I'm not sure it will ever be beaten with the ticketing arrangements these days. I was glad to be there. I felt lucky to be there. I felt privileged to be there. I just wanted to see a goal.....

BJMAC - Seville...sighhhhh...Wonderful wonderful experience. Sadly it was my Dad's last game and that is my abiding memory of Seville. Of spending the day in a wee square in the city, a couple of beers, nothing too heavy – for once I wanted to remember and enjoy the experience of the game, despite being very nervous. The chaos trying to get into the stadium, the odd fan breaking through and making a run for the steps into arena, but always seemingly caught agonisingly close to their goal.

The intense heat in the stadium, wearing denims as my only lair of shorts brought with me were unwearable following being thrown into the pool earlier in the day and my Dad using the match programme to fan me, when he was struggling to cope with the heat. The joy, the love, the heartache, the pride.....no regrets, they'd given their all, defeated by a team who I couldn't watch if they won matches playing in that way. Across Europe that night, every neutral that watched that game wanted Celtic to win, we as a family did win, we just didn't bring back the cup.

On return to our hotel, which we shared with the riot police, there was an entirely different attitude from them, one of respect and friendship rather than suspicion and guarded, shaking hands and being commiserated by some of the nastiest men in Spain demonstrated some of what the Celtic family had achieved. A party was started by my brother on return, with the rPod (RebelPod) connected to the hotel sound system, what a night!!!!

A magnificent experience I will never forget, my last holiday with Joe. My last game with Joe before he left us all to early at 55 years old. He brought my brothers and myself up in Celtic, let us understand through

Aye yull see some exterminatin'
if he knoaks err ma pint!

his example what Celtic was about, it wasn't just football, it was more than that.

Poignant day, thinking of very happy and very sad times, as I now type through glazed eyes.

A SON OF DAN - Never been so emotionally drained as the day after that game. I will also never forget the bus journey back into Portugal where we were staying.

TONY DONNELLY 67 - I have the CD of the game. Why do I have it? I haven't a clue BUT I have never watched it. I probably haven't watched it because of the great times and laughs we had that week lump in my throat as I type this. The CD will be staying where it is. As for the result Porto just edged it but the time wasting and diving left a bad taste in my mouth.

ARRANMORE BHOY LXV11 - Seville memories...The sorrowful ones first...Screaming at Bobo for diving in to a challenge - as they'd been diving all day...Screaming at Rab for not catching the ball better. ..Smacking my wrist hard on the ground when they scored their third!

The glorious ones...Rushing home from work to sit as a family, 3 generations, in my house to watch game...The joy at Henrik's goals...The joy at our immense support...The joy at being a Celtic supporter...The joy at MON (Martin O'Neill) signing my Seville Celtic book.

SEVILLE67 - I was promised 3 tickets and was let down (badly by an ex mate) on the weekend before the game.

I was then faced with a decision to go alone with 1 ticket or to watch the game with my 2 sons who now did not have tickets – the boys were in their early teens.

In the end I did not want to go through my life having not shared it with the boys. I wanted to be able to talk to the boys about Seville like my Dad and I still talk about watching the Lions on a Black and White TV.

So I gave away my ticket to a very happy mate cancelled the flights (as

I did not want other Celtic fans not to get and there be empty seats on a plane) and stayed at home. We had a BBQ in the light rain, painted the faces of the kids in the street. My oldest had his first beer and decided that for me Seville was a family experience.

Two days before the game my mate from Porto called and asked me where we meeting for dinner – I told him the story and he immediately offered me 3 tickets for the Porto end – cue a mad scramble for flights but none were available.

At the start of extra time I got a text from a Rangers fan saying that only one team was going to win it and it was not Porto.

When we lost my youngest son was crying and at that moment I knew I was right to share it with him – I told him not to cry but to be proud of the team and of the future he had as a Celtic fan. He is now a fanatic.

To this day I do not regret sharing the game with my sons. I even selected Seville67 as my CQN name to show no regrets.

!!BADA BING!! - After all good ticket sources were drying up by the day, the elation of Boavista was being drowned by despair. The biggest Celtic game in my lifetime and I (along with thousands) didn't have a ticket until a flash of inspiration. I knew ex Scotland Manager Andy Roxburgh worked for UEFA in Switzerland so I tracked down the address and cobbled a letter together.

I enclosed the wee CL Wallet we got that year along with SB insert and a blank cheque and sent it registered post. I got a reply about 4 days later (which I still have). I saw the word "unfortunately" in the first paragraph. I threw the letter on the floor, took a wee walk to the shop, facing the reality that I wouldn't be at the game. After a couple of hours I thought it was very decent of the guy to reply to me, so the least I could do was read the letter.

It said "unfortunately" he couldn't attend the game as he had a coaching seminar booked that week. He said I could have his 2 tickets free on 2 conditions: 1) Don't sell them on and 2) Don't tell anyone he had more tickets because he didn't. He gave me his PA's number and told me to phone her. The tickets were mine. I have never met Andy Roxburgh to this day.

BROGAN ROGAN TREVINO AND HOGAN - Henrik Larsson scored the perfect strikers goal that day. One chance, one defender to shake free, one leap, one touch, just one spot where he could possibly put the ball out of the keeper's reach, one movement to achieve all of that– and one goal. Perfect. Perfect. Perfect.

MIGHTY TIM - We arrived in Seville on the morning of the game in a convoy of coaches that had travelled overnight from Benidorm. Went to meet a guy from Clydebank at his hotel who was selling us 4 tickets for the game at a small fortune. He never turned up so no tickets. We went to the square for the big screens and could not see the pitch properly as the sun shone on the screens. Headed back to a pub and watched the game there. Met so many people that I knew and guys I had not seen since school, priests that I knew from way back.

After the match finished we headed over to the train station to meet up with the rest of the guys from our bus. Our bus left at 3 am to take us back to Benidorm. On the flight from Alicante to Heathrow we got in tow with a crowd of Bhoys from Cork. Pretty sure we drank the plane dry and sang the whole way home. My abiding memory of Seville is one of a great feeling of family. The Celtic family at its very best. Although there were 12 in our party, I was there with my 15 year old son and my best mate. I will never forget my trip to Seville.

MALEYS BHOY - Memories of Seville.

I had just changed jobs before the semi final. A few good Tims in the new workplace so was happy. Sensibly took the day off after the game...or so I thought. By the time I went back to work everyone had booked up and I couldn't get a flight or ticket for love nor money. Ah well...I will just watch it on tv I thought.

But as the days went on I knew I had to get to Seville. Everyone I knew was going. This was my generation's Lisbon and I had to be part of it.

Brilliant! Ah love Tripe!

I started looking for flights again and contacting friends and former work colleagues to source accommodation and a ticket. I was going to have to travel alone as everyone else was already booked up. I eventually managed to book a flight from Glasgow to East Midlands on the Tuesday evening and an early morning flight to Malaga. I couldn't get a hotel room in either East Midlands or Seville. Also there were no hire cars left from Malaga.

On the plus side I got a call from a fellow CQN'r the day before the game... he had got me a ticket. All I needed to do was phone him on my arrival in Spain. On a high I headed off to Glasgow airport wearing a sombrero and my hoops with pride. The flight to East Midlands was pretty empty except for about another 30-40 Celtic fans and some bemused looking businessmen and flight crew. We sang and drank merrily on the short flight. Made some friends on that flight. Dumbarton CSC.

We sat in the bar til closing time. No-one had a hotel for the night so we brought all the beer we could from the bar before it closed and drank through the night.

Got on the flight to Malaga and ended up sitting next to a big Irishman. First thing he asks is...do you have transport to Seville? Nope...good he says. I've got a car but need someone to navigate and share the cost. A mother and her 12 year old son also joined our crew. Picked up car in Seville and I then began to wonder how I was going to navigate our driver to Seville considering the amount of beer I had consumed. I needn't have worried. We joined the Celtic Convoy and followed it on the 2 1/2 hour drive waving to fellow supporters and spotting people we knew on coaches and in other cars.

All the way there I am trying to phone Kev to arrange pick up of my match ticket. But as everyone knows, telephone networks were in meltdown. Couldn't get a hold of him. Every call and text just bounced back.

Arrived in Seville and we all went our separate ways. The next 12 hours or so was a joy...Celtic fans everywhere and everyone was so happy. Met loads of people I knew...but still couldn't get hold of Kev.

Thone wee Stewardess telt me the Pilot's oan 120k a year! Am gonnie get oor collection back!

I made my way to the stadium...It began to sink in that I was not going to get to the game. Not far from the stadium I bumped into some bhoys from my new job and tagged along. Soon our numbers had swollen to a couple of hundred and none of them had tickets either and we knew that the big screen was already full and we were too near the stadium now to make it back anyway.

We needed to find somewhere to watch the game. Everywhere in the outskirts was closed. However a local bar owner appeared. Like the pied piper he led us to his establishment and led us in. €3 a drink in a plastic pint tumbler...no matter what you were drinking. We looked around for the big screen tv....none. There was a tv mounted in a corned and as we got our first drink the teams came out onto the pitch. As the camera panned round we couldn't believe the amount of fans in the stadium. The atmosphere in the pub was electric and I will never forget the fact that a few hundred fans travelled all that way to watch the game in a pub on a 32" TV.

After the highs and eventual lows of the game we headed back to the centre for food. No one was despondent. We were proud of our team and our fellow supporters.

Shortly after midnight I realised I had nowhere to sleep and no means of getting back to Malaga for my flight home. I spent the night in a hotel on the floor of a work colleague's room who was travelling with his Partick Thistle supporting pal who wore his strip with pride too. In the morning I got a voice mail from Kev...he had been trying to call me too. My ticket went to a good home. I managed to get a lift to Malaga from the bhoys in work and made my way home. Tired but not sad.

I remember those 2 days as if it was yesterday and have never experienced anything quite like it. I dream it will happen again soon and this time I can take my 2 bhoys so they can share a truly special occasion they will remember for he rest of their lives.

JOHNNY CLASH - Seville – Went on a chartered day trip from Glasgow to Seville. Glasgow Airport was like an Ellis Island of excited Hoopsters. At Seville Airport there weren't enough staircases to get people off the plane, so we were stuck on the plane, on the tarmac, with the doors open to provide a bit of ventilation for about an hour until a staircase became available. A few beers with pals in one of the fanzone squares and then the long hot walk to the stadium. High fived Owen Coyle (without his Gran) and met the great Hughie McIlvanney outside the ground.

The sight as I walked up the steps and out into the stadium, 3/4 of which was covered in green and white and saltires is the moment that will stay with me longer than the game itself. The only stadium entry that comes close for me is atmosphere when I walked into Celtic Park in 1980 for my first European night match against Real Madrid.

Straight to the airport after the game and back home in Glasgow by about 6.00am. An unforgettable experience.

TAURANGABHOY - Seville was a highlight of my life. I hope that I can get that pure Celtic feeling one more time before I die. The city was green and white. I had booked a family holiday to Gran Canaria so had to leave Mrs Tauranga and the girls and take an internal flight to Seville. Lucky for her we lost or she would have been waiting more than a few days. I didn't get to the game. First night I watched a big group of Porto fans feeling scared in the middle of a plaza and decided to make them Celtic fans.

I approached the patriach of the group and asked him who were the singers in his party. Many pints later we were all singing and dancing and partying in the long hot night before the game. We were swapping tops and the Portugese television crews were celebrating what it means to be Celtic. After a couple of hours sleep I woke up to find to my cousin who had the tickets. Well you all know how impossible it was to get through on mobile.

I even walked to the ground and then walked back to the city when I knew I wasn't going to get the golden ticket. By a small miracle I met a whole bunch of friends again and we watched the game from their hotel room as the big screens failed in the plaza nearby, some of the group had flown in just to watch it on a TV in Seville. After the game I went out with young John Paul and we drank and sang until there was literally nothing more to drink or sing and the sun came up.

An even younger Porto fan joined us who didn't drink or sing but wanted to be part of that special night. I could go on, a thousand small funny moments and stories and every one proud to be a Celtic fan. Who said we didn't win that night. We should have had a medal for Henrik, for sure, but we all made this final more than a memory. I hope I get another chance to experience such a day.

HENRIKS SOMBRERO - Wasn't there a story about some guys sneaking into the stadium the night before the game and sleeping in an air duct?

One of my memories was having to go into a chemist and explain that me and my mates needed a cream to sooth our sore bits after wearing a kilt for 3 days. Then when applying said cream behind a block of buildings (to ourselves, not each other…), being chased off by a cop who must have been wondering what the hell the guys in skirts were doing!

…On the plane from Glasgow to Malaga. Plane was rocking, singing all the way with beach balls being passed along and bounced over our heads.

SOUTH OF TUNIS - I took my time going home and when I got home I received much commiseration. Fitba people wanting to talk about the game and the behaviour of the Porto players. I remember a Juve supporter telling me how disgusting Porto were. Quite an achievement!

SCOTT MCAULEY - My brother and I returned to Seville for an Easter break this year. The city was teaming with the Semama Santa festival and his wife and my girlfriend (who were both still in school and not interested in football 10 years ago) remarked that the city was crammed full of people. Sean and I laughed and told them that this was nothing compared to 10 years ago when Celtic descended on the place.

Every street you turned into from one end of the city to another had Celtic fans everywhere. I remember seeing groups of Porto fans walking through the narrow streets and turning into the piazzas then looking amazed at each other as if to say "there are still MORE of them!" I also remember Celtic fans forming an impromptu guard of honour to welcome the Porto marching band coming through a street. I remember the Daily Record double decker getting footballs booted off of it and fans trying to topple it before the driver thought better of it and moved on.

The heat outside the stadium was staggering but the stadium seemed to have a greenhouse effect. I couldn't help but wonder what the Porto fans, players, UEFA officials and sponsors and all the neutrals thought of the sights and sounds of the Celtic fans that day and night? We must have gained a lot of fans and friends on the back of that single event!

JIMBOB71 - My Da died a couple of days after we beat Blackburn at Ewood Park. 56 years old to bloody cancer. He was diagnosed on 1st July. Our last game together was the previous season.

We shared the joy of the earlier away games on TV and I still went to the home games with mates. He wasn't able to watch the Ewood Park game.

When Seville came round my sister and I decided to go even without tickets.

We were about to buy 2 tickets for £500 outside the stadium for Porto end when a wee local with a moustache offered us 2 for 500 euro in the Porto end.

We bought them, had a great day in the city then headed to the match. Took our seats when a Porto fan told us that the stewards on the concourse were letting Celtic fans through the barrier into the Celtic end (Health & Safety?). So I sent my sister down, (better looking than me!!) and she waved down that we were getting through!

We watched the game on the steps and a great guy beside us handed me his mobile to phone home and let everyone know we were in and in the Celtic End!

HENRIKS SOMBRERO - Going for a midnight swim post pub crawl in Torremolinos while two unknown wummin watched our kilts and then walking into a beach bar wearing nothing but our sporrans. And getting served.

DONTBRATTBAKKINANGER - Seville team rightly regarded as the strongest for many years but on the bench-

Hedman, McNamara, Laursen, Sylla, Fernandez, Smith and Maloney!

GLASGOWBHOY - My Seville started on the Saturday prior to the match. I went to Waverley Station in Edinburgh to see off my brother (the lucky winner of 6 tickets in the UEFA ballot) who had a full week booked in Torremolinos. He was on the 9:00 to London and as soon as he boarded I headed round to the Celtic shop in Hanover Street to buy my brand new strip and also a sombrero. The guy in front of me got the last sombrero though –gutted!

My own trip (with Glasgowghirl) started on Monday 19 th with an early taxi to Edinburgh airport. Taxi driver – where to? Me – Seville. We flew to Gatwick then we went to check in for our BA flight to Seville. Bad news - no record of us on the flight. Along with 8 others, our booking company had re-sold the seats the previous night for over £600 each – one of our group had seen them online.

We then had a nervy 3 hour wait to see if they could squeeze us on the flight – the poor wee girl sent to help us was convinced it would be fine, as it had happened before – but she had never seen an airport so full of Celtic supporters, so we weren't so sure. In the end, 6 of us got on, including us. Two flew instead to Faro, which suited because they were staying there, but 2 had to fly to Valencia – hope they got to Seville in time!

So, we've made it to Seville. Next, though, we could only stay in our hotel the first night – we had to move out to Cordoba for the next 2 nights, then back to Seville the day after the game! On match day, we joined the express train from Madrid, which only has one other stop – Cordoba – so a wee bit of luck there!

I'll never forget climbing off the train and climbing the stairs with hundreds of fellow Celtic fans singing Hail Hail the Celts are Here. Match day itself was everything everyone else says it was – just brilliant, even with the heartache. We got massive hugs from some old Porto fans as we left the

HENRIK'S GOAL THAT TOOK US TO SEVILLE!

L Monaghan

L Monaghan

SEVILLE – THE CELTIC MOVEMENT

L Monaghan

L Monaghan

SEVILLE – THE CELTIC MOVEMENT

L Monaghan

L Monaghan

SEVILLE – THE CELTIC MOVEMENT

L Monaghan

L Monaghan

L Monaghan

SEVILLE – THE CELTIC MOVEMENT

L Monaghan

L Monaghan

SEVILLE – THE CELTIC MOVEMENT

L Monaghan

SEVILLE – THE CELTIC MOVEMENT

SEVILLE – THE CELTIC MOVEMENT

SEVILLE – THE CELTIC MOVEMENT

SEVILLE – THE CELTIC MOVEMENT

SEVILLE – THE CELTIC MOVEMENT

SEVILLE – THE CELTIC MOVEMENT

L Monaghan

L Monaghan

SEVILLE – THE CELTIC MOVEMENT

SEVILLE – THE CELTIC MOVEMENT

SEVILLE – THE CELTIC MOVEMENT

SEVILLE – THE CELTIC MOVEMENT

KING OF KINGS

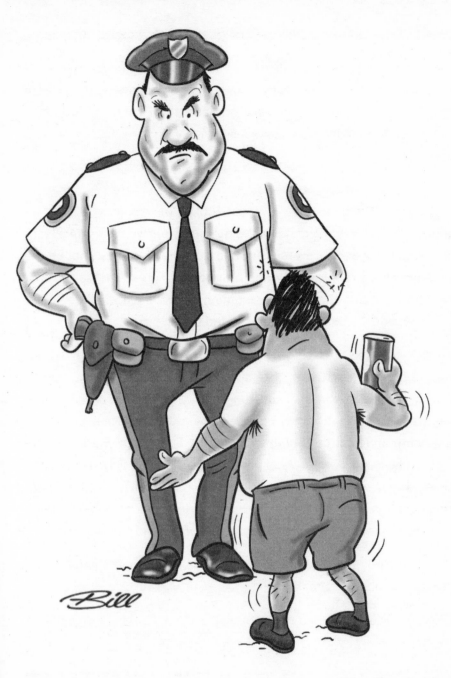

Okay okay Manwell, if yer the Polis where dae ah report a missin' bus?

stadium, then started our 2 hour walk (and some) to the train station – only this time we were hoping for a taxi back to Cordoba.

With a big queue forming, only some excellent queue jumping from Glasgowghirl would do the job – she grabbed a taxi just as he arrived at the station and we ran for it – apologies if anyone reading this remembers us!

Thoughts of a wee kip on the journey back to Cordoba? No chance, the guy drove like a banshee at about 160kph the whole way. Then he stopped at some waste ground on the outskirts, and we thought we were going to get mugged, or worse. Turns out he's a good guy, though, he was getting his street map out and dropped us right at the door of our hotel. By now it was about 3 in the morning, so we had a wee beer in our room, then bed – knackered, disappointed but so proud!

Next day – back to Seville again on the express train! As we arrived, we were greeted by the masses of Celtic fans who had slept in the station, including the big guy from Elgin who used to sit in front of me in 405 every week blocking my view! We spent the rest of the week in Seville, flying home again on the Sunday, during the final league games of the season. The captain was under strict instructions to only give us the scores if Celtic had won. Eventually he came on to tell us,,,Rangers are champions again. Thanks mate. At least I didn't have to watch it, never have, and I'm really glad I didn't know we were ahead at one point.

Seville was one of the highlights of my entire life, I'll never forget being there. In the "neutral" stand!

STEVIEBHOY66 - Tears in my eyes again! Great stories, remember as if it was yesterday.

Went to game, walked from stadium in morning walked to game then walked back. Me & wifey decided to stay instead of heading back to Benalmadena....bad move!!! Slept on a bench next to river, eventually got a taxi from bus station, cost us a fortune :)

You wonder what it would have been like if we had WON!

CONNAIRE12 - What great stories! My experience was less exciting because I went out by plane the day before and returned after the game. Did have a fabulous night in Jerez and met many of the Lisbon Lions that were staying there. Managed to tell Tommy Gemmell that I had seen him play as a striker in a game in Jersey USA in 1966. Of course, he insisted he was a world beater in that position.

Incidentally, how many of you will own up to telling family and friends that you would meet them in front of the Cathedral? Well, I did. Never found them. But the atmosphere was incredible. Yes, a day when one was proud to be a Celtic fan. Just one among many proud days in 125 years.

I was at Lisbon also and had the privilege of getting to visit Mr Stein's room and hold THE CUP in my very own hands. A moment never to be forgotten.

MONTEBLANCO - When I went to Seville my neighbours at the time had Shih Tsu dugs and one was pregnant. When I came back from Seville I had a Shih Tsu.

'If you can spend awe that money on a day oot at the fitba, ah'm gettin' a dug!'

POGMATHONYAHUN AKA LAIRD OF THE SMILES - I was in Seville with a great wee guy whom I knew but eventually became great friends with and we travelled together after Seville to Barcelona, twice 0-0 and 1-1, Munich, Teplice, Villarreal and back to Scotland for numerous home games. He was also a regular visitor to the Munich Oktoberfest with me and always wore his hoops with pride.

Unfortunately, John did not get a ticket for the game but watched it on the big screen and was rather stocious when we got back from the ground. Didn't stop him though. He bought me a programme for Seville. In fact he was always buying me things when we went away, football tops, souvenirs from our visits, an incredibly generous man. We had some great times when he was alive. Unfortunately, he died suddenly at the tender age of 57, three years ago. Gone but never forgotten.

MORT - I hate you all!!!

Ok, not really but reading all the stories makes me sad that I didn't make it to Seville. A few days before hand we were offered flights for £500 for a one day trip but no ticket. As just out of uni and only a part-time job, sensibly at the time turned it down as couldn't afford it.

In hindsight, should have just whacked it on the credit card and worried about the consequences later.

BOURNESOUPRECIPE - In the Cathedral holy mass was being celebrated almost continuously throughout the day on two separate altars and services. Celtic fans mingled with the locals and Porto fans alike. There was a side altar with a monument of the resting place of Christopher Columbus.

WIKI - The exemplary conduct of the thousands of travelling Celtic supporters received widespread praise from the people of Seville and the fans were awarded prestigious Fair Play Awards from both FIFA and UEFA "for their extraordinarily loyal and sporting behaviour".

WEERON - I was fortunate to spend a week in Seville. 5 days before the game and a couple afterwards. I experienced the whole thing coming together. From 60 Tims at Flaherty's to the complete takeover of a beautiful city. Bumped into dozens of friends from all over the globe.

Missed our train back to Madrid, but all in all, a wonderful time in our lives.

BOURNESOUPRECIPE - Before the match UEFA Cup chief of security Rafael Carmona said:

'I don't believe 50,000 fans will travel to Seville, that is madness, it is an exaggeration. I think a fair number will be around 4,000. We are talking about a final to be played on a Wednesday, a day when people normally work'.

LIVIBHOY - The heat was unbearable. How players could run around for 120 minutes was beyond me. I was struggling to catch a breath and

After analyzing the air inside them,
even the beach balls are pissed!

I was just sitting watching it. The window above the Porto fans was just streaming the sun into the ground and onto the pitch and must have been like a greenhouse! The players did not let us down in Seville. They gave us everything. We scored two great goals and we could not have asked for anymore. If that game had been played north of Paris I believe we would have won the UEFA Cup. If the referee had been stronger we may well have won it in Seville but Porto were a very good side. It was a pity the antics they resorted to when Celtic started to get on top in the match.

MATT E - The night after the game in Seville my mate and I were sitting outside a bar with a mad Stirling crowd when a couple of suited guys with their wives asked if they could sit and listen to our stories. It turned out to be David Will, at that time vice-president of FIFA and the other guy was vice-president of UEFA. They told us then that the Celtic fans would win every Fair Play award going, as Lennart Johanssen had said to them that he wished Celtic could make it to a final every year as he had never seen a festival of colour like it!

I was back in Seville a couple of years ago and the main street by the Cathedral has been transformed, now pedestrianised with a Tram system. I remember thinking its amazing what u can do with Celtic fans beer money!!

MALCEYE - This sounds pretty daft but one of my memories of the game was the excitement and anxiety leading to the kick-off in the stadium – Las Ketchup were playing their one and only hit, (The Ketchup Song, obviously). The song is on one of my girls' Wii games and never ceases to bring a tear to my eye.

The high hopes, the deflation at their goals, the exultation brought by Henrik's goals. The reality that we had lost. If we were supporters of any other club, the final would have been a disaster. While we probably all harbor regret at not winning, we emerged from Seville as the best supporters of the best football club in the world. Not that we didn't know it already. It's just the rest of the world found out.

PARKHEADCUMSALFORD - I have watched the game again. Once. Just had to see how we had played, as in real time, it just flashed by, between moments of deep misery and sheer joy, and a lingering sense of anger at Porto's behaviour.

Of the match, my abiding memory is of longing for any sort of drink to quench the raging thirst. The stadium ran out of all liquids, certainly by half-time.

Never seen anything like the sea of support inside the ground.

Wouldn't have missed the experience for the world.

LEN BRENNAN – I remember arriving at Glasgow airport at around 6am and we were queued at the end of the walkway over the road with a few hundred Celts in front of us singing the conga. The plane was totally rocking and the cabin crew looked like rabbits in the head lights as they had to tell us that they could serve any booze :)

We arrived in Malaga with the temperature hitting high teens as we were herded into a bus park were we eventually found our bus and then tried to communicate with the driver to see if he could stop at an offie on the way out of town and after a lot of hand signals he smiled and nodded. We settled into the 3 odd hour drive, which saw one of the strangest things I've probably ever witnessed.

We stopped at a huge service station which had the flags of every European country flying outside and found about 100-150 buses full of Celts singing doing the huddle and generally taking the over place. The cafe served the most dodgy food but no-one was that interested as they also served beer and had a few toilets (which was lucky as the ones on the bus we're now backed up).

When we finally arrived in Seville the first thing we saw as the bus rounded onto the drop off point at the square was the huge fountain, which had about twenty shirtless Tims dancing about in the water while others posed with a happy smiling policewoman, as her male colleague took their picture.

We walked up passed the cathedral with mouths open in awe as the streets were packed with green and white. Huge flags on poles were being waved further down the street and tricolours and hoop shirts were hanging out of windows of hotels above our heads.

The sight itself was something but the noise and buzz was amazing. As you walked along you got caught up in about 7 different songs dancing with strangers as they walked passed. At one point we walked passed Danny McGrain who was trying to walk down the street with his family but he was being mobbed with everyone wanting to shake his hand as he was being followed by a huge group who sang his name over and over.

We were all starving but finally found a McDonald's by the river side and were settling down to munch when some eagle eyed Tim spotted John McKay who was there reporting for Scotland Today. Not sure if he was doing a live report or a recording but he basically had to pack it in as he got dogs abuse from the several hundred fans on the street. His face was a picture.

Five of us had travelled and none of us had tickets so we decided to get out to the ground as early as possible. However when the bus dropped us at the stadium we realised we weren't that early. The place was mobbed and basically all the touts were realising that they could name their price and someone would pay it so we soon realised that we weren't going to get into the game and resigned ourselves to heading back into town to watch the game.

We had passed the big screens but felt we'd be so far back and wouldn't see anything, so we ended up in a bar which was in a wee street behind the bullring. The place was tiny and as we found out was a Betis bar but every Spaniard in the place was cheering for us. We went through all the highs and lows together and shared beers and tears at the final whistle.

On the walk back to the bus we met dozens of Porto fans who were brilliant with hugs and scarf/shirt swapping happening everywhere. When we got back to the square where we were due to be picked up I just slumped to the ground and just stared up at the sky. I think I was in shock but my old mate hit me a kick and told me to cheer up as no matter what the outcome, we had shown the world what a great club and great support we were and no amount cheating would ever change that fact.

The bus ride and flight back to Glasgow were filled with stories and songs and I cemented some life long friendships.

I have since then been to a large number of our European excursions and experienced some highs and way too many lows but I will always remember Seville.

PRINCE ALBERT KIDD OF HAMILTON - I had the best forgery in Seville by a mile. BlantyreKev and Monteblanco allowed me to get so drunk I never got anywhere near the ground. I never got any of the tapas either.

BROGAN ROGAN TREVINO AND HOGAN - On the day before the Seville final, 3% of the entire world's air travellers were Celtic fans - the biggest flying support in sports history!

"Approximately 80,000 Celtic supporters, the largest travelling support in history at that time"

The Independent 2003

WINNING CAPTAINS - We arrived at Glasgow airport around 5am on the Monday morning – we were flying to Portugal and making our way to Seville from there. The airport was brilliant – a mixture of confused business types and Celtic fans - one with a ghetto blaster with the Willie Maley song playing and the beers – even at that time – were being enjoyed.

We watched the 1967 Final on the plane – there were so many Celtic supporters that they agreed to our request and I remember thinking that every time you see that match you are surprised at how much of a doing we gave Inter Milan. It should have been 7-1 not 2-1. When we arrived in Seville there weren't too many Celtic fans around, so we were there from the start and watched as more and more arrived over the next three days.

We headed to the stadium, which was fairly deserted and the one person we did meet was none other than Billy McNeill – so we got some great pics with him. Then we went back into Seville (on the bus, way too far to walk although we had to there and back on the Thursday). The Cup was on display in the centre of Seville so again some great pics.

The number of supporters kept increasing - it was like a massive green and white tide coming in. I remember walking to the game – and most of the supporters were going in the opposite direction, these were the unlucky ones without a ticket. Another memory was a bus driver on the Thursday afternoon in the centre of Seville – the city was gridlocked due to the sheer volume of Celtic supporters. Anyway he simply parked the bus and told everyone to get off and off he went to enjoy the occasion! For those who reckon there were only 80,000 in Seville then I say that is a massive under-estimation.

The walk to the stadium was long – it was even longer on the way back. Anyone who wasn't there just could grasp what it was like in that stadium – the heat and the dry air was horrible. They ran out of water too and there were lots of supporters struggling – dear knows how the players managed to play in those conditions – it clearly gave Porto a massive advantage.

We were sitting in the perfect spot to see Henrik's goals and before that big Rab's first mistake. To me the game turned when Jackie Mac was fouled and that rubbish ref failed to give the free kick at the edge of their box, instead they broke and Bobo brought down their player and was sent off. Even then you could see that Porto had settled for penalties then our goalkeeper presented them with the trophy.

The walk back was long – it was well after 2am when we got to the hotel and no-one really wanted to go to bed. We sat around, stunned but proud. Then when we went to our room around 5am. I turned on the TV and they were showing live pictures of Porto arriving back with the cup – OUR cup.

Next day, back at the airport in one of the shops there was a dummy displaying a Porto strip and a security guy standing next to it. A Celtic fan brushed past it and as it fell the security guard caught it, whist drawing the Celtic supporter a dirty look. The Celtic fan quick as a flash said –

Are ye no a wee bit embarrassed
huvin' that brolly in yer Guinness?

"I never touched him – it was a dive!" The guard laughed – he was a Sporting Lisbon fan and wanted Celtic to win. Like many on here have never been able to watch that game – don't think I ever will.

MRS WINNING CAPTAINS (by special request!) - I remember taking Winning Captains and his friends to Glasgow Airport very early on the Monday morning to catch his flight to Faro for the final. It was a lovely clear morning - a perfect day for flying I guess.

We didn't live far from the airport and got there around 20 minutes. We parked the car then went into the Terminal 2 building for check-in, which was completely packed with supporters all heading to the game and mixing with rather bemused business people at the start of their working week. Everywhere was green and white and the atmosphere was quite special. It wasn't particularly quiet as you would expect with a crowd of Celtic supporters – But it was in fact quite civilised with a real sense of anticipation for the forthcoming match. I stood with my husband in the check-in queue so I could soak up just a little bit of the Seville atmosphere and I was listening to all the chatter around me when the funniest thing happened. The guy in front of us in the queue took out a portable CD player, placed it on the floor then pressed the 'on' switch. It was at this point I noticed a shift in the atmosphere as the song 'Oh Hampden in the Sun' started to belt out from the aforementioned CD player! The sense of excitement amongst the supporters was palpable and I really hoped that the team would do the supporters proud and bring the cup back to Glasgow. Although I wasn't able to go to Seville, I'm glad I was able to experience a moment of that very special atmosphere Glasgow the airport that morning. And I never realised that the Celtic supporters could start drinking for the day at 6.00am!

WEET WEET WEET - Four of us drove to Heathrow to get our flight to Zurich then another to Malaga, a hire car to our hotel in Cadiz only to find that the hotel was in the town of Cadiz 50m back at Gibraltar. Sod it we said. Just get blootered and sleep in the car. Next day Seville, wonderful, wonderful Seville.

After the game we were heading back to find our hotel. The next day we got to the hotel, checked in and went straight over to Gibraltar and got blootered.

Never been the same since.

MARK DERRY BHOY - Didn't make it to Seville. My good lady wife was pregnant after our final attempt at IVF and had just lost the baby. She was in hospital for the D and C operation the day of the final. She went into surgery early around noon and I had heard absolutely nothing till after 6pm. Apparently there were complications.

The doctors told me her first words on waking were "How soon can I go home? My husband wants to see the game?" The doctors were not having it but my wife told them she was a midwife as was her mother and that she would be ok. We were allowed home and after a mad rush home to Hamilton, we got to see the final. Was just relieved my wife was ok and sad at the previous few weeks events that much of the game was a haze. Don't remember much of it apart from Henrik's goals and Porto diving.

TEUCHTER ÅR LÅ - Your recollections of the city being seriously depleted of food and drink made me smile. After the game, I managed to find a small café which "only" had a line of around 20 or 30 people outside. I ordered a pizza and some time later a box was thrust into my hand.

Upon inspection outside, I noticed that the toppings were corn and carrots – I didn't care as I was Hank Marvin'. I took a bite out of the first slice – It was rancid. I tried another bite…just the same. A Tim in the queue asked me "you finished wi that big man?". I replied that it wasn't particularly good, but he was welcome to it. As I turned to walk away, I heard him say "Hey blue cheese – That's unusual. I just couldn't bring myself to ask for it back:)

UNCLE FESTER - 10 years ago today, myself, 3 mates, my then girlfriend's Dad and his mate made the pilgrimage to Seville.

Only two of us had tickets but that wasn't really the point, was it? We were going to the biggest Celtic party ever. That was good enough for me to make the trip.

I'd be here all afternoon taking you through the experience so I'll keep to the highlights -

* Sharing a few beers with hundreds of fellow Tims, bedecked in green & white, at Glasgow Airport at 6am in the morning.

* The pilot, both at the start and end of the flight, shouting Hail! Hail! over the aeroplane intercom and wishing us all the best.

* Arriving at the Cathedral, singing, dancing and drinking all day until kick-off. The atmosphere was sensational. * Being filmed by a local TV crew playing keepie-uppy with my mates in the Square.

* Meeting & having a photo taken with the guy from UEFA (cannae mind his name) who said we'd only bring 4,000. I'll never forget the look on his face.

* Finding a BUTCHERS selling ice-cold, 1 litre bottles of beer for £1.50.

* Looking along the 'Green Mile'. A finer sight I've yet to see.

* Hearing my Da call out my name. Didn't know he was going. He booked last minute and took my sister for good measure. Probably still paying it off today!

* Continually interrupting Raman's news piece for back home. Priceless. Celebrating Henke's two goals with 10,000 others at the big screens. His first was particularly special.

* Whilst celebrating his 2nd, someone knocked off my glasses (which I need for everything). Never saw them again. Mate had to talk me thru the rest of the game.

* The feeling of pride, not dejection, at the final whistle.

* The joy at finding my fellow travellers (who I had been separated from) at the bus park after the game. Barely being able to see 10ft in front of me, it's a miracle I found them!!

Am new but even Ah can see
that there's nae photies oan here!

And that bhoys & ghirls, was my Seville experience!

THEMIGHTYQUINN - I didn't make it over. Or to a single game on the lead up. I was a poor broke bum in those days. But I had watched every single game in O'Neill's on Sauchiehall Street, in the back room, with my mate Hogan.

On the day of the game we got to the pub in plenty of time only to be told by the bouncer tat the pub was full and they weren't for letting us in. No matter how much we begged and pleaded fearing a jinx on the game the bouncer didn't shift. Across the road The Garage nightclub had a queue from the front door, along the street, round the corner and all the way up the hill to the Art School.

We feared that we'd have to grab a carry out and watch it in the house.

As a last ditch attempt we grabbed a taxi west to the QMU.

Arriving there only to be told they weren't showing it.

This time I was not to be denied though. Hogan and I along with a few other few lads managed to convince the staff that there was a goldmine ready to be tapped as there would be hundreds of punters in the same situation as us and that they would fill the place no problem.

The staff saw sense and the game was put on the big screens on Qudos. We even helped put out hundreds of seats so that the masses who were now arriving in droves as word had spread that the game was being shown could watch in comfort.

I remember the game all too vividly and the pain of losing but the atmosphere in the QM was spectacular that night. But the pride I have in knowing that I helped many a Celt find a crowded room to watch the game is also still with me.

I wept after the final whistle.

I still blame myself for the defeat, no matter how ridiculously superstitious that may be.

If only I'd got to O'Neills sooner….

BLANTRYETIM - TheMightyQuinn. Glad to see at least you don't blame the keeper…Douglas was one of eleven…

BOOKER T - Seville memories,

On the outward flight which was scheduled for Seville airport, being informed by the travel rep "we're not landing in Seville, it's Faro airport instead" ok says I. Is that nearby?…This was quickly followed by the guy behind us roaring "It's in Portugal!"

Singing The Celtic Song in a bar with Shug Keevins on a link up back to Radio Clyde at lunchtime.

Seeing a guy I went to school with standing at a bus stop…went over stood beside him and casually asked "is the 44 due soon?"…cue his face when he turned and saw me!

The heat in the stadium…or should I say the lack of fresh air…head was burstin' everytime I tried to sing!

Would do it all again tomorrow! Thanks Martin, 'Twas a lovely journey!

SAINT STIVS - Everytime I try to type about Seville, I get another wee memory, and want to add it. Needless to say, it was the best day of my life. Other than the result. Also not winning the league that weekend, I felt seriously dejected for months after, with what ifs and might have beens. It did take me a long time to get over getting beat.

CITYBHOY - The 21st of May 2003 for me and the CitiBhoys really started on Friday the 25th of April. Flights Gatwick – Malaga were sorted out for 19th May. A hotel booked in Puerto Banus to meet up with some Dublin friends and engage in a bit of pre match acclimatisation ; Car hire for the final push to Seville was easy; a hotel in Seville for the nights around the the game was slightly more difficult but "happened"… Ah right, all we need are the tickets….. so various web-sites "contacts" and other sources official and unofficial were tried, all to no avail.

Two weeks pass and we are getting nowhere, quite a few tickets on e bay seemed to be coming from the Malaga area and I'm getting desperate so I posted an online request on the Malaga FC bulletin board – and amazingly got a call that same evening. Did they have tickets...? eh Si!! How many?...How many do you want...Well there were 8 of us so I wasn't hopeful. I need 8 ...Perfecto he says. I have 8. Ok how do we do this? I wanted to see the "goods" and he wanted cash (a lot of cash).

Our negotiation was getting bogged down in my poor Spanish and his equally poor English. At this point I told him that I would get a Spanish speaker to call him back shortly. So Citighirl, a native of Spain got on the phone... called the guy and was on the phone for what seemed like hours..."Dinero , Madrid, Manana" were the gist of it.

So next day I find myself flying to Madrid on the first flight out of Heathrow. A visit to Citibank to pick up the "Dinero" and then off to the "meet" at the Ritz hotel. Carlos was already waiting. A colleague of mine from our Madrid office (big chap) agreed to play minder. Ray-Bans and all. So there we are sitting on the terrace having a San Miguel checking the "merchandise". It all looked kosher – tickets issued to Malaga FC. Carlos claimed to be a family member of an FC Malaga official. Was happy to provide us with a photocopy of his passport.

It was still a risk, a big risk, and one that might not become a reality until we got to the turnstiles... But there was no room for doubt – the "Dinero" was handed over... and do you know Carlos never even counted it. Just stuck the envelope of 500 Euro notes into his inside pocket, shook hands and off he went. I thanked my colleague and headed straight back to Barajas for the 5pm flight to London. The Citibhoys met the next evening to examine the merchandise and it was the consensus that they were genuine! Seville Bring it On! God how slow were the next two weeks... TBC.

RICHIE - I was at the game and haven't watched it since, but I remember seeing the winning goal on telly and was it not a nick off Laursen that put the ball beyond Rab's reach?

I've no desire to see it again but always thought the Big Man wasn't at fault for that goal.

DANNYGALL - Before heading off to Seville I was comparing the date with that of Lisbon & realised that my 3 1/2 year old son was the same age TO THE DAY on 21/5/03 as I was on 25/5/67!!!!

Surely it was an omen, I thought...

JC2 - Edinburgh - London - Zurich - Malaga

All you lot talking about drinking at 6 o'clock in Glasgow airport. We were in Zurich with all business types at 6am. They ordered expresso we ordered "NO the Big glasses please." As a wee wifey dressed as if she was going to the Darby and Joan club ordered Double doubles at the bar. The Barman thought the circus was in town.

PANDYHANDS - I haven't posted in ages (lurk daily) but all these recollections of Seville has stirred up my own memories.

The day before the final we, myself and 3 others, were due to catch an early flight from Belfast. Things didn't get off to a good start as I was sitting in the driver's seat of my car at 5am saying the Rosary that my car would start on this the 3rd attempt! Success.

After picking up the rest of the crew a few beers were consumed pre-flight and to Luton we went. Sitting consuming another few beers waiting on our next flight we noticed Monica McWilliams (was then the leader of the Women's Coalition party in the Stormont Assembly).

We begged her to give the boul Gerry Adams a call to see if he could use his 'influence' to get 4 Belfast Bhoys tickets! She took this as good humoured and even posed with us in front of our 8ftx10ft Tricolour on the promise that we wouldnt pass the photo to the Sunday World :-) To Alicante next after a delayed flight then in to the hire car.

Carry outs purchased at the 1st available stop, old skool tunes blaring, we set off on the 500km journey to Seville. We stopped off just after midnight at a roadside taverna in the hope of a room and were ecstatic to find two rooms left and only 25 euro pp. Result. The journey in to Seville the next morning was great. We passed bus after bus of Celtic fans with the customary horn blasting and scarf waving antics raising our spirits even higher than they already were.

We set up in the square, right next to the Tony Mowbray CSC flag visible in most of the photos of the square and the drinking, singing and dancing started. I have to say that those few hours in the square were the best craic I think I've ever had. With no tickets we set off to find a wee bar that was packed to the rafters with Hoops and the banter, craic, beer flowed right up to the final whistle. Although deflated I can still remember feeling so proud as the locals applauded us as we passed on our way back to our car.

There was so many wee things about that trip that stick in my memory that make me smile – The bagpipe player marching into the square like the Piped Piper and hundreds of us dancing to his tunes in a big circle and taking turns to take the centre to perform our party pieces.

My cousin falling asleep topless on a newspaper to wake up with the print of the sports page readable off his back. The chants towards the Daily Record bus! The slagging we gave two women in the airport cause one looked like Sideshow Bob – even her mate was crying with laughter.

I could go on and on but I'll end by saying that undoubtedly that 3 day round trip was by far the best craic I've had, I could only imagine what it would've been like if we'd won! I know our crew had suggested that we'd stay for a few unscheduled days and max out the credit cards – the result probably saved a few marriages.

MARGARET McGILL - Apart from the game, my favourite memory of Seville was my brother wearing a Porto top in Carmona on the night of the defeat. Got some dirty looks from 3 hooped tims (2 Glaswegians and a Dundonian) in a street cafe where we ended up. He had learned some Portugese and went over pretending to commiserate in broken English. "Ah Henrik Larsson #1", "Ah Henrik Larsson #1," "Celtic good team no?" Then we both broke out in " Big Bobos gonna get ye" "Big Bobo's gonna get ye" . 5 Tims stoned out their minds in the Parador de Carmona is how it ended.

TIM TANIUM - Some harsh words on here about Rab Douglas in the final. He was one of the reasons that we reached the final. His displays throughout the run were excellent.

THE TOKEN TIM - Having a brilliant time reading the post re everyone's Seville memories.

The stories just re-iterate what that trip meant to us all and reminds me how much fun it was. I doubt any city anywhere in the world has seen the likes of that day.

I remember heading away from the cathedral area to meet up with some of my brother's mates. the bar they were in – like most of the bars that day – was about to run out of beers. In fact the only alcohol they had left in the entire bar was a bottle of Midori, which a guy next to me bought happily when I said no thanks. Don't think I've ever seen a bar owner look as happy as the guy in the bar did that day!

The walk from the city centre up to the stadium that evening will stay with me to the day I die. That priceless ticket was zipped in my wallet, which in turn was zipped up in my shorts pocket which was then buttoned into the bargain! That great majority of that ticket is sitting in my desk drawer to this day – the guy at the turnstile ripped off only a tiny part at the top corner.

TALLYBHOY - Today I am proudly wearing – as I often do – my commemorative Seville polo shirt. White, with the Celtic crest over the left breastie. Over the right one – UEFA Cup Final –underneath the UEFA Cup Trophy – and on the bottom, Seville 21-5-2003.

!! BADA BING!! - What happened to the Seville money?

SOUTH OF TUNIS - Saint Stivs - "It did take me a long time to get over getting beat "

Me too - it bothered me for a long time. Bothered me more than any other defeat. I had no doubt that Celtic would beat Inter. I wasn't convinced we'd beat Feyenoord as I'd watched them hump a very good Milan team in Rotterdam. There was a lot of hubris after we beat Leeds. I felt like a voice in the wilderness as I told people - Feyenoord are a right good team. Being beat came as no surprise. I accepted it and moved on ...

Losing in Seville bugged the hell out of me. Porto were a very good team but their antics sickened me. It also really bugged me that 2 Celtic players I really didn't rate proved me right.

BJ MAC - Fantastic!!!! Reading the posts and seeing the pictures is very poignant indeed, especially knowing where I was sitting, who I was with and the fact that was the last time we had done what we'd done on hundreds of occasions...

CQN, at times, is an amazing, warm place ;-))

WESTENDTIM - Don't post regularly however I believe that on very rare occasions and in relation to very select organisations such as our own, winning is not the most important thing. I was in Seville with my daughter, sister and nephew and was incredibly disappointed not to have won however the manner in which we handled the occasion was, I think, an extension of the very ethos of our club.

We were inclusive, gracious, truly dignified (not some brown brogued version of dignity) and above all sporting especially when we arrived at the airport 4 hours after the game and were warmly acknowledged by the Porto fans. I truly believe that the greater powers plan was that after that defeat we would achieve our reward for the fans not the team but also we could be held up as a direct comparison to a dead teams shame in Manchester. The Lord does move in mysterious ways for those who believe that sort of thing!

LIVIBHOY - The guy at the turnstile never ripped my ticket at all. Still have the whole thing intact in a drawer with the official programme, unofficial programme and my flight stubs and other wee keepsakes. I think the tickets for the final were the cheapest tickets I bought that season. I think they were under £20 with the exchange rate at the time.

VMHAN - Seville memories, I left CP the Wed night before after beating Dundee 5-1. I was worried about that late goal they scored and hoped it wouldn't hurt us in the chase for the league. I remember that

No even if ah put it
roon ma neck?

disappointment but quickly forgot as we partied on the way back to Blackpool that night. The next morning we left for Manchester airport to head out to Faro. I could go on for hours but Coorslad has already mentioned the guitar I bought and the impromptu tunes in a wee English bar in Albufeira. The best bit was being with 80,000 friends and family in Seville.

SPARKLEGHIRL - Seville – I couldn't believe my luck when I got the ticket, Took a week and flew from Newcastle to Málaga then back to Manchester. I spent the week in Granada, a favourite place of mine, with one day and one night in Seville. As many have said, I just had to be there...Reading some of your stories I realise how lucky I was to get such convenient flights...

TWISTS N TURNS - Seville. Glasgow airport at dark o'clock (must have been about 4am I think). Met and had photo taken with John Higgins. Shuttle bus across to the plane seemed to be sitting forever. Mild panic at the thought the plane might be goosed. Jubilation and relief as the flight took off. Had 3 tickets for the game and didn't meet a single passenger on that flight who'd managed to secure one. Sat next to an ould fella who told me this was the first Celtic game he wasn't gonna see for donkeys years. Felt somewhat of a fraud that his dedication didn't merit a ticket yet me as a part timer had got 3. One of my sons couldn't make it and we had given his brief to a mate. I wish I'd still had it on the flight to give to the old fella. Cadiz the night before the game. Hotel emblazoned with Celtic flags and scarves. Little bar outside the hotel opened for business and the owner thought all his Christmases had come at once.

Must have made a fortune. Played all the reb tapes for us all night and into the early hours. Coach to Seville on match morning. Blistering heat and my son dying of a hangover. The atmosphere that day in Seville – well documented now. Realised I had only 1 fag left as we entered the ground. Hung on to it as long as I could. Lit it up....Henrik scored. Fag went flying.

The rest you all know. Score disappointing but the experience was awesome. Amazing day, amazing people, amazing team. (One thing I will never know is how I found the coach post match).

JIMBOB71 - The pilot on our plane when we landed in Seville was a hoot!

He started telling us about his friend who owned a wine shop near London City Airport, how to tell a good wine etc etc then he meandered onto how his friend flies to Seville and picks up wine but that he also picks up the local ladies and that he picked up something from one of them!

He was telling all us gentlemen to be careful of this situation especially as we all probably had wives or girlfriends back home!! Telling us to make sure as well as visiting the bars and restaurants to also visit the chemist!! All this in about a 10 minute speech with the poshest of English accents and a massive dose of humour amongst it!

He had everyone in stitches!

LIVIBHOY - Our flight had a hat for the pilot. Someone also sold a football card and the pilot won it. He has had worse days!

BHOYLO 83 - Ah Seville...I was a poor 19 year old in my first year at University and unfortunately didn't have the money to travel the whole way to Spain.

On the day of the final myself and my Celtic loving mate who was living in the dingy student flat with me decided to have our own wee Seville party. We went to the shop and bought every newspaper / magazine that had any mention of Celtic, took them back to the flat and proceeded to cut out and stick up as many Celtic pictures, jerseys, flags etc that we could find to add to the atmosphere for the night ahead.

We watched the first half in the flat but decided to head up the Falls Road to find a bar to catch the second. Booking a taxi we asked the taxi man to take us to the best Celtic bar in west Belfast. To this day I can't remember its name. Anyway the bar was rammed packed with Tims with sombreros and the sangria was free.

At the final whistle I broke down in tears as my mate consoled me and we continued the party long into the early hours…

I was up at 8 the next morning for my final English exam very tired and still extremely emotional!

DESSYBHOY - My good lady and me went with no tickets and booked to go to Seville with Jim Doyle. He called us on the Friday before we were due to leave on the following Monday morning to say we were flying to Faro with a bus transfer to Seville.

Our plane had loads of guys from Partick and Drumchapel, many of whom were in the same hotel just across the street from Seville FC's stadium. The hotel staff could not believe how many were there and the city was not prepared, expecting only about 8k.

Night before the game was spent in the Prado de San Sebastian in the company of Charlie and the Bhoys. Brilliant night. My brother arrived from another part of town. Don't know how he knew where we were. We found one of those kiosks that sell food and drink. Were there to dark o'clock. Met folk from Manhattan CSC who had tickets and were apologetic that we didn't.

Next day out and about, the cathedral etc. Watched the game on the big screen over the river. Walked back into town over the bridge and traffic was at a stop. Sevillians looked on from their cars. Didn't know what they thought. Found an 'abbierto' bar which was 'cerrado' until he saw the hoops. Another late night. Home the next day via Faro. Our bus rep was a Porto fan and he agreed they were diving but that is what happens in football there.

JUNGLE JIM - CQN is a very pleasant place. The fact that this excellent atmosphere has been created to celebrate the anniversary of a defeat makes me begin to believe that, once again, we really don't "care if we win, lose or draw". Because there WAS a show and the Glasgow Celtic WERE there.

THOMTHETHIM - Heat and cheating Porto players did it for us in Seville. Every Celtic player was a hero that night. No need for scapegoats, especially ten years later.

79 CAPS - One thing that is hardly ever mentioned is that Mourinho kept the Celtic players waiting for 5 (?) minutes before letting his Porto team onto the pitch for the second half. The Celtic players were all standing in the heat and waiting. The referee should have yellow-carded every Porto player but he was weak.

SAINT STIVS - so, I was in the unusual situation of having got 4 tickets via UEFA, that with 3 weeks to go, I still didn't have travel booked.

I was looking at all sorts of solutions, and Catman, of this parish provided the fix with his old dad having airline contacts, and 3 of us got booked on a day return from Prestwick.

Catman's parents were an absolute joy to travel with, lovely people.

Picking up Jimbo and Stiv, I can still see them coming out the houses in their hoops with the biggest grins. We left the Port at 4am, our flight was 8ish. Prestwick was unbelievable, thousands ready to go, planes lined up to the very end of the tarmac. The flight itself was strangely subdued. I don't know if I expected more like a supporters bus but it wasn't. Everyone quiet, reading the papers, general chit chat.

We got to Jerez a couple of hours later, then the coach up to the Stadium. The bad part of the day was the coach park. We got dropped there, then set off for the town. Took a fair bit of walking and melting already. Next big challenge, how to find cousin Patrick who was already in a hotel.

Had a beer at first place we got to, then taxi to find Paddy.

Getting to the centre, I really couldn't believe it. Hoops everywhere, and I mean everywhere! Coaches, cars , trams, all the pavements. Tricolours out hotel windows. 80,000 my bahookie!

We got Paddy and the square beyond his hotel was just packed out. We diverted into another pub, met Willie McStay, talked about his tackle on the tin man.

Then in one of those mad coincidences, we got talking to a few auld tims. "Where you from?" - "The Port" - "That's where I am from,' says the auld guy, 'but I moved to Canada 30 years ago'. Unbelievably, he went to school with my father in law from Kelburn, and knew my grandparents as well for good measure.

I really wanted to find more of the family, particularly the Blackpool connections but the mobile phones just didn't work. We had a McD's next to the square and took some pictures. Years later, looking at them again, I spied Allan and Brian, right behind where we were, 10 feet away. !!!!!

Mid afternoon we were in another bar and the chat turned to Touts, Forgeries, and Police checks, and the problems that would happen at the stadium. Those who had been in Seville for a few days said if you have a ticket get there early.God knows why but I was paranoid about getting the bag with the tickets lost or stolen.

We decide to go out to the stadium then.

We took a tram out, it was filled with Porto supporters. It was only about 4pm by then but at the park their crowd was already there, parked up behind their end, eating and drinking out of their cars. No hassles walking through them.

Got to our side and as soon as the gates opened, we went in.

We were genuinely among the first few hundred into the ground and the big stand above the dug-outs was empty. We were in the back row, brilliant seats,

The heat was unbelievable and having had a few beers, we were seriously dehydrated, and schoolbhoy error on our part, we had nothing with us. Went downstairs, nothing opened, nothing to buy (I actually thought the stadium and its catering were rubbish, seriously rubbish).

Within half an hour, the Porto end was filling up. The rest of the stadium slowly more and more, but it was all Green and White and Tricolours. Spied some guys I knew, spied some others, spied even more. It was one of those nights. Special mention for big Frank Tweed of Greenock. Tweedy, a wee bit unsteady on his feet and a wee bit unable to talk and a wee bit red from the sun, nearly broke my back with the hug, and an emotional "canny believe it ".

Murdo was a little in front of us. We can debate about ex-players and their feeling for us, but he really was acting like a fan.

Big John then came out and took interviews. In those minutes alone he was melting in front of us. But a sad sight.

Then the entertainment and the arrival of the cup onto a plinth. It must have been over 100 degrees. I went for food and drink the choice was …water, crisps and hee haw else. I met Dominik Diamond in the queue.

Then the game itself. Our crowd were just unbelievable. A sight to behold in full voice. Amazing spectacle.

Martin and the players were nearly legends on the night. Nearly.

Henrik proved what we already knew - he was world class.

I wore a Kearney CSC baseball cap that night. It was a gift from uncle Pat Higgins, retired president of the club. He gave me it one night in Perth at the beginning of the season in 97/98. We had lost two games previously, but that night we won 2-0. I think Henrik and Jackson scored. Pat said, "That's a Celtic team. We are on our way back. Fergus's plans will see us go on to great things" and we did.

I had the hat on yesterday with a black Lisbon Lions t shirt - the one with Chalmers scoring the goal. I love it. The match itself whizzed by. I have watched the game again, only recently. I don't know if we were beaten by a better team. It was a game played in Porto's environment. We came very close.

After the match we couldn't find our bus so we said cheerio to Paddy, In a panic we jumped on any bus that had Jerez on it. Back at the airport it was surreal. Thousands again, duty free raided by others, but everyone quiet.

Tales are told of how people got to Lisbon, and cars left behind. Two guys on our flight had driven from Kerry to Prestwick to go on a day trip!

We got home about 9am.

The most amazing day out. Memories forever.

The next weekend at Kilmarnock though, that loss and it all sunk in, and I felt very cheated by the season's end. All that work and nothing to show.

A question was asked, Champions League last 16 or UEFA Cup Final? I would be happy with another final.

Our time will come and when it does, we will all be there and we will win. Keep it lit.

YORKBHOY – Seville. Does anyone know what happened in The Bill that night?

WILLIEBHOY - 10 years ago….surely not! Seems like just last week!

I eventually arrived in Madrid the night before the game, booked into my hotel then decided I better go and book my train for next day to Seville. Sauntered down to find it very busy and when it was my turn, told the guy I wanted a return to Seville next day about 2.00pm. LOL.

Then I was told ALL trains full tomorrow so I asked when was the next available…an hour that night 9.00pm or something. Had to go back to my hotel and settle up then headed to train which was packed with Celtic fans.

As I wandered through the station I thought about grabbing a bench but was quickly put right by local Police. On exiting the station I stood for ages in the taxi ranks…got to the top and told the taxi driver, Hotel… which one he said – ANYONE says I with a spare room !!! Guy looked at me like I was mental, ALL full, Celtic everywhere – no hotels.

So I camped down outside the train station with a few hundred others for the night. Must have slept soundly as I awoke early to find lots of broken bottles all around me and not a single scratch. Apparently some local Moroccans (?) had tried to steal our bags.

Decided to head early to the stadium about 11.00am when a huge English guy asked me at the bus stop if I had a ticket. "Yes" - "Is it genuine?" – "Think so"...Did I want to compare with his...No way Jose. Nipped across the road (I was on the wrong side anyway) got to the stadium after a long walk...incredible heat. I had 2 cameras with me to take lots of pics, bumped into some guys who knew me from the Grangemouth bus who came from Falkirk...took pics of each other under the big adverts and plenty more during the game.

Recall Porto fans selling tickets (mostly fake for ridiculous prices) a wee lad grabbed one and ran chased by about 6 Porto fans shouting Celtic fan in trouble and was quickly swallowed up by the crowd.

Went into the stadium as soon as it opened, dreading the thought I might have a fake...but it was fine (Cost me plenty from a guy in Glasgow). No idea how many cold drinks, ice lollies I had...not enough anyway. After the game I asked a policeman the way to the station and he just pointed ahead...walked on to find myself in Porto Bus area...walked back - asked another Policeman and he pointed other way...eventually found myself back at the train station for another sleep on the pavement, guarding my programmes with my life.

Two biggest regrets apart from losing...I went in too early, before the UEFA vans opened and never got an official hat. Then back home at Boots chemists I gave the girl a camera and watched as she opened it, so I did likewise...then recoiled in horror as she said..Ooh might have exposed the film, don't worry If they are ruined we won't charge you !

Damn right lady...alas they were ruined both of them...

Thought we had to win in 90 mins due to the heat, incredible performance, a truly awesome support and despite the lack of pics – memories that will never fade.

I've been very lucky to attend 5 CL Finals & 3 UEFA Finals but none come close to Seville. Was unbelievable and proud to say I was there.

TWISTS N TURNS - I decided to wander in Seville and grab some food. Any food. Passed a Celtic fan lying non compos mentis at the side of the street. Very much the worse for wear through drink.

Turns out however that although he was clearly bladdered, some portion of his brain was working perfectly well.

As he lay there and a couple of fellow hoops fans approached him asking "Are you alright big man – have you got a ticket?"...he responded "Aye – and you're no getting near it so get lost!"

Not so drunk after all eh!

SOUTH OF TUNIS - DBBIA "Dianbobo and Rab carried the can"

Yes, I fully acknowledge that both played their part in the run to the final. (Proving me wrong). My problem was my conviction that both were prone to dreadful decision making and error. I was convinced that Porto were just the team to cash in on those weaknesses - and they did. (Proving me horribly right).

THE TOKEN TIM - re the flights, I took a chance and booked my flights (Manchester – Malaga) the morning after we beat Liverpool. £60 return!!

Managed to persuade 2 of my brothers, the youngest unfortunately had one of his Highers on the day of the game and wouldn't / couldn't go – still gutted that he missed out on that trip – and a couple mates to also take the chance. How glad were we all that we did!

Also booked hotel in Seville at the same time.

One of my more inspired decisions.

One of the funniest moments was in a bar close to the cathedral the night before the game and they had run out of glasses to serve the beer in. Some of the bhoys'n'ghirls were getting a wee bit frustrated at having to wait till others finished before they could get theirs, until one of the staff had the inspired thought to start serving the beers in tupperware dishes!!

I got a beer in what looked very like a 1 litre ice-cream tub. Still only charged me 5 euros, the same as they were charging for a pint ;-)

CORKCELT - I love the stories of the events surrounding the game and will never forget the trip but like many, I never watched a recording of the match and don't think I ever will. I remember thinking at the time that Bobo was hard done by for the 2nd yellow and I see where Lenny said that there was a bad foul on Henrik in the lead up to Bobo's sending off, which the Ref missed. We could and should have won that game. Whilst I'm loving the stories strangely enough for the first time in 10 years, it's making me angry that we didn't win. I need to take a break from reading this and go and cop myself on.

BOOKER T - Paranoid about losing your ticket…had mine in a sealed sandwich bag in my trainer.

THE EXILED TIM - Ľuboš Micheľ was the main reason we lost the final. As weak a referee as I have ever seen.

MHARK67 - Thanks to all for the Seville stories. The funny bits have made me laugh out loud and some of the poignant bits would bring a tear to a glass eye.

As I'm on the iPhone in the cab, I won't try to type all of my memories but here are some of the selected highlights:

1. The weeks leading up to it winding up the Darkside.

2 Being accused of harassment by one of the Royal Mail's finest trying to find out if her uncle Frank had got a ticket (stalked the poor person all round Blackwood!).

3. Glasgow Airport with thousands of others including an ex polis mate from Blackwood dressed in a green Mohican, kilt and Doc Martins (he has his picture in the official Seville book).

4. Arriving at our hotel and finding all the Celtic supporters given one accommodation block to themselves away from the tourists ….24 hr party time!!

5. Packing out an "Irish" (ma backside it wis) bar in Puerto Banus and giving the barman a Charlie and the Bhoys CD to get the place rockin'

(he changed it to euro pop music after an hour and we left, silly señor!)

6.An amazing day in Seville on the day of the match. Gutted but proud sharing my seat / step inside the stadium with God's finest fitba supporters.

7. A very scary trip back to hotel over the top of the mountains (including the driver getting told in Glaswegian to " slow doon and get a grip thurs weans oan this bus or yer gonna get a doin' pal!" I was genuinely bricking it.

8. The next day in a beach bar with many other Celts having a pint and sharing experiences and laughing my heid aff at some mental bhoys from the Duntocher CSC (I think!) chasing a goat down the beach which had been fully dressed in a new set of hoops including shorts.

There are other highlights but on my phone wi fat fingers this is the best I can do for now.

It was a privilege to be there bhoys. Here's to the next one!

CORKCELT - Just to mention an incident, which many forget, a Porto fan was drowned in an accident before the game. His friend quite obviously distraught did not go to game and gave his ticket to a Celtic fan. Refused to take any money and just said say a prayer for my friend.

LEN BRENNAN - Biggest cheat of the night – Victor Baia!! His rolling and crawling about trying to con the weak ref when nobody touched him still makes my blood boil to this day.

CELBRIDGE CELT - Got my ticket from dodgy London ticket touts in hotel in Seville… tried to give me two for the Porto end… no chance! My big mate was downstairs – could have gotten ugly… he went back and got our "Silver tickets" in the Celtic end/corner.

Paid a few bob and still wasn't sure it was genuine until we got into the ground – when the barcode machine went green… it was like scoring a goal!

We stayed in an old apartment, thanks to a fellow Tim's wife in Madrid who went to College down in Seville… I met a couple of guys who slept under cars. One slept in a cardboard box!

Some good stories in the Official Book… and mine is in there too!, I always knew they'd be so many good ones missing…

Never watched the DVD of it I bought either. I remember my partner at time crying down the phone and my son spoke to me on the phone, he said "How can the Man of the Match, spend half of the game rolling around the ground?"

I wonder if other teams who made finals from Scotland talk about fighting with other fans, police and general ransacking… But who would do anything like that?

ALLY HUNTERS GLOVES - don't often post but wanted to share my Seville memory.

I got 3 tickets through the ballot. You had to collect them at Celtic Park. Had a miserable boss so sneaked off to get them. Queue snaked from ticket office into the stadium (they opened the gate at the Rangers end) stood for hours and got back undetected, only to find my photo at the front of the queue in the next day's Record.

Went on a trip organised by Ricky Fearns (an absolute legend). Flew to Torremolinos for 2 nights then down to Seville. The trip had a very mixed bunch on it, lots of supporters from Ricky's home ground of Garngad but also a pre CEO Peter Lawell, Tommy Coin and Simon Donnelly.

Torremolinos was great. We were met in the square by thousands of Celtic fans and a lot of Spanish Police with Rottweiler dogs, however after about an hour or so the Police tied the dogs to a tree and played football before heading off. Ricky had decided we should all head off to a nightclub near the hotel that night. We entered to see the hip and trendy strutting their stuff, not sure they knew what to do when 500 pissed up Celtic fans arrived. They certainly knew what to do when Ricky persuaded the DJ he should play Trisha Fern's CD of Celtic songs instead of that "techno rubbish". They left…I don't think the song about being from Garngad appealed.

We drove down to Seville next day stopping at the infamous service station that was a sea of Green and White. When we entered Seville (around lunchtime on the day of the game) it was like Janefield Street before the game - there were Celtic fans everywhere from the outskirts to the city centre, every open top bus was rammed full of Celtic fans as were the horse and carts that took you round the city.

I had a spare ticket and I was determined I was giving it to a Celtic season ticket holder and not a once a year fan. I texted all my mates etc and incredibly they all had a ticket. Simon Donnelly didn't and was eyeing up my spare but I resisted. On the way into the game I met a boy outside the ground who sat near me in the South Stand and I gave him the gift of a lifetime.

The game was brilliant apart from the lack of water. My boy nearly passed out and I missed half the first half queuing for water. Heart -breaking in the end but our flight left at midnight straight after the game. It was good to get away at that point.

Fantastic memory and in recognition of 10 years since the trip I have finally had my genuine Seville program (They reprinted and sold in Glasgow after the game) and my ticket stubs framed.

BANKIEBHOY 1 - Memories of Seville…

The heat and the humidity…the long walk to the stadium leaving a saltire in a wee bar on the way, half tired, half drunk…

Hoops everywhere. I bumped into a guy from school hadn't seen in years – hugged like maniacs and in the process bust a pair of Ray-Bans just purchased for the journey – didn't care a jot.

Seated amongst the Porto fans who were civilised and relaxed – can remember feeling anything but relaxed…especially when they started to talk animatedly about Derlei…

The trip home was downbeat and I've never watched the game since but

I've never been prouder of a Celtic performance and never prouder of our support.

HAMILTONTIM - One of the biggest regrets of my life is not getting to Seville.

My memory floods back to Henrik's goal in the semi final and me lying on a living room floor in Halfway with my mate and his son on top of me.

The second leg of the Boavista game was on a Thursday evening and my work was closed on the Friday and the Monday. On the Tuesday morning my first port of call was my boss' office.

"I'd like to apply for a couple of days unpaid leave please".

"What's it for?"

"To go to the final in Seville to see Celtic."

"No bother but I'll need to check that it's ok with headquarters".

I'll never forget her face that afternoon when she walked into my class, I knew that it was a "No" immediately. She knew what Celtic meant to me and it can't have been easy for her to pass on the news. GCC had issued a blanket ban on all teachers looking for time off to go to the game.

I was genuinely devastated.

Instead I made arrangements with those other unfortunate souls who couldn't attend to meet up in Trader's Tavern in the Barras on the day of the game.

The time ticked slowly by and I could have sworn that there were several occasions that day when the clock actually stopped. My phone had been lighting up regularly throughout the day from friends who were lucky enough to at least be in Seville on the day of the game, some with tickets and some without.

On the stroke of 3 the weans were released and I made my way to the Calton, safe to say it was one of the quickest journeys I'd ever made!

The Gallowgate was a sea of Green and I took my time to walk through the pile of sand which had been placed at the doorstep of Bairds Bar, just to kid myself on that it would almost help me believe that I wasn't in the east of Glasgow but in fact in far off sunnier shores.

My da who lived in London at the time had decided that he wanted to watch the game in Glasgow and so he and my sister's partner (a Chelsea fan) flew up on the morning to partake in the revelry.

Around 6.30pm a wee bhoy from my class appeared in the pub with his dad whom I knew from coaching the school football team. I have to confess that I was a little apprehensive upon seeing him as it would mean that I would have to curtail any celebrations etc. I shouldn't have worried. His father took me to the side and let me know that whatever happened that night in the pub would indeed remain in the pub. It was typical of the spirit that this game provoked in the Celtic support.

I won't take up much more of your time as this should really be about the people who were actually in Seville that day. However, for the rest of my life I will remember standing with a pint of Guinness in my hand at 1-0 down, closing my eyes and praying for a goal, just one goal. It wouldn't matter if we still got beat, I simply wanted to watch Celtic score in a European final.

My final thought is of my da that night. He had been to Milan in 70' but didn't have the money to go to Lisbon. At the final whistle the place was awash with grown men and children in tears.

I came back from the toilet and stood in admiration as he walked around consoling strangers, putting an arm around them and telling them,

"Be proud of our team, be proud of Celtic. What we have achieved just to get here is incredible and we will be back again one day".

I hope that he's right.

If I'd gone to Seville I wouldn't have shared that night with him. In hindsight I'm thankful for that opportunity.

TINY TIM - Over the years there has been a lack of praise for MON (Martin O'Neill). MON made Seville possible. God bless him.

BLANTYRE KEV - Somewhere around 5am and Glasgow airport is only open for Seville flights and is a sea of green and white. I've 80 Euros, my passport, boarding pass and a ticket in my shorts, Celtic top on, no baggage of any description.

The happiest queue of all time has formed, I swear some of these people have tattooed those grins on. Albert Kidd has the biggest sombrero rim of all time - must be a metre and half across.

There's a lot of joyous cheering at the front of this queue. As we get to the front we see that each person is being cheered as they go through the metal detector with no beep.

Better still the security staff are in good spirits and are taking each beachball and passing it through the x-ray machine. In it goes along the conveyor. Everyone holds out their hands, waggling their fingers in anticipation of it coming out the other end with a low "wooaaaa...", Absolutely nothing shows up on the machine screen as it's just air inside and as if by magic it pops out the other side and all the hands are raised to the air with a shout of "Ole!"

Happy, happy days.

!!BADA BING!! - I remember standing in a bar in Seville and SSN (Sky Sports News) showed guys with buckets and spades in the sandpit outside Bairds the pub. I collapsed with laughter.

CORKCELT - Just after the final whistle when there was a tremendous rendition of " We are Celtic Supporters". That's when I started to cry.

TONTINE TIM - have never watched Milan or Seville even though I was at the former game.

I had Seville on tape but taped over it the following weekend.

Someone posted the Feyenoord game on the Huddleboard a few weeks back...nae chance.

Prior tae Seville I had for a few years suffered from an atrial flutter, medication wisnae helping so the Friday before the game I was in the Toronto General Hospital for a 5 hour procedure tae correct it.

On the day of Seville I faked a follow-up doctor's appointment (was only a few months in the job) and went home tae watch it, after Ghod's amazing equaliser I told Mrs. TT that if it had happened a week earlier I would have had a heart attack.

Still cannae watch it and cannae read about it. Still blame Bobo and Shirley Douglas for our loss as well as wee Shawnie for a poor free kick at the death.

A few years later we were in Madrid tae visit one of our daughters who was teaching there. She asked if we wanted tae see anywhere else so I said Seville. Walking along the front there was a sign for the stadium. Mrs. TT enquired did I want tae go and see it...naw.

Went tae the Alhambra in Granada after that then over tae the souks in Marrakesh, back tae Madrid and toured the Bernabeau as well as the cultural spots such as the Museo Del Prado and palace but Seville haunted me then and still does.

Incidentally on the on/off bus in Madrid, I passed by a sign that indicated the Estadio Vicente Calderon was down that street. Mrs. TT pointed it out to me, my response under my breath may have cost me a few venial sins.

Talk about Lisbon on Saturday.

MINX1888 - I had booked flights from Glasgow – London, London – Madrid. My travelling companion at the time was off sick from her work and it was the only way she would make the game. Something about a blanket ban for her profession (I won't mention the number of holidays they get a year!) Her task was to book the train from Madrid to Seville!

Arrived in Madrid the night before the game. The centre was covered in Green and White and party tunes were coming out of every Taverna we passed, and pass them we did. We only wanted to get to the hotel and get ready for the match. Our hotel had a few Porto fans staying and they could not believe how many Celtic fans had travelled to the game. I wonder what their faces were like when they got to Seville the following morning!

Madrid train station was more like Queen St Station and all we had to do was collect our tickets! My companion, bless her, did not bring the card she booked the tickets with and without them … no train ticket! After a few heated exchanges and along with a few Celtic fans helpfully telling the Manager the lassies better get on that train, we had our tickets!

Met a chap from Boston on the train who had never been to a game in his life but his Granda had told him all about Lisbon and the famous Glasgow Celtic. He came over just to savour the atmosphere! Met up with John Hartson's pals in the drinks carriage - what an atmosphere in there! Only one of them had a ticket but they still wanted to come and savour the atmosphere like BBJ (John Hartson), they were now confirmed Celtic fans.

My Dad and Uncles had booked a week in the Algarve and after seeing the gridlock outside, I was worried they wouldn't make it.

I walked into the stadium and I made my way to the top of the stairs, turned round and there in his seat my Dad, the man who had given me Celtic. The tears started then! I got to see my team in a European Final and I got to see my team score not once but twice in a European Final and best of all I got to share it with my hero!

And for that I thank every one of those players that took us on the most amazing journey!

LEFTCLICKTIC - ONE of the many memories I have is walking back to find our bus after the game, After crossing the bridge and making our way towards the buses I looked up and saw a large banner draped across three houses in what looked like a tenement block.

It was being held jointly by the local residents. Those who were not holding the banner, men, women and children were cheering and applauding.

The banner simply said:

"THANK YOU CELTIC"

TEUCHTER ÅR LÅ - After the game, Mrs Teuchter and I headed back to our hotel in Praia da Rocha in the Algarve. Don't know if it was the drink our the lack of sleep, but was struggling to keep my eyes open and my heid was doing the auld noddin'. Decided, after a close call to pull over and sleep for a while.

We found a walled in area – right next to the main road, parked up and went to sleep. The heat was unbearable – even at night – so I got out and lay down outside the motor and fell into a deep sleep. I awoke the next day to a policeman kicking my feet. I stood up and looked around at the 20 or so police cars parked up beside me and dozens of cops walking into a rather large building I hadn't noticed the night before. His mate showed up with 2 cups of coffee, mentioned something like "Celtic fantastico" and bade us farewell. Great times.

BOURNESOUPRECIPE – From Celtic Wiki…

When the Hoops fans held an impromptu going away party at Ibrox on Beach Ball Sunday they would set the tone for the whole Seville experience – whatever the result, the Celtic fans were going to have a party. And so they did.

An army of 80,000 supporters travelled the long road to southern Spain via any means possible. Not before or since have so many travelled so far in the name of football. It was like the friendliest of invasions. Large quantities of alcohol were undoubtedly consumed but the mood was never anything other than festive.

Locals and Porto supporters happily mixed with the Bhoys supporters in the squares, bars and clubs of Seville. Hugs, huddles and handshakes were the order of the day as new friends were made and old pals reunited. As kick-off approached the Celts danced and sung in the sunshine and even when the Bhoys suffered the agony of an extra time defeat, the partying continued.

Not even defeat could sober the mood of a support who had come to realise in recent days just what a unique and special club they belonged to. Although the team lost the final, the support had won the hearts of the people of Seville as well the respect of the football world. Awards in recognition of the fans behaviour followed from both UEFA and FIFA.

UEFA Cup finals are annual events. They come and go. What happened in Seville however was a once-in-a-lifetime experience. An experience no other club is ever like to repeat.

LEFTCLICKTICK - Shortly after arriving in Seville we were just standing about trying to take in what we were witnessing.

When from down the street came a demonstration by local teaching staff about education cuts (I was told by a local).

The teacher at the front would shout through one of those loud hailers and the children who were holding long Green & White type banner the length of the procession would shout back.

As they approached as they stopped at the junction and the kids were gifted with flags, tammies, scarves and their collection buckets were loaded with money from our Bhoys & Ghirls.

As they moved on the teachers at the front could hardly talk through the tears and the kids, now draped in the colours were now shouting "CELTICA" as the moved on. I knew then I was involved in something special.

CORKCELT - I remember being held up for ages in the bus carpark whilst they let all the Porto buses go first. It was pretty frustrating as we were facing a long drive to Benalmadena. Suddenly a large group came striding across the park and passed just alongside our bus. It was Billy Connolly plus entourage surrounded by about 10 minders. He got a big cheer and gave a clenched fist salute as he went past.

BOURNESOUPRECIPE - Good stuff – there were more Celtic supporters at mass that day than normal. It was an out of body experience. The whole day was specially made for Celtic and the result of the football match was inconsequencial.

UNCLE FESTER – Bournesouprecipe - I felt that about the game too. I wouldn't say it felt inconsequencial but I barely gave it a thought until about 45 mins before kick-off.

It was about being with the Celtic Family and showing the World that we are fantastic Club with a wonderful support. I'm convinced we did that. . .

DANNYBOY 67 – Seville. Memories are made of this, never to be forgotten.

It all started over a curry and a few beers 10 days after Boavista. My pal Jack and I talked the other halves into it and a mad scramble for flights and hotels and a couple of days later we were sorted - but no tickets.

Monday before the match, dropped off at Glasgow Airport 7 ish on our way to Faro via Stansted. Stansted was fairly quiet but a few hours and a few beers later the place was swarming with the hoops. Met a guy I worked with who was booked on the same flight and same hotel in Albuferia. We managed to beg a lift from them from the airport. There must have been 10 of us in a white transit van…happy days.

Next morning lying at the pool having a few beers, I couldn't believe how many hoops were around the place so far away from Seville. More and more were arriving every minute and 3 Irish guys sat next to us, bought us a beer and managed to secure us a ticket within 10 minutes of meeting them …Wee Sean will forever be in our memories - he even got us seats on the Irish bus to the match and return free of charge. We took over Albuferia that night with non-stop singing and drinking and we even did a huddle around a cop car on the strip.

Day of the game, wee Sean, a big carry out on the Irish bus and heading for Seville, the wee man knew the words of every Celtic song in English and Latin. On our way to Seville the motorway was just a trail of cars, buses and vans all with green and white. We stopped at a service station and it was like a swarm of ants all with hoops on - even bumped into Curly Watts from Coronation Street.

The first person I saw getting off the bus was Tommy Burns, standing in the bus park welcoming everyone but taking it all in himself. We headed straight to a 5* hotel in the centre, secured our tickets and started one of the best days of our life. A few beers later, a bite to eat we headed early to the stadium but we all got split up and of course mobiles down, we made our own way there.

Upon arriving at the stadium and waiting on the rest, I met my brother in law and a work colleague and was offered 2 tickets free on 2 occasions from 2 different sources...unbelievable but as I had one, I told them to go and give them to one of the many hoops who weren't so lucky .

I was nervous going through security but when that wee light lit up green I felt I had landed. The sight when I entered the stadium will live with me forever. I was in the main stand and looking across to that wall of green and hoops brought me to tears. A few minutes later Jack arrived and we were ready. Photos were taken and the rest is history.

I was so proud even in defeat but annoyed at the antics of Porto as they were a good side and didn't have to resort to those tactics.

It was with a heavy heart we headed back to Albuferia, without wee Sean on my bus. The next day we had another party on the strip before heading home, missing our flight from Stansted and having to get a bus up the road on Saturday morning. We got picked up at Hamilton, still in the hoops, smelling bad. Jack's feet had swollen up to twice the size but we had the time of our life and memories never to be forgotten...C'mon the Hoops!

MARRAKESH EXPRESS - I managed to get a ticket from a mate but gave it to my son who was an apprentice at Dundee Utd at the time. At the last minute McCall gave him a couple of days off to go so I did what any dad would do. I'd blagged my way into many games over the years, 4 times at Wembley and numerous Oldco games. So with that in mind I bought a snide brief for £15 in Alfredos West Nile Sreet. It was the worst fake ever seen but it gave me a fighting chance.

We flew from Alicante down to Malaga the day before the game and then had to get a taxi to the Costa del Sol. As I waited in the taxi queue a jacket appeared on top of my bag, and it wasn't mine or any of the mob I was with. I picked it up and there was a wallet inside. I opened it and inside was a passport - name P. Murphy, 62 from Dublin, a few hundred Euros and a ticket. One guy shouted to keep the ticket but no way could you do that to a fellow Tim.

Anyway I found the guy in five minutes, he was blitzed, crying like a wean and being held up by two Spanish cops. He was that drunk he probably won't remember me giving him his wallet. I think God must have been watching me because the very dodgy ticket got me past the first police check, and from there let's just say I got past the turnstile operator, in a very nerve wracking manner. I've never experienced an atmosphere like it, and that includes the Leeds game 1970.

CATMAN - Having driven to Gatwick from Glasgow for a 6am flight to Malaga with a mate who had got my boy's ticket due to his maths Higher being on the day of the Final, we arrived at our hotel in Marbella in time for the FA Cup Final. The following days were spent watching the increasing number of Hoops gathering in the bars and restaurants along the front.

On the day of the game I boarded a supporters bus which had been arranged prior to leaving Glasgow and which was picking up at hotels in Torremolinos. At one of the hotels a lad got on the bus who I recognised from years earlier when my bus, the Johnstone No1, shared with his bus, St Brendan's from Linwood, to away games. We immediately struck up a conversation and it turned out that both of our brothers were travelling over to the game from Australia.

About 30 minutes into our journey I got a call from my brother and nephew who were on a train down to Seville from Madrid having arrived from Melbourne. Amazingly, sitting next to them was the brother of the guy I was sitting next to on the bus up to Seville!

Later that day we all met up along with my other brother and my Mum and

Dad who had flown in on a day flight for the game. It was, I believe, one of my Dad's proudest moments to share this amazing Celtic experience with his wife and 3 sons. It really did pay off having faith in the team and buying the tickets prior to the Liverpool game. I carry the ticket stub to this day in my wallet.

I would love to think that I could one day share the same experience with my wife and son.

MIDFIELD MAESTRO - Around this time 10 years ago, I walked the stairs to stadium with my son & daughter, having a good chat with Joe McBride. I wanted to get there in plenty of time due to horror stories about fake tickets. So much joy when our light turned green, so much disappointment for the kids when the steward checked my bag & took the 4 bottles of water from me - so much joy for me that he allowed me to keep my 6 cans of Cerveza. As I mentioned this morning, my son's tears of joy at the 1st of Henke's goals will live with me for ever. Cheating, diving, time wasting players of Porto and referee. They were the biggest disappointments.

GRETNABHOY - My program and ticket are still proudly displayed in my house to this day. Left Glasgow for Faro a few days before the game on what I thought was a normal Algarve flight. Surely most folk would not stay that far away from Seville. Anyway there were a few hoops but when we landed someone shouted Hail Hail and the whole plane erupted. Then onto the hotel in Praia de la Rocha and it was like a Celtic holiday camp. Flags, singing and even crates of Buckfast! How did they get that there? Hired the car (bedroom suite) and into Seville. The rest is history.

THE MOON BHOYS - After the final whistle is my own favourite memory of Seville. None of us left the stadium - to a man we all stood and sang We are Celtic Supporters. We made more noise than the Porto fans during the presentation of the trophy so much so that Mouhrino instructed his players who were celebrating to go over to the Celtic fans and salute them. That's when we all stopped singing and started booing them instead. We got beat but standing there alongside so many defiant Celtic supporters - it felt like a victory.

50 SHADES OF GREEN - Day of the game.

Wanted to take everything in so decided not to drink too much until we got to the park with the big screen.

You had to buy tokens from one place and then exchange them for beer at another.

Me and my mate got 40 euros worth of drinking vouchers and as we made our way over for a beer, we bumped into half of the Greenhills pub. After much hugging and catching up and with kick off approaching, my mate took some of the vouchers and headed for a few beers to do us to half time.

He got lost and I never saw him again till tea time on the Thursday.

So I watched the first half stone cold sober without a drink and in warm weather. Half time arrived and I decided to join the queue for a drink wondering what happened to my mate. Anyway being a kind soul I got 4 beers thinking that James will surely be back by the time I get served.

Got the beers and just got back to my spot and Henrik goes and scores, cue mucho celebrations and my tray with the 4 beers disappears without a drop passing my parched throat.

I must have been the soberest guy out of the ten thousand at the park.

PISTONBROKE - Ahhhh Seville! What an absolutely sublime few days it was. I was working in Aberdeen back then and managed to get a ticket along with my two younger brothers. I remember having to work till about 3am on the Wednesday morning so I could take the time off. Anyway got on the 7am train to Queen St and sat down hoping for a couple of hours sleep before the inevitable party in front of us. Guy sits down opposite in his hoops. "Where you off to mate" says he. "Seville" says I sleepily. "Me too" says he twitching with excitement and promptly slaps 12 beers on the table between us. Needless to say they were gone by the time we reached Glasgow. The first of many new friends I made over the next couple of days.

There then followed a drunken, song filled, journey via Glasgow airport, Birmingham airport and a night out in Madrid from which there are still pictures of my kilt adorned youngest brother hanging upside down on a pole on stage in a nightclub beside a drag queen!!! We got back to our hotel 2 hours before the express train to Madrid on the morning of the game.

That Madrid-Seville train journey was in itself fantastic fun. Again I sat down hoping for some sleep only for the guy sitting next to me to produce freezing cold cans of Grolsch. "Want a beer", "No I really need to sleep thanks", "Go on, they're cold"…nuff said…I believe we drank the bar car dry on that train!

Arriving in Seville itself was just incredible. What a sight. What an atmosphere! I could go on and on but I really must get some work done…

THE BOY JINKY - Seville 2003 came a few weeks after I had flown home from the USA to bury my beloved son.

My wee mum was even more distraught than I… so the offers to go to Spain were rejected.

Family first.

A friend of my sisters was going and she agreed to take my sons ashes and scatter them at the stadium.

I gave them a lift to Glasgow Airport… parked the car and we went to the bar upstairs.

The place was a sea of green and white… songs and chants and laughter.

I wished them well and waved them goodbye. My boy made it to Seville and there he rests in peace ;)

BLANTYRE TIM - TBJ I never knew that mate. God bless.

SAINT STIVS - TBJ. Thanks for sharing. The stories that people are willing to share on here, in relation to a football match, of family loss and remembrances of those who had passed on are humbling.

TOMMYSBHOY - Some fantastic stories of the pilgrimage to Seville. After a wee drink in the Gallowgate my mate and I headed to Glasgow Airport for our lunchtime flight. Never seen anything like it - it was as if the airport was our stadium. We managed to get into the first bar and met my brother's mate then we proceeded through passport control into the other Celtic lounge. It was mobbed.

In the lounge a beach ball was being banged about in the air - as you do - next minute it hit the guy in front of me who was sitting supping his beer. It was Blink McDonald, the guy my brother had introduced me to previously…you should have seen the look he gave the guys who were responsible…ohhh dear and they knew who he was! It wasn't until later that I was told who he was…anyway flight delayed till 14:50 on the day before the game was no bother. Landed in our hotel in Matalascanas in Huelva region about 10pm.

The hotel lounge was like Bairds before a big game. Absolutely jumpin' till 3am - up for 9:30 breakie then outside for the buses to Seville. What a sight that was - a sea of green and white all with brand new Carling strips on ready to invade Seville. We landed at the stadium at midday, walked over the bridge to the first bar in the searing heat. 90 something and met Porto fans all sitting quiet then I burst out wi' the Jorge Cadette song. What a reaction - they were in shock and all the bhoys surrounding us joined in. This went on for about ten minutes.

Then we all mingled with them it was such a great time - never had a ticket and I didn't care for one either - watched the game later on in a bar full of tims and we still partied well on after the game then missed my bus back to our hotel. Two of our party did the same at a cost of € 200…not me…met a couple of guys later from Glasgow in a bar about 1am told them my plight and they gave me a bed in their hotel just round the corner. What a relief! After seeing dozens sleeping rough on walls on the pavement etc…I was bricking it…no way was I doing that!! Breakie in the morning…bus station was 15 minutes walk away and there were still guys sleeping all over the floors of the bus station decked in flags for covers.

Got a bus to Matalascanas at the second attempt – first one filled in 3 minutes with young ones heading to the beach. Arrived at the hotel to a cheer by my mates at the poolside…bumbag aff an' straight into the pool…Yaaaa beauty!!! We partied all day and never got downbeat until we boarded the jumbo to take us home. I'd do it all again tomorrow if I had the chance. A big thanks to the guys who put me up that night!! Special fans indeed.

STAIRHEEDRAMMY - TBJ- puts it into perspective for the rest of us.

Me - I arranged to meet my 2 mates on the steps of the Cathedral having flown out myself - "We will be the ones wearing the hoops" they said- cue my mobile's battery failing as I try to locate them - never saw them till I got back to Greenock- did meet plenty of other people I knew though- a pilgrimage.

TALLYBHOY - The Boy Jinky

Of the many 'Seville stories' that have appeared on CQN yours is the most poignant, the most moving and the most touching!

YNWA!

GOOGYBHOY LOVES CELTIC - @OfficialNeil: 10 years today since we were walking out at Seville…One of the best experiences of my life… Fans were magnificent.

THE BOY JINKY – Stairheedrammy - Perspective…is a word I learned the meaning of in 2003

Tallybhoy - Thanks …Celtic are a bond from father to son. In my heart I know my boy still sits with me at every match.

CORKCELT - The Boy Jinky - I thought I couldn't cry anymore about Seville, till I read your post. That puts so much of the nonsense we all go on with into perspective.

BURGHBHOY – Seville. First there was the ecstasy of qualifying for the final. Never thought I would see that in my lifetime. Then came the panic about travel and a ticket . Then came the horror when the letter duly arrived from Celtic saying I was unsuccessful in the ballot for a brief. Then came joy when a ticket was secured from an unlikely source. Then came the anticipation of the biggest game of my life. Then came the pride, seeing how many Tims had made the pilgrimage. Then came the tears when the bevvy kicked in. Then came the awe to see Henrik score those majestic goals. Then came frustration at the cheating antics of Porto. Then came the party…Oh what a party!!

God Bless Fergus. We would have thought that experience unthinkable 9 years prior. Thank you Martin. You fulfilled a lifetime's ambition for me.

HOUL YER WHEEST - Arriving in Aldergrove airport I spotted two guys wearing kilts. I assumed they were Scots but then realised they were in our group (two idiots). We flew out of Aldergrove at 8am on Tuesday to Gatwick where we met up with friends from Edinburgh and Glasgow. We boarded a flight for Malaga in mid afternoon after an impromptu party.

Once in the hotel in Malaga, efforts were made to erect the Randalstown banner across the street. After half an hour a Spaniard threw a brick attached to a rope across to us and the banner was duly raised. A police car arrived and the occupants had photographs with the banner as a backdrop. There were 54 in our party all with tickets but at least another 300 Celts were in the hotel that night. We boarded the bus early and arrived in the centre of Seville before midday.

We watched the bathers in the fountain, drank some beer and met Dermot Desmond. I met one of my sons and his pals, none of who had a ticket. I was tempted to give him mine but he wouldn't take it. I've just looked at some photos. The atmosphere was electric. One thing I remember is seeing four mature Seville ladies on the street with their eyes agog. Because of the noise they were missing their siesta. Five minutes later they came into the bar we were in, having purchased Celtic jerseys from one of the street vendors and determined to join the party.

The walk to the stadium seemed to take hours as we had a guy with us who had some years earlier been hit on the head with a plastic bullet and had mobility problems. One of our group hived off to find a loo. He never went to the game and pulled out a complete ticket the following night, claimed the steward hadn't removed the stub and allowed him to stand in a passageway (bollix).

This annoyed me greatly as it was at my asking he got the ticket. He hasn't had a match ticket since. The walk back to the city centre seemed to take twice as long as the journey out. About twelve of the party including our no go guy missed the bus back to Malaga. We stayed until Friday when the mood became a little lighter. About 20 of the group went to Kilmarnock on the Sunday to watch Celtic win 4 – 0 but more disappointment was the order of the day as Dunfermline accommodated Rangers. Another quiet trip home. Three of our group had attended every game home and away. The best stories are from the Lithuania trip.

BILLY BHOY - Reading all these posts has brought the memories flooding back. I've just remembered that the "coach driver" that took us up from Jerez ended up coming off the main drag and we ended up in a farm. He then had to reverse about 200 yards back on to the main road. It was at this point he explained in broken English that he had never driven a bus before and if anyone fancied reversing us out he would be very grateful.

Not surprisingly we all lost confidence in him. I was never so relieved to get off a bus! At the end of the game I walked back to the bus park alone as I had lost my two mates. Getting there I suddenly realised that I had not paid ANY attention to the bus. I didn't even know its colour!

The scene was chaotic! There were hundreds of buses lined up as far as the eye could see. I was starting to panic a bit and them I saw a sight that reduced me to tears. A typical wee Glesga guy; drunk, sunburnt, topless and hopelessly lost staggers up to one of the policemen patrolling the park. The guy was massive and just standing still – like Darth Vader – surveying all before him.

Wee Guy; "Hey! Manwell, huv ye seen the Baurheed bus? Darth doesn't even blink! Wee Guy; Well, huv ye? Tumbleweed rolls passed. Darth still hasn't even blinked. Wee Guy just gives him a mouthful and staggers away into the night. Just at that I recognised my driver among the throng and made my way over to the bus.

Next problem; you had to specify if you were returning at midnight or 4am. It was quite obvious that I was not alone in deciding I had had enough. The scene was Pythonesque. The driver was going up and down the bus trying to check names. He would eject people off the front of the bus and they would just go back on via the rear door. I thought we were going to be there all night.

Eventually he just gave up and we had about 100 on a 70 seater coach. I remember looking out the window and EVERYBODY that we passed for nearly an hour was wearing Hoops. I don't think I saw a single Porto fan the whole day except in the stadium. Like many, I have the Seville DVD but it's still in the cellophane. But as Rod would say…maybe…Tonight's the night! Hey, why don't we all lose our virginity together? Put it on at 7.45 and we can come on later and chew the fat. It's either that or River City or the Chelsea Flower Show.

CAN I HAVE RASPBERRY ON THAT CHAMPIONS LEAGUE ICE CREAM - Still got my full ticket too. Was defo there!!!

Too many tales but highlights being: Fleecing a tout with some funny money. Going show shopping with the wife before game…best shopping ever done. The game…still never watched again. My first beer after the game bought for me by my ma's old classmate, king Kenny. The joy I had with my nephew and father in law and mates was amazing. Oh and the wife!

TWISTS N TURNS - TBJ - Of all the Seville stories, yours will live in my memory forever. I just wanted to say thank you for sharing it. Sometimes we get so wrapped up in our own selfishness we forget to count our blessings for each and every day we are given.

God bless you and yours.

HUGH BONKLE FAE DALLAS - Seville remains my only foreign trip with the hoops. Never had a chance of a ticket and didn't care. It was enough to be there. Hire car to Manchester Airport. Flight to Madrid via Brussels. Bullet train to Seville.

I said to my mate on the car journey to the airport this is going to be mental. I'd never seen so many cars filled with the hoops and this was just going to Manchester. Met a couple of young guys in the airport, flying to Alicante and they had no idea how to get to Seville. A quick phone call and my mate arranged for them to be picked up by a bus from the Shamrock Bar in Benidorm.

Got the first train from Madrid to Seville. Don't know if these trains were supposed to tilt but this one did. The train manager threatened to stop the train because of the crowd in the buffet car. Draft beer - what was that all about? The two girls working in the car told him to get lost as they were making a fortune. What a singsong! Big respect to the Buchan CSC - some stamina bhoys. Watched the game on the big screen - fell asleep standing up. I never knew Bobo was sent off till the following day.

The train station that night was full to the gunnels so slept outside. Back to Madrid in the morning. The best trip I've ever been on in my life and I'd do it all again tomorrow even if they told me the result would be the same. There are football clubs and then there is Celtic. Believe. Always have done. Always will do. Thank you to everyone who was there, absolutely the best of days.

CHE - TBJ I wish it didn't have to be under those circumstances, but Seville is a richer place for the gift you have given them.

Special thoughts for very Special people. Yours in particular. YNWA.

TINY TIM – TBJ - A wonderful place for your Bhoy to rest. When I think of Seville, I will always now associate it with your Bhoy aswell as OUR final. May he rest in eternal peace.

WINNING CAPTAINS - Talking about the Scotland squad on the radio. Ten years ago a Scotland squad gathered to watch the match in Seville – and cheered when Porto scored. Never been back to see Scotland play.

WHINHALLKEV - Flew from US to LHR then to Madrid. Two days in the Celtic pub there met the fellow from Chewing the Fat …Hemphill nice guy. Two hours in the Madrid train station on Monday afternoon and was lucky to book the last train out of Madrid for Wednesday. Yep it was drunk dry: conga line and guys drinking wine spritzers which was the last booze in the train.

The scenes in Seville were as described. Cathedral: Irish pub; walk to the stadium — no ticket and then off to the park. Couldn't see the screen due to the sun. After the game I hobbled off and slept on a park bench. Up at 5 and walked back to the city. Breakfast - Churros? And then Cathedral for a wash and then to the train station. I slept and snored the entire way back. A Celtic fan had to wake me when we arrived. When my father died a few months later — he had a copy of the game taped and on the TV. The last Celtic game he ever saw.

Loved it.

RALPH WALDO ELLISON REMEMBERS ALS VICTIMS JIMMY JOHNSTONE AND JOHN CUSHLEY - Got the Seville Celtic fans poster framed in my Huddle Room. Still astonishes friends here who think it must have been photoshopped in some way.

GINCHER67 - My permanent framed reminder of Seville. The weird thing was I was kind of swithering whether to go or not! Mental. Gave my sombrero to a wee laddie at the game. He's probably about 20 now….

TRUTH BEAUTY AND FREEDOM - Hi The Boy Jinky. Out of many amazing reminiscences of Seville, yours immediately brought tears to my eyes. (As did the tale of the Porto Supporter who drowned before the match.) God Rest his (their) soul(s) and God Bless you and your family.

My own story is much less poignant. From the Liverpool Game I thought, "If we can beat Liverpool, we can go all the way…" and so I managed to get 2 tickets from UEFA; I wish I had bought 8. My now ex-girlfriend and I had an amazing week staying about 12 miles just outside of Seville on a campsite and bussed it in to town every day.

The support on matchday was just unbelievable; definitely a history-making day, everywhere we went there were just Celtic Supporters… and more Celtic Supporters.

I am fortunate enough to have seen wee Jinky at his Red-Star-Belgrade best, and I remember with fondness Tommy Gemmel's thunderbolt against Benfica. However I am now also blessed to have witnessed not one, but 2, World-Class goals from Henrik. Memories like those are to be cherished! :-) (I have a signed Celtic top with only 2 signatures on it; Tommy Gemmel and Henrik Larsson. The only 2 Celtic players who have scored 2 goals in European Finals; how cool is that? :-)

It is incredulous that there was not one arrest. Much more edifying was walking through Seville after the match, (still wearing the Hoops of course), and coming across a beautiful School Month-of-May procession where the kids carried a statue of Our Lady on a stretcher-type arrangement. I just grinned from ear-to-ear and applauded as one of the kids just couldn't stop himself from shouting out "Celteeeeec!!"

Similarly, whenever we passed a bar we were met by a raised glass and an invitational shout of "Cerveca?!" I like to think that the locals were keen to talk to some of the remnants of the magnificent Celtic support that had so joyfully taken over their beautiful city for a day. Then again, it may have had as much to do with the gorgeous hoops-bedecked ghirl that was strolling along with me.

JIMMY QUINNS BITS - Let down with tickets by friends of Spanish in-laws who had tickets and then suddenly didn't – in-laws weren't chuffed.

Train to Bristol day before the game. Evening in the Bristol CSC pub (can't remember the name) and off to the airport for a 5am flight to Faro. Airport chockers with hoops and couldn't get a sleep for the bams.

Hired a car and mad Belfast wummin' drove us to Seville. It was on the road from Faro to Seville that it struck just how big this thing was going to be. It seemed every second vehicle was rammed with hoops. There were cars, vans, buses, camper-vans, even a fleet of scooters. Magic

Seville was even more jawdropping and I do remember the guys with the green Mohican. He was wandering about with a set of plastic five a side goals last time I saw him, looking for players – he didn't get many takers.

THE COMFORTABLE COLLECTIVE - A guy I know very well, a season ticket holder at Celtic Park, was offered the chance to fly with the official Celtic party to Seville, with hotel and ticket included. For a very, very reasonable price. (i.e. regular price for flight to Seville, face value ticket and hotel room at whatever rate Celtic had block booked them at).

He was married to someone who worked for Celtic and they (the staff) were taken over for free by the club. They had the chance to bring their partner for, as I said, for a very reasonable price.

This offer was made in the week before the final when tens of thousands were doing all sorts just for the outside chance of a ticket.

He knocked it back as he didn't (not couldn't) want to take two days off work.

BAMBOO - I estimate the Celts in Seville to be at least 100,000. There seemed to be 6 ticketless for everyone lucky enough to have a ticket. And in the stadium it seemed be at least two thirds Celtic fans.

TROON TIM - What a fantastic place CQN is.

I feel as if I'm in a huge hall full of Celtic fans, one-by-one sharing our individual Seville stories, as the rest of the Bhoys sit quietly absorbing every word.

If we were all together, we could give TBJ a huddle-sized hug for his bravery before joining together in a heart-felt rendition of YNWA.

It's been an absolute pleasure – far better than watching the DVD.

THE SPIRIT OF ARTHUR LEE - Another good tip that came out of the Seville. Don't ever drink Cruzcampo.

BAMBI - Some fantastic stories today and brings a lot back.

My Seville story started before we played Liverpool. I had a feeling we would make it to the final - don't ask why, I just did. We booked 4 tkts via UEFA website just in case and the rest is history. Me, my late mum, my dad and a good mate were going to go and we decided to make a holiday of it and booked a week in Fuengirola. Loads of mates had no tickets but decided they were going anyway.

Decided to book the week as well. There were thirty of us in all and only half with tickets. Didn't matter as everyone just wanted to be there. Couple of nights before the game we all met in Puerto Banus as friends have a flat there and some of the boys were staying there. Fantastic night out with Patrick Kielty and his mates - all massive Celts.

Got to Seville the morning of the match and it was just a sea of green - car horns tooting wherever we went as the citizens really took us to their hearts. The heat was unlike anything I'd ever experienced. Was unreal. Taxi took us out to the big hotel near the park where a friend was staying so we got in there for a beer and it was like a who's who, Davie Moyes, Big Roy, Rod Stewart, Roy Keane to name a few. Then someone shouted, "There's Paul McStay!" so I just had to get a photo taken with my hero. Doesn't get much better than that for me.

Another roar goes up and its the Porto team leaving to go to the game. Some good natured booing and ribbing takes place but Mourinhos face was a picture when he saw the Celts in the hotel. I think at that point he knew how big our support was going to be. We met a few mates outside the ground by chance and one of them still hadn't got a ticket. We wandered up to the ground and he managed to get past the first cordon. He got to the turnstile where his brother stuck his ticket into the machine, green light and he was in. He then passed the ticket back to his brother who tried it on and red light, nightmare, he's not going to make it but for some reason the guy looked at his ticket and passed him through. Magic! We were all in.

That sight will live with me forever; green and white everywhere. Everyone knows what happened next. Henrik's goals were just genius.

After the match we made our way through some Porto fans coming the other way; handshakes all round and they seemed sort of stunned that we'd taken defeat so well. I was of course disappointed but the main feeling I had was pride. Proud of the team and the fans. Proud to be a Celt.

TOMMYSBHOY - unlike some posters on here I have watched the dvd several times…with no shame, no regrets and total pride in my Bhoys who gave us one of THE most amazing nights of our Celtic supporting lives. A few years later I bought Henrik's limited edition framed picture of his 200th goal…his second of the game that night, signed and has Seville ticket in the frame…nearest I got to one! No.67 I picked and well worth the £175. Watched the recordings of the game when I came back from the trip to get it out of my system and felt it was the best thing to do as the more you put something off the harder it becomes.

ANDYCOL IS YET ANOTHER NEIL LENNON - My mates and I took a punt 3 months before the final and bought 6 tickets direct from UEFA. Best investment ever. We flew from Glasgow to Amsterdam to Madrid then caught the bullet train to Seville. Apart from the Tims enjoying themselves, the highlight on the train was the naive young American couple sitting across the aisle from us.

After asking us what the green and white uniforms were about and us carefully explaining where we were going and its significance, the girl turned to her partner and suggested that they would maybe take this event in. We left them in blissful ignorance but wondered afterwards what they made of Seville and how it fitted in with their vision of Spain. We had booked into a hotel on the outskirts near the conference centre thinking the facilities nearby should be decent and that there would be a taxi rank on hand. Both guesses worked out so we were sorted. We got to a position just before the river from the opposite direction to the bulk of the support and settled down to have a few beers outside a friendly little bar.

A carload of Tims arrived with a load of parched Bhoys inside. They wanted to know how far they were from the stadium and when we told them it was a reasonable walk away, they piled out and settled down with us. After the game we headed back to our hotel where there was a few Porto fans staying.

A couple of guys in the lift apologised for the theatrics but we told them not to worry about it as we were off out to party. Round the corner were a few bars which stayed open till late. (So late we never found out when they closed). These bars seemed to be inhabited by a young crowd, maybe students. Anyway when we walked in, still wearing out strips into a large bar/club where we were the only non locals and the entire bar stood up and gave us a standing ovation and the owner came over with drinks followed by plenty more. I have a vague memory of the bar closing around 3 and when we expressed disappointment we were advised that this was the early night for that establishment and to move to the place next door. Cue repeat of applause drinks etc. A great week for all of us and one the spiteful references to Seville calculators by radio pundits will never diminish for those of us who were there.

DAN - Regretfully could not manage to get to Seville due to being skint at the time. Reading the blog this evening lifts the spirit. Many fine individual stories with the main theme of folks enjoying a once in a lifetime experience.

Despite the disappointing result, the true Celtic spirit coming to the fore, this is what makes me proud of being a Celtic supporter.

Special thanks to TBJ for sharing his special story.

ESTORILBHOY - Not sure if it has been posted already or not but for those of you who have not viewed the official DVD there is a quote from the commentator (Jim Rosenthal I think), where he states that, in 25 years of covering European finals, he had never experienced an atmosphere at a European final like the night in Seville. Always good to hear a neutral's view of our fantastic support.

VHMAN - For those who never made Seville, like a lot of Celts that night, I never got a ticket but I did have two lovely Celtic lassies along with me just outside the stadium in a fan's area with large screen TVs etc. If the screens went bust we would have made our way to the stadium and sang the songs in support of our team.

SALTIRES EN SEVILLA - Ahhh Sevilla - is it really 10 years ago?

Glasgow flight to Belfast - hire car to Dublin, stayed overnight in Swords then afternoon flight from Dublin to Madrid on eve of match. Met gang of mates in Madrid, nite out on town with Celts everywhere and great atmosphere with locals all wishing us well.

Match day took 'Ave Maria' train at what felt like the speed of sound to Sevilla - train jammed with Celts arriving around 10:00am. The first thing I noticed was the stifling heat - jeezo how was Lenny going to play fitba in that ? It occupied my thoughts for most of the day as we sauntered from Cathedral to bar after bar -piazza to fountain, all choc full of hooped fans and a fair amount of happy friendly Porto fans.

Around 2pm we headed outside the city centre for the hills around Betis (I think) where we found a small taverna and were made very welcome - across the road was a Police station. In no time we had the banners up and song/beer/sangria was flowing- soon the police station had emptied as the local Gardia Civil decided to join the party

The landlady produced a steel box attached to a large iron chain – each cop took his gun off and popped it in the box- landlady locked box with a key hung around her neck (gulp!) – then poured large measures of a lethal tasting spirit for the cops who all toasted the 'Fantastico Celtics Glasgow '- cue a hastily composed response and more singing and dancing.

A wonderful experience as more and more stray Celts appeared in the bar - including two lads from Cork who wanted to display their Basque flag. Thankfully they were politely discouraged as we had visions of that gun box being opened up muchas rapido ;-)

A very, very, very long walk to the stadium with locals parked en route with makeshift bars in the boot of cars - black bin liners, bed of ice and bottles of water and cervecas – not charging the earth either!

Two glorious goals from Henke and grown men in tears – surreal feeling and still feel let down by antics of a highly skilled Porto team – the isolated Porto fan and his mother sitting beside me apologised for the behaviour of their team. I told him to fully enjoy the victory, wished them both well and gave them a club badge. It wasn't their fault after all and I remember the feeling of pride in my club when I saw them looking at each other in awe, as Walk On was belted out by the fans around them. They had clearly never seen or heard, or felt anything like that before and they loved it. Two more converts secured.

Eternal memories of the entire Celtic family on tour and an unbelievable affinity with the big-hearted natives of Sevilla.

The trip home - jeezo…that is another story…

TIME FOR CHANGE -Ten years ago I had the daytrip of a life time after letters from the ticket office saying 'sorry you have been unsuccessful in the ballot'. I had no hope of a ticket for the final and then lo and behold I got one. I had less than two weeks to get flights and was skint into the bargain! Never mind. Made it via Malaga . Back home they had a party with all the neighbours in attendance…

WGS - Seville finished for me when I left that stadium. Still not watched it yet.

Why MON never signed Broto at the start of the season rather at Christmas when he was cup tied probably comes back to haunt him. Broto in goals that night for me or another keeper, we would have won that even with 10 men. The look on Mjallby and Larssons' faces at the final whistle looking towards the Douglas goal stays with me. Although Sutton and Larsson was always my preferred partnership. I think Harston would have battered Carvalho.

TAGGSYBHOY - Fantastic reading all the Seville stories. Never mind losing the game, even losing the league the following Sunday couldn't dampen my spirits. So many highlights from those couple of days. Meeting Barassiebhoy at Seville airport. He'd left his honeymoon in Cuba. Dirty rotten scoundrel selling our tickets. Seeing 'the chosen one' touting tickets for 700 euros each. Another Dirty rotten scoundrel selling our hotel room! Watching the game with a Hearts fan on the big screen. Hearts fan supporting us. Staying up all night (again) with a fine group of fellas. Hair of the dog with Barassiebhoy in a fine Sevillian boozer. Carnage at Seville airport. Ryanair shutting check in early, getting on plane without checking in. Guy next to me getting on plane without checking in and without a ticket! Meeting old mate in London taxi queue and staying up all night again. Darn the hair we cared that we never won, but we had a great time. That's the Celtic way.

CROPPYBHOY - As one whose employer made it perfectly clear that no leave would be granted for Seville, can I just say how amazing today has been! The stories convey everything that is good about our support. Warmth, humour, love and respect – for themselves, our club and our opponents and hosts. Thanks a million guys for all the stories.

EMUSANORPHAN - Sitting in bar at our hotel (Sol Melia I think?) 90 mins to kick off. "We better head," says I. Someone in our company says " It's only 3 stops in the Metro to the Stadium. Metro station is only 2 streets away". OK then cue another slab of beer! Finish beer and out we go. Met two young women. "Where is the Metro?" I ask in my best Spanish. "Barcelona or Madrid?" they respond. PANIC! Rush to a taxi rank. Huge queue! MAJOR PANIC!

I'm thinking after all the hassle getting tickets, including buying one at Glasgow Airport for £500 off someone masquerading as a Celtic fan… We are gonna miss the game!

Out into the middle of a dual carriageway I dash flagging down bemused drivers. "50€ if you drive us to Stadio Olympico?" 2 young students in a wee banger thought they'd won the lottery!! They even sparked up a joint! Arrive at Stadium to meet brother who was travelling over from Algarve.

As anyone who was there will tell you, mobile phone coverage crashed! What chance of finding a guy wearing the hoops among 50,000? Just about to give up and give ticket to some lucky Tim when a voice from directly behind me sitting on a wall shouts my name! Wee bro with a bag of warm Portugese beers! Into stadium we go. Guys throwing their used tickets out from stadium in plastic bottles to fans below. Amazing the number who got in with them!

PETROVSCHEF - Might as well join in. Stayed in Marbella with my Dad. Had been having a rough time of things, so was a welcome break. Hotel full of Celtic fans which wasn't supposed to be a football type hotel but certainly turned into one! Managed to hire what seemed like the last mini bus on the Costa del Sol for a small fortune. Atmosphere in the city was amazing. Watched the game on a big screen in a park, like T in the Park for football, only better.

Will never forget our goals and celebrations. Somehow managed to find the bus at 1:00am to get back to the hotel, how, I will never know. My old man seldom gives much away but I knew he was proud. He seemed to know everything going on on the pitch, even though he had lost his sight and the noise made it difficult to commentate to him! Like P67, never watched the game since on DVD. Prefer the memory even bittersweet.

MAJESTIC HARTSON - I travelled to Seville with my whole family, brother, 2 sisters and Dad in a car with another car in convoy containing cousins, uncles and wives. Only 2 had tickets but none of us could miss it.

We spent a few days driving down stopping an hour past Paris, Madrid, where one car broke down, then on down to Seville. We all swapped cars all the way down so the laughs never got tired.

Camped out in Seville and enjoyed the city for a couple of days. A beautiful place. We bumped into many old faces and generally had a smile on our face from start to finish.

The only downside was the "Bhoy" in the pub we watched the game in saying we didn't deserve to be there after Porto scored their second! Why travel all that way to be negative?

We left the next day to head back home again laughing and joking all the way. Stopped off in Leicester to watch the Killie game…. and then home. I also got to fly out with my old man a week later to pick up the repaired car in Madrid. Nightmare;)

It was one of the best weeks of my life and was great to spend it with my family and extended family. Reading all these stories has brought it all (that I can remember) back, and has caused a few tears to well up. Love it.

COWIEBHOY - Back to Seville. An afternoon visit to Cathedral, and like many, the bell rings, and Mass starts, in Spanish. I couldn't concentrate for the singing from Flanagans outside. Young miss Cowieghirl, due to arrive on last flight out of Glasgow, and no idea where she is being dropped off in City, she is 17, and like most others her age, in middle of exams, planned to fly back on 1st flight back, as she has an exam next day (22nd) at 9. Who now remembers the entire mobile phone system collapsing?

So search party out to find miss Cowieghirl, no luck so return to square, and there she is sitting with mum, without a care in the world, and no idea where she is to be picked up for return to airport – I saw her school report, even passing exam, comment in school annual from friends, she slept through exam. Brings me back to 21st May 1979, and as a 16 year old heading to the game, the bus breaks down at Stepps – still managed to get to game though – 1- 0, down by the time we get in, what a night that was, and O Level next day.

How hot was it inside that stadium? And how did the hoops do so exceptionally well in that heat? Also easy to remember the 25th May, ma old Celtic daft Da's birthday.

JIMBO67 - Been in from work 45 minutes and have been catching up with Sevilla stories. Lump in the throat stuff especially TBJ – I knew it had been special but not quite how much.

I hope we get to another final before I am too old to go but nothing will ever be better than Seville.

MURDOCHAULDANDHAY - CQN shows only a fraction of the personal, the humorous and at times emotional story of the 80,000 plus who shared the Seville experience, not forgetting those millions watching worldwide as well. It truly was a one off and Celtic and its fans are the only football club on the planet who could have pulled it off and shook the world while doing so.

DOUG C - Loving the memories - so many routes to Seville. I went via Manchester / Frankfurt / Madrid, had a great night in Madrid, a lock in that ended with a stand-off with the polis. All ended well. Early morning train to Seville, what a journey, draught beer on a train. That's the future!! What a day in Seville - one big party.

God it was hot! The highlight for me was walking out to my seat and seeing the green and white everywhere; was nearly crying then. Was crying at the end. What a wonderful few days, with a million good memories. I could write a Brogan Rogan length post about them.

SIPSINI - Seville...I went with a crowd from work and a couple of my mates. They all got booked into hotels in Torremelinos...me and my mate ended up in a hotel outside of Torremelinos. The best description I could give of the hotel was that it was up-market and full of Spanish pensioners other than a few Celtic fans...Cocoon springs to mind.

A few days of madness and it was time to head to Seville. Tagged onto a lift with a really nice couple who were driving through and squared them up. Us three blokes bought a couple of slabs for the journey as the girl was driving. None of us had tickets so we got to the stadium and opened the boot and were swarmed with fellow hoops and passed out the remaining cans...unknown till later they were alchohol free. The car park attendant came over and unbelievably...the company went by the name of Proddi Parking. A bad omen...we had a great time in the arena and wouldn't change a jot of it. Other than the result...I could say a lot more of our experiences; another day maybe;-))

PALACIO67 - Seville put Celtic back on the European map. My brother has lived and has had a pub in Costa Brava since 1991 and all the Spanish know him well. Always sporting the hoops whenever possible. Putting Barca out of the UEFA cup in 2004 was great for him being a local. But he has always stated his proudest moment was walking down the promenade and seeing all the shops and markets displaying the Hoops rather than the Milans and Barca tops. Seville opened a lot of eyes around Europe.

FANADPATRIOT - As it was my birthday, I refused my family's attempt to pay my way to Seville, no ticket no way. My night was spent in the company of my family, minus my youngest son, who was in Seville. I was fortunate to be at Lisbon and Milan, but to experience the joy to be in a major European Final with your family is something special. We had a great party, full of joy and laughter, song and music. That is why we are special. We love to be part of something good, win lose or draw.

GEDHED7 - Seville . Some amazing stories extolling all that is great to be part of the Celtic family. Remember being outside the pub opposite the Cathedral when the priest strolled through the crowd as the throng opened up like the Red Sea and gave him an ovation. He was waving like he was the Pope…hilarious! Then an even bigger cheer when a lorry load of fresh beers arrived at the pub. As for the game, I was obviously gutted at time up but equally proud of the performance of the hoops. I have a wee sneaky feeling we are destined for another final in the not too distant future.

EXCATHEDTRA44 - I can't believe its 10 years. Pal and I with our sons arrived day of game with 2 genuine tickets for TV gantry (don't ask) and 2 forgeries.

Boys refused the offer to use the genuine tickets as they feared we would get jailed, real reason was they fancied the Big Screen area.

Visited Cathedral where Christopher Columbus is entombed and went to top of the Tower just as bells peeled. Was deaf for next hour.

Although Hartson would have made a difference, Broto in goal would not have spilled as Douglas did.

Real disappointment considering the support but what a memory. I have the book but have never read it and I have the DVD, still in cellophane.

For all those who wished us defeated, our memories have outlived your hatred.

SQUIRE DANAHER - What a marvellous place this is, so many stories covering the whole spectrum of emotions.

My own Seville story is rather mundane. During a particularly foul January 2003, Squire-ess and I decided we'd book a Menorca holiday in May –

as you do – between 9th -23rd.

Thought no more of it until after the win at Liverpool then consoled myself with the thought I wouldn't get a ticket even if they made the final.

Lo and behold we get the supposedly easy SF tie v Boavista, while Porto eventually horsed bookies favs Lazio.

Watched the SF 2nd leg in Kelly's in Pollokshaws Road with timmy7 - noted and other assorted lurkers. The most agonising game I have ever watched. All's well that ended well – while everyone was goin' ape, I resigned myself to going on holiday.

Until the large A4 letter arrived from CP. I knew instantly what it contained

Dear squire Danaher

As the club reaches the end of of our greatest European journey in 33 years, we are delighted to offer…

I did the decent thing, went on holiday and gave my ticket to my best man.

Watched the game with 200 other Celtic fans – men, women and face painted weans – in Cala n Forcat, Menorca – the Hoops were out in force all week and plans were made for all the Hoops in town to watch it together – can't add anything to the accounts already posted except that BBC Match of the Day coverage was very complimentary to Celtic (Barry Davies got the gig). At kick off a pitch side thermometer showed it was – at 20:45 – over 100 degrees Fahrenheit.

Squire junior got home and on going to his bed, broke his wee heart sobbing and started his old Bhoy off.

The thing I hold on to is that the best man went with two other mates of ours from school and got the ticket on condition he used it.

I have the pictures he took from inside the stadium. His family lost a rock and the world lost a good man when he died in 2011.

Particularly enjoy reading the stories regarding the response of the locals to the Bhoys - we really are more than a club.

EX LUDO - 10 years already? My abiding memory of Seville isn't the game itself but one of those wee moments, which will be with me for a long time. I had met 2 friends who had my ticket in the hotel next to the Real Betis stadium on the afternoon of the game. About 5 pm we went out to get a taxi to the Olympic Stadium.

It was a gloriously hot evening and there were about 25 people waiting in the queue. The taxis were fairly efficient at picking people up and we were moving slowly down the queue. We were about half down the queue when a wee murmur went up and the guy behind me tapped me on the shoulder and told me Billy McNeil was at the back of the queue with a couple of his pals.

When the next taxi arrived everyone stood back without being prompted and indicated to Billy that the taxi was his. He politely declined at first but eventually gave in and walked over to the car with his pals. There was an immediate loud round of applause from everyone in the queue as he got in the cab. The look of amazement on the drivers face was something to behold.

LENNYBHOY...SUPPORTING NEIL LENNON AND CFC UNTIL I DIE - Never watched the DVD yet despite having it. Bought two official programmes; both still in pristine condition including postcards inside them.

Got my Seville top signed by the squad with a few extras including Tommy Burns. It hangs proudly framed in one of my rooms. Inside the frame also is my match ticket, reminding me for eternity of the Seville Season.

For all the Final and the experience was fantastic, being in Porto the night we beat Boavista was the highlight of our European journey in 2002/2003. To be in the Boavista end as well.

LUCKY CODA - Just been out for dinner with my son in London and we reminisced about Seville. I was in Dublin at the time, on the corporation tax game living in Malahide Marina.

Anyway I decided to go to Seville when Henrik did the biz against Boavista. Problem was no ticket. So phoned one of my younger brothers to sort it. He spoke to Paul McBride RIP who he hired quite often as a QC, to sort it. He then put pressure on Jim Traynor as the Record's legal guy for a ticket. Traynor delivered so that was part one sorted.

My brother sorted flights (he couldn't make his due to some High Court case) although he turned up later. I sorted the penthouse apartment in Seville for a week thru my Spanish contacts. The bar in the area was full of Real Betis fans and one had spent time in Derry. They were a hoot. The Spanish girls were all on the tic; and it was a great time.

I was one of the first arrivals and saw the one nasty incident involving a Celtic fan on the hill full of restaurants. Moments later as I recall the nuns walked up the hill with Spanish school kids all singing Celtic Celtic ...it was unbelievable. Our pad was a little bit outside town so during the day we got a bus in and the old Spanish ladies having a laugh with us was brilliant.

At night I remember now locals giving us a lift back. The night before the game was laugh with all the Glasgow lawyer crew now in attendance and a chorus of Adeste Fideles sticks in the memory. The day of the game was the sweltering heat and last minute ticket stuff. Amazingly we had a spare ticket and we ended up giving it away to a mate's brother.

The game passed and we left the stadium; bumped into a Kirkie bhoy who was a right good player who had been in the Porto end (he got a ticket at the last minute for face price from a Porto fan).

We went back to our bar beside our pad. The Spanish crew were all waiting for us. We didn't know what to expect. I said we lost...they said NO CELTIC WON TONITE...people will only remember Celtic. We proceeded to enjoy the nite with a flight to be negotiated the next day.

Later in the week on Friday I had an Irish Wedding at Dalmahoy Golf Club. I advised my good lady if Celtic won I would be in Seville for at least a week. Somehow I think this has something to do with the final outcome.

Anyways it's good to look back.

Looking forward is not so easy for Celtic. We all want another day in the sun. Somehow I don't see it happening especially in the SPL, which is on a life support machine. We should never stop trying to be successful in the European arena. However with each passing season it becomes more difficult.

JONNY THE TIM - Went to Seville with a mate I hadn't seen for about 10 years. Day trip, arriving at about 8.00 am. As the plane came in to land, we flew over a campsite. WOW, it was wall-to-wall, fence-to-fence green and white! Bussed into the city, every car and bus seemed to be decked in green and white. Made our way to the Cathedral, and it was like being at Celtic Park, only hotter!

There was a bus in the square (The Sun I think!), and STV were broadcasting from it, can't remember if it was McKay or Raman Big Man, but they were getting pelters from us all. This was obviously the business centre of Seville, and every office had staff out on the balconies just watching in awe and disbelief, at the sheer numbers, and good time we were all having.

Neither of us had tickets and I had no intention of denying a more deserving fan of one, but we were approached by a fan who offered us 2 tickets for 1200 Euros! He was told in no uncertain terms where to go and the thought did cross our minds of relieving him of the tickets. Disgrace of a so-called supporter.

We went to some unofficial car park near the bus station where there was a bar set up; the kind where you paid in advance and got vouchers/tokens for drink. Not for me, so, as it was approaching kick -off, time to look for a bar which had the game on. Decided to go for a pee in the bus station, and hey, waddayaknow, there's a waiting room with a bar and a TV, and 2 wee Spanish wummin waiting for their bus! Bingo! We shouted out to a group of passing Bhoys, and within 2 minutes, the place was mobbed!

The place went absolutely mental when Henrik scored and the locals were awe-struck at the atmosphere in that place. The toilets were insufficient to say the least; 1 cludgie, 1 urinal, and 1 wash basin - the wash-basin was being used as a urinal and at times had 4-5 guys peeing in it at the same time!

I could go on about the after-game atmosphere but it's already been mentioned many times.

Never thought I would ever get to see Celtic in a European final in my lifetime. One of the most memorable days of my life!

Thanks Celtic, MON and the players and fans who made it so!

TBJ

Was very moved by your memories, I can only imagine the turmoil you were experiencing at the time. I hope that time has helped heal your wounds and that you'll make that pilgrimage one day! God Bless.

VOGUEPUNTER - Seville…after match ended, tears in my eyes, pride in my heart for our team and our fans.

BAMBI - The morning after the game we drove from Seville to Malaga and stopped of en route in a wee village in search of food and drink. Walked into a wee non descript bar only for us to realise it was a Sevilla supporter club. We had the hoops on so got a great welcome. The barman said, "Do you want to see the back room?"

"Aye ok." we said so he took us through to a shrine to their team, signed photos of past players including Maradona, Suker etc. Brilliant to see this stuff and they just wanted to talk about Celtic.

Went out in Benalmadena that night. the 24 hour sq was rocking. Got talking to two Swedish brothers, Hammarby fans, who were travelling round Europe and decided they wanted to be down there for the final to see what the atmosphere was like. They couldn't believe the noise, the atmosphere and the party despite our loss. They were massive Henke fans and just loved the party.

CELTIC CHAMPS ELECT - Great stories guys. It's a pleasure to read everyones' adventures. Ours started when we beat Liverpool. We booked to stay in Cabanas, Portugal for a week which is 1hour from Seville. We were 2 couples along with my 2 year old son who is now incidentally, in the intermediate academy at Celtic. On our flight over 1 of our cases got lost and our boy's buggy went missing. Anyone who has had kids knows that the buggy is a lifesaver so we needed to go buy a new one for Seville :-). This was on the Tuesday.

Off we headed, parked up and then all you hear in the distance was the singing as u got nearer the cathedral. It was jumpin'. There were hoops everywhere singing and dancing and it was awesome. You just can't explain in words how happy you are to witness such happiness in so many people. My mrs and my mates mrs and my son got sent to get a new buggy.

My mate and I had a few beers (cruzcampo) and soaked up the atmosphere. We met guys we knew from school and I met my cousin and my cousin's husband. It was so surreal at times and the heat was stifling but I was so proud to be here knowing I had a ticket for game. Was offered 1000 euros for my ticket but there was no way I would have sold it. Anyway the girls returned with buggy. They had a few drinks and we headed back to Cabanas. The next day me and my buddy set off early for Seville and get there around 10.30 and party right thru until game time. I bought a small bandanna from a guy who was selling them next to the cathedral which I still have to this day.

I vaguely remember walking to the stadium. I saw Tosh Mckinlay and Darren Jackson outside the stadium. Sat bevvying till the gates opened and went in early. Then met all our mates who had tickets. We were high up at the end where Henke headed his wonder goal and the thing that sticks with me is that there were a number of empty seats behind us. Then the stadium started to fill up - the banners all getting laid out the fields and boom, the tears start to flow.

My dad was having his lung removed having been diagnosed with lung cancer but he wanted me to go to Seville and not to worry about him.

Old school you know but the emotion of it all had me in tears. I finally got my act together and the game started. Thought we played okay up until Porto scored. That changed the game imo. Then we lost a bad goal and then equalized. There was only one winner. Surely it was our time again. Even down to 10 men my heart sunk. But no, we deserved a pen shoot out.

Then Big Rab's dreadful error. I have watched the game a few times and Rab's mistake was criminal. But that's fitba. You take the good with the bad. Anyway me and my buddy were too gutted to party so we drove back to Cabanas. When we left on the Sunday, as we boarded the bus to the airport we were champions. When we got off the bus, Dunfermline had lain down. Sorry for rambling on but the memories of Seville are with us to our grave. Ps my dad passed on 1 year later but loved the stories we had about Seville.

ALL GREEN - Seville is the greatest Celtic memory I have. We went without tickets and the laughs and atmosphere started as soon as we arrived in Benalmadena. The day of the game I couldn't believe the scenes in Seville. I met folk I hadn't seen for years, everyone had to be there.

We had arranged to meet more friends at a pub near a roundabout, too hot to walk and no taxis, it was a horse-drawn carriage for the 5 of us. We arrived at the pub to total abuse. A few of us didn't have tickets so we started to make our way to the park for the big screens. We stopped for a beer at a bar right beside the river full of fans when two motorcycle police waked in.

The first thought was oh no this looks bad. Next thing one of the police has his camera out getting photos and swapping scarves. My pal got a shot of one of the bike helmets, when he put it on he couldn't see out the front and was staggering around the pub like an out of control dalek.

We got to the park but one of the screens had a poor picture so instead of rioting we got a taxi back to town and watched the game in a pub with fans and locals. At one point I was behind the bar trying out some local liqueur made from oranges, my only vitamin intake for 5 days. The

Celtic fans and team excelled themselves in a way even I didn't think possible. The whole trip was a joy apart from the result.

COLOUR BLIND BHOY - Don't post much but logged on to site about 2 hours ago and have read every single Seville story with a wide range of feelings and emotions and the overriding one is pride. I paid significantly over face value for 2 tickets for the Fondo Stand and it was the best investment I have ever made. The memories will last forever – just wished I had spent an extra quid to get a bottle of water!

The Boy Jinky, on a day of very high standards for the best blog on the web, your emotional story stands out as a highlight. God bless and Hail Hail.

CHAPTER 23

SEVILLE – THE SPANISH OVEN

Views on the intense heat in Seville for the 2003 UEFA Cup Final, as expressed on Celtic Quick News in January 2014…

BLANTYRE TIM - there was a lack of water inside the stadium so we had to drink beer to stay hydrated…honest!

Goldstar10 - I was fairly close to ground level and can remember watching the players' warm up routine (ha) thinking there is no way they can think properly never mind play in this furnace. And the insects- huge dragonfly types, thousands of them swarming all over the pitch.

Burghbhoy - It was pigging boiling!

Leftclick - We were in a taxi in Benidorm on the Monday from Alicante airport. The driver asks where we are eventually headed: "Seville" said I ,"Ahhhh THE OVEN OF SPAIN" he replied. We looked at him and wondered what he was talking about. We left Benidorm on the Wednesday night in a fleet of buses. The Bhoy who organised them initially ordered one, I think there were about 20 buses by the time we left.

When we arrived in Seville 9 hours later, we were not long in finding out what the taxi driver was talking about. I'm a tea-totaller and can't remember how much I spent on Ice packs(was warned not to drink it) for the stay at one point there was 15 of us under a massive tri-colour pleading for the sun to go down.

The Exiled Tim - What was the temp that night in Seville, mid 30's?

Leftclick - to a busload of peely wally ML5rs it felt like the high 300s:))

Gretnabhoy - My mate and I hired a car from the Algarve and drove to Seville. The first night, we slept in the car, which was far from comfortable. After the match we were wandering around the City. There were so many people sleeping everywhere and anywhere, they could get comfortable. We woke one guy sleeping on a bench with his wallet, half out his pocket and suggested that he put it somewhere safe! Eventually met another mate who had a hotel room and five of us, three on the floor, stayed the night there. Blankets were not essential as the heat was incredible even with the window wide open. Even with the drink it was hard to sleep, what with the noise from outside and especially the heat. Still what a great experience!

Cowiebhoy - Like BT, without the beer, how about the absolute bedlam in the concourses as the water ran oot, and that was before kick off in the area I was in. Fondo, puerta H, sector 229, To be exact.

Bobby Russell - Everything was going well in Seville until the big screen cut out, then all hell broke loose and riots ensued!...youreinthewrongmoviecsc

Billy Bhoy - It was like being in a sauna with jeans and the Hoops on. I walked to the stadium alone from the Cathedral. I had got detached from the guys I was with and being on my own without the distraction of chatting along the way I was acutely aware of the heat. I thought I wouldn't make it – and I was a fit 43 year old. It was SO hot during the day I hardly had a beer – and if you knew me you would appreciate how hot it must have been!

Burghbhoy - I was with a crowd of about 10. We briefly lost one of the ghuys for about 20 minutes. He'd fallen asleep in a stupor and now looked like a lobster. Really badly blistered the next day! Sair!

Cowiebhoy - We stayed in the city until around 3 in the morning, still having a party. As we left, we passed through and around the train station, still taking everything in, before heading back to Islantilla (Huevla). Flying home from Faro 2 days later, the flight was still absolutely full of Hoops. 2 of the Bhoys (they are brothers) would talk about Celtic 24/7, as we sit at airport, next thing our names are called out, flight about to close and last call, they still wouldn't stop talking about the Bhoys. Awesome experience!

Leftclick - Weather Overview for Seville. Seville, located in the South West of Spain, is known for its stifling hot summers and mild winters, making it a fairly typical Mediterranean climate. Seville is one of the warmest cities in Europe. In 2003 the city experienced a heat wave which reached uncomfortable highs of 46°C. The all-time hottest European temperature ever recorded occurred in Seville in 1881, when on 4th August it hit a blistering 50°C! (122°F.) Pre air-conditioning, this would have been hard to endure.

In the height of summer sightseeing in Seville can be somewhat of a challenge; one of the most popular sights, Plaza de Espana, is known as one of the hottest points in the city.

Bamboo - If Seville had been located a few hundred miles further north I think Celtic would have won.

Natknow - Where were you thinking, like? Glesga? :-)

Tommytwiststommyturns - don't know about the temperature inside the stadium that evening, but it was definitely 42 degrees C in Seville during the day. They had a huge display near the park that the party was in the night before the game. We couldn't believe it could be that hot in May, especially as we had just enjoyed the environment above the southern coast at Ronda for 2 nights.

Due to a monster hangover and the oppressive temperature, I only managed a half pint of lager during the day prior to the game! It was water, water and more water. I actually had to leave my mates and take the wife back to the hotel for a cold shower, as she was overheating and feeling unwell. We then met up with our friends and started the Tenko march out to the stadium. In my opinion, the host city didn't get enough criticism for the lack of decent transport.

I think we managed to get a couple of water bottles inside the stadium before taking our seats high up across from the main stand. I can definitely remember the mutant dragonflies that someone mentioned earlier and the feeling that I was sitting in a sauna with clothes on! It wasn't comfortable at all.

After the game and another lengthy trek, we found an internet cafe near our hotel. I bought about 8 small, cold beers for taking back with us. Just as well, the hotel bar was shut! We sat in the room, guzzling the beers and talked about what could have been.

I'd like to go back to Seville, but maybe in March or October!!

The Exiled Tim - I was just looking at some stuff re temps in Seville, it is one of the hottest cities in Europe, and mild in the winter, their top temp of 50 deg is not unexpected where I am, we had about a dozen days last summer over 50, and twice that the year before, July and August would never drop below the mid 30's at night, and mid to high 40's during the day, brutal in a house, not a bother in the cave, Being at nearly 1000 metres above sea level accounts for the extremes in the temp.

Adi Dasler - It was roastin' going to the Seville game. I remember a guy with his pyjamas (he had just been released fae the local hospital after falling from a tree nickin' oranges) and his partner asking for anyone who could give him a tic top for the game! Also after the game we walked back towards hotel and over the bridge at the river to find a kiosk that only sold ice cream (they had run out of booze)!

Gerald766 - My wife and I, along a friend of ours were booked into the hotel that was originally meant to be for the team! They were moved to another hotel, because this was a 'Complex Site', which had a golf course (designer, one Jack Nicklaus), and a 'go-cart' racing track! Celtic thought that the noise from the track would be too much, so they put the players 'families' in to this one – a beautiful Hotel! Hugh outdoor pool facility, Chris Sutton's, sons' and Allan Thompson's boy gave it some wellie! Heat!

I had a shower 0815, came out after drying myself, was back in having a cold shower at 0817! The room temp at that time of the morning was 33 degrees, and that was with the 'picture window' open to the max, door to the room wedged open to give catch any possible draught! I had a 'heated' conversation with the Manager about air-condition, and he apologised, but he assured me it was fully ON! He asked to liase with the other guests as what to do at mid-day, when the temperature would be in the region of 45 degrees!

However, we coped! Wouldn't have missed it! The Stadium was equally as bad that night, just how our players performed that night, in that arena, in that heat, well, is something that will live with me forever, they were magnificent, to a man! The only thing that really irked me about that 'forever' experience, was the fact, that the player for Porto, who scored their winner, had been STRETCHERED OFF, on three occasions! ' Special One' my ass! The whole Celtic Mission, were the 'Special Ones', that particular magnificent night in Seville.

Gerrybhoy - One of the painful things I remember about Seville was going down to the bars in the stadium at half time looking for water. 5 or 6 deep at the bar and they had completely run out of water!! We walked a couple of miles after the game and there were loads of Tims outside petrol stations etc lining up for water. Dying of thirst I was. A very hot day.

Lennybhoy - Seville, Fr. Sweeney, PP St. Patrick's and his Pal, Fr. Towery (spl) were room next door. We had to get a shuttle bus into Seville town. So the two Padres, wearing Hoops, shorts and bandanas came on to the Bus. Fr. Sweeney says we will say a wee prayer that God looks after us. Heads bowed and caps removed by all those assembled waiting for him to begin….to our amazement he launched into Hail Hail, the Celts are here…

Billy Bhoy - I travelled with the Irvine club to Malaga and that was our base. We got the bus up on the day of the game and parked outside the town. The walk in was tough as there was no shade. After the game I couldn't find the bus and slept on the pavement beside a fan from Troon.

At 5:30 we both got a lift on a milk van to the railway station, which was mobbed with fholk like me who had missed their transport. I thought the hospitality in Seville after the game was really horrible: no buses or taxis at all. Had a fantastic time and would love to have an opportunity again.

Bada Bing - The 2 hour walk back in to Seville after the game was a nightmare, how they got a Final like that with non existent transport is a complete mystery! We found a bar and the owner stuck up 3 beers and 3 shots for us. The BBC reporter Chris Hollins was in there and I asked him his thoughts on the match. He said he had never seen anything like us at any event he had been at and probably never would. A nice guy btw.

Bobby Murdoch's Ankle - it was roastin! I remember there was a thermometer in the stadium, which was showing 39 degrees just after kick off. As BT said there was no water, my cousin went down to get water and came back with 4 beers, ach wit the hell we drank them. It was hot for May.

Nakasammi - I had two tickets for Seville and have two sons. Guess who ended up watching the game in the Big Ben pub in Seville on a TV on top of a cigarette machine! The bar owner a boy from London and his partner were brilliant as they just kept pouring shots of whisky every time Celtic attacked and were giving us plenty of water too. Only three of us at the bar liked whisky!

My 4 flights cost me £24.70 in total along with air miles as the girl in the British Airways call centre was a Celtic supporter! I had to get a train back to Madrid the following morning at 7.30. I couldn't believe the number of fans in the station but fair play to the police. They just ensured walkways were kept clear. I would love to know who was the last Celtic fan to get home from Seville!

Granny Macs Bhoy - When we arrived at the stadium in Seville under an hour before kick off we phoned one of our mates who was working inside the stadium suited and booted. He was complaining about the heat and commented that the players might find it hard going as he had just been told the temperature at pitch level in the shade was 35 degrees C.

When we got in to the park there was no water left for sale in our section. After the game ended we waited in the bus park for over an hour waiting for lost souls and gasping for a beer but any re-hydration would have been fine. Then a hooped figure in the distance carrying large bottles of water caught my eye. When I marched over and asked where to go to get the water he said no chance mate these were some of the last the shop had and the queue was massive.

When I offered to buy one to share round the guys on the coach he said forget it you're having a laugh if you think I am taking money off you big man. Just take one he said and buy me a beer next time you see me. Probably sums up the spirit of Seville. Never saw him again to buy him the beer but the water hit the spot with the Bhoys.

Praecepta - Seville and the HEAT – it was 21°C (mid-day) when I visited recently, after this year's Barca away game (December 2013) – hot! 2003 after ET – on that night we walked back to the city (extremely long trudge). Our route was parallel to the river and brought us into the city at the railway station – handy for where we were staying – Rue de la Catholicas (catchy name)!

There was a large electronic signboard displaying; time, date and temperature – it read: 1:00 am – 22nd May 2003 – 31˚C!

Visit – www.celticquicknews.co.uk

CHAPTER 24

THE SEVILLE POEM ON CQN

This Seville Poem was posted on Celtic Quick News in January 2014…

A true story about the Seville trip, about a guy I know who went to Seville to see Celtic.

The Heartbreak Of Seville

The baby is due, all is going well,

But Dad is worried, everyone can tell

Tam has a problem, a real sticky wicket,

CELTIC in Seville, and he's not got a ticket

Convincing his wife the birth would be late,

Tam booked his flight, and phoned up his mate

His schoolmate, his pal, his friend for life,

Kevin, get a ticket, I sorted it with my wife

Tam, – the birth of a baby- a joy to behold,

A wonderful experience, or so I've been told

Kevin, forget that, I don't care what you say,

I am going to the final, come what may

Tam's search for a ticket was in vain,

As Kevin teased and taunted, again and again

Then finally Kevin sent this message to Tam,

The Eagle has landed, try and be calm

Tam's plea for the ticket fell on deaf ears,

You'll get it over in Spain, confirmed his fears

They all thought that Tam would stay at hame,

If baby was born on the day of the game

Glasgow airport was full to the brim,

But things then started to get really grim

Ticket desks sent Tam from pillar to post,

Indicating his flight booking was probably lost

This information aroused Tam's ire,

Blood pressure going higher and higher

When the idiot admitted the ticket was there,

Tam caught his flight with minutes to spare

SEVILLE, for oranges, paella, and the runs,

80,000 Celtic fans, but no any *uns!!!

We're gonnae win the cup, the choir sings,

Cos we've got Henrik, the King of Kings

A call from Kevin, to meet at his hotel,

Tam starts to think, things are going well

But in a maze, no hotel can he find,

Needle in a haystack, springs to mind

Meet at the stadium, right away,

This is definitely not Tam's day

He takes a flakey, and starts to cuss,

He can't find a taxi or a bus

Tam jumped into a car, asked him to dash,

The hijack was quelled with the offer of cash

A Spaniard, bewildered, as off he sped,

Amigo, you loco, was all he said

The phone network crashed, contact was gone,

Low and behold, Tam met his pal John

The look on John's face, he didn't need to say,

The words that Tam dreaded, his ticket was away

Traumatised, distraught, forlorn and defeated,

This paragraph ought to be deleted

Full of expletives, not to be repeated,

Well maybe just one, – B******s

Not enough money to satisfy touts,

The dirty thieving Spanish louts

Give us your money, your camera and phone,

Tam knew he couldn't beat them up alone

A young girl took pity, as she saw his despair,

My dad's got a ticket, standing over there

His price also too high, touts began to deride,

Tam's only option now, was to commit suicide

Take the money I have, Tam wailed pleeeeeese,

Ok, stop crying, and get off your knees

Thank you, God bless, Tam said to the man,

He ridiculed the touts as off he ran

(ram the tickets up your arse as far as you can),

ESTADIO OLIMPICO, a wonderful sight,

Everywhere was covered in green and white

Tam starts singing with all his might,

And praying his wife won't give birth that night

A big ugly Porto fan accosted wee Tam,

Right in among them, he didn't give a damn

You in Ze Big Trouble, if Porto no win,

I hope its deep shit, said Tam with a grin

Out you go, said a Polis with a gun,

Tam pleaded innocent, what have I done

Into the Celtic end, beside your own kind,

A seat in the press box, Tam did find

The magnificent Henrik keeps them in the game,

But blundering Rab, is mainly to blame

Bobo's sent off, into extra time,

A 3-2 defeat, it really was a crime

Fans land in Glasgow, the media do grill,

First up to comment, was Tam from " Harthill"

The ref was a joke, I've no more to say,

I need to get hame, there's a wean on the way!

A girl called Megan, born two weeks late,

She's so beautiful, it was well worth the wait

If Celtic can get to a final once more,

Tam will get his own ticket, before he leaves the front door.

PS Tam was not from Harthill, God forbid, he was from Uphall, the media got it wrong, as usual.

Courtesy of CQN contributor St Patricks Day 1956.

WHAT HAPPENED TO THE SEVILLE MONEY?

Paul Brennan thought he knew the answer, so started a blog. Celtic Quick News was born…

We returned home from Seville, beaten but unbowed. Just six months earlier, ahead of the game against Celta Vigo, only the most optimistic of us believed we would progress to the last 16.

It has been 23 years since Celtic were in Europe at Christmas, a generation of meagre failure which had conditioned us to expect the inevitable. On the road home from Seville our expectation were reset. Celtic were a respected team in Europe once more.

We had beaten Celta and Stuttgart, before winning away from home in the quarter and semi-final against Liverpool and Boavista respectively- a remarkable achievement.

European exploits in the following season still burn in the memory. Two almighty games against Bayern Munich, who celebrated a 0-0 draw at Celtic Park, after scoring two late goals to recover in Munich. The home win over Anderlecht had the stadium bouncing, although we suffered an ignominious defeat in Belgium, but it was the games against Lyon which remain most vibrant in the memory.

Celtic's best Champions League goal, to date, was scored by Liam Miller, but the manner of defeat in France still stings. Lyon were awarded a controversial penalty three minutes from the end to rob Celtic of the chance to qualify for the knock out stage for the first time. Celtic were left with the compensation of the UEFA Cup, where they achieved one of their most remarkable aggregate results.

Barcelona were beaten by sheer heroism, not only from our established heroes but notably from David Marshall and John Kennedy, who were drafted into the team for cover.

Porto, meanwhile, progressed to the Champions League Final, which they won with far greater ease than their win over Celtic a year earlier. A complete rethink of our place in the world was needed.

A year earlier we pushed the newly crowned European Champions to extra time, we knocked out a Barcelona team who had just achieved a club-record nine consecutive wins, and we had witnessed the sight of Bayern Munich player jump around like part-timers after drawing at Celtic Park.

Of course, we also waved goodbye to Henrik Larsson in the summer of 2004. An enormous hole opened up in the club at the precise time we felt that, with just a little more, we could bring some really special times back to Celtic Park.

Then it started. "What the Celtic fans want to know, is where did all the Seville money go?"

It was impossible to walk (virtually) any street in Scotland without seeing someone out wearing The Hoops, and there was all that gate money, surely Celtic had a pile of money in the bank ready to splash.

That was the version of events that was delivered by our media. Reality was a little different. Celtic lost £7m during our Seville season. The club was gambling right at the edge of responsibility. "All the Seville money" went into the pockets of the players to took us there, and more still.

Debt was escalating, we were involved in an arms race with a club who were on a path to liquidation, facing some dreadful choices. Do we follow them on the same path, hoping that something turns up?

Do we say enough is enough, and suffer the consequences on the field of play? Celtic pushed as far as they thought appropriate. Decisions on debt and spend will forever be subjective. There can be a case for a small change in budget but subsequent events have shed a different light on the madness that was, and in many places remains, football governance and finances.

Celtic's finances were not secret. They published accounts on the club web site, posted a copy to Companies House, and to circa 20,000 fan-shareholders. It was widely available information, but it wasn't news. The 'news' was Celtic had a pile of cash from the run to Seville and were unprepared to use it to recruit the players required to push them forward. This message was driven relentlessly, it was pernicious poison, designed to provoke turmoil in the heart of our club.

I was going off my head at this. "Where was all the Seville money?" I was shouting at the radio but in 2004 there was not really much more you could do. Football accounts might have been posted to tens of thousands of fans but most of them never read company accounts, so had little knowledge of the format.

The football media in Scotland consisted of a couple of radio stations, a few TV journalists, two daily and two Sunday newspapers. The top journos worked across all platforms, ensuring their interpretation of events, and of Celtic, achieved maximum exposure.

I arrived at work one morning and bemoaned the toxicity to Celtic of "What the Celtic fans want to know, is where did all the Seville money go?" to a friend, who happened to be a Rangers fan. "Why don't you start a blog and explain it?" he suggested.

"What's a blog? I answered.

He sat me down in front of a computer, brought up Blogger, and talked me through setting up a blog. Over the next four weeks Celtic's accounts were dissected in granular detail.

Thousands came to Celtic Quick News, mostly to tell me what a dick I was, but some to share their hunger for genuine information about our club.

A decade later the mainstream media have thoroughly lost control of the football agenda in Scotland. Fan-based media is all pervasive, so much so the Scotland of 2004 was more like modern-day North Korea in media-message-management terms than modern Scotland.

The clowns who rag-dolled Celtic are now seen for what they are. Largely ignored by the bulk of the population, they prey on a diminishing demographic, with a broken business model.

Fans, through new-media, held Scottish football to account in 2012 when the established powers tried to change the rules to accommodate Craig Whyte's outrageous business plan.

Citizen journalism is far from perfect, in fact, it is mostly absurd, but it is democratic in access and most importantly, it's ours.

Written by Paul Brennan, founder of Celtic Quick News.